What People Are Saying About *Fix It*

"You will not be disappointed with the next chapter in *The Oz Principle* accountability story introduced in *Fix It*. Roger Connors, Tom Smith, and their colleagues have truly hit another home run!"

—Gail Ciccione, Worldwide VP of Operations,
Medical/Diabetes Division at BD

"*Fix It* is a powerful, user-friendly must-have guide for taking the next step in creating a Culture of Accountability."

—Greg Wasson, Cofounder and President,
Wasson Enterprise; Retired CEO, Walgreens

"Understanding customer and employee expectations has been crucial for us as we build a more accountable culture. The tools in this book . . . enabled us to consistently achieve our Key Results. A must-do process."

—Bob Eckel, CEO, MorphoTrust USA

"I loved the innovative way the book flows, ultimately delivering many valuable lessons from real-life executive examples of what works. . . . *Fix It* is a powerful sequel to *The Oz Principle* and the logical next step to greater accountability for results."

—Ian Baines, CEO, Cheddar's Scratch Kitchen

"*Fix It* provides the essential road map to create a Culture of Accountability and shows the how-tos to get that job done in a way that can be truly transformational."

—Janee Harteau, Minneapolis Police Chief

"The powerful insights in this latest book from the authors of *The Oz Principle* will help you take those crucial first steps toward building a Culture of Accountability in your team or company. The results will astonish you!"

—Carla Cooper, Former CEO, Daymon Worldwide

"*Fix It* shows you how to build a Culture of Accountability from the ground up, with concrete examples and proven practices to create greater accountability for results."

—Larry Miller, CEO, Sit 'n Sleep

"Every leader who is serious about improving their results by identifying what's wrong in their culture should read *Fix It*!"

—Debbie Bowles, General Manager/Plant Director,
Ocean Spray Cranberries, Inc.

"*Fix It* is a fantastic guide to navigating the what, why, and how of accountability. A must-read book for aspiring and current leaders."

—Marty Smuin, CEO, Adaptive Computing

"*Fix It* is a powerful guide to getting accountability right!"

—Steve Binder, Executive VP, Hormel Business Units,
Hormel Foods Corporation

"Over a decade of experience with these principles convinces me that *Fix It* is a great tool for anyone who wants results and aspires to making lasting changes."

—Elaine Thibodeau, VP Strategy and Deployment,
Consumer Medical Devices, Johnson & Johnson

"The principles presented in *Fix It* have made me a better leader, a better spouse, and a better dad. I highly recommend this book to anyone who is ready to differentiate and lift themselves and their company to another level!"

—Tom Day, Group VP, Refrigerated Foods,
Hormel Foods Corporation

"Whether you've been working to get Above The Line for some time or you're just beginning your journey, *Fix It* provides targeted guidance and recommended practices—a chance to learn from others' successful accountability experiences."

—Pete Hammett, Managing Director, HR, OGE Energy Corp.

"*Fix It* . . . delivers down-to-earth proven practices that you can use right now—practical ideas for creating your own Culture of Accountability, where people are engaged and desired results are happening. *Fix It* works!"

—Tami Polmanteer, Chief Human Resource Officer,
Daymon Worldwide

"From assessment to concrete solutions in just thirty minutes—*Fix It* provides real solutions that you can put to work right away as you build a Culture of Accountability."

—Boyd Blake, Senior Director, IT, Nu Skin Enterprises

"If you are interested in developing or sustaining agile, collaborative, innovative teams and organizations that consistently get top results, *Fix It* is your go-to guide."

—**Kim McEachron, Senior VP of HR, Genomic Health**

"We won't stop using the tools in *Fix It* until we have the highest save rate in the country. . . . These traits and principles have become essential to how we operate. Fixing it for us means lives saved. This works!"

—**Mike Niblock, Fire Chief, Salem Oregon Fire Department**

"*Fix It* is simple and straightforward, laying out the hard truths on how culture and performance intersect—a must-read for CEOs looking to transform their company and results."

—**Stuart Schuette, CEO, American Tire Distributors**

fixit

The Official Sequel to *The Oz Principle*

ALSO BY ROGER CONNORS AND TOM SMITH

The Oz Principle

Journey to the Emerald City

How Did That Happen?

Change the Culture, Change the Game

The Wisdom of Oz

fixit

GETTING ACCOUNTABILITY RIGHT

The Official Sequel to *The Oz Principle*

240 SOLUTIONS TO YOUR TOUGHEST BUSINESS PROBLEMS

ROGER CONNORS ◇ TOM SMITH

Craig Hickman ◇ Tracy Skousen ◇ Marcus Nicolls

PORTFOLIO / PENGUIN

Portfolio / Penguin
An imprint of Penguin Random House LLC
375 Hudson Street
New York, New York 10014

ISBN 9781591847878 (hardcover)
ISBN 9780698194359 (ebook)

Printed in the United States of America
10 9 8 7 6 5 4 3 2 1

Set in Minion Pro

We dedicate this book
to the Partners In Leadership team.
Each of you inspires us, exemplifies these Accountability Traits,
and causes ripples of excellence, achievement, and service throughout the world.
The world is a better place because of your contributions.

Contents

TAKE THE *FIX IT* ASSESSMENT

LEARN ABOUT THE ACCOUNTABILITY TRAITS

PUT THE ACCOUNTABILITY TRAITS INTO ACTION

CONTENTS

CONTENTS

Foreword

Whether you are leading a team, a project, or a company, the ability to deliver results is what it's all about. I faced this reality early on in my career.

I became a CEO in my thirties. I knew I didn't have all the skills I needed to lead a global organization in trouble, especially one experiencing an upheaval in both the regulatory and competitive landscape. Yet the title on my business card, "President and CEO," made it unlikely that I would get much-needed feedback and coaching from those around me. Lucky for me, I met Tom Smith and Roger Connors at Partners In Leadership and learned about the power of a culture built on open and honest feedback. They gave me a framework for thinking about how to move people, to SEE IT, OWN IT, SOLVE IT, and DO IT—what they call The Steps To Accountability.

Partners In Leadership has nearly thirty years of experience teaching individuals, teams, and organizations worldwide how to effectively engage and lead others to deliver exceptional results. Doing this is *much* harder than it sounds.

Like me, you have likely experienced a business culture that is satisfied with a compliant "tell-me-what-to-do" level of engagement from employees, rather than a culture that looks to truly engage its employees' hearts and minds and unleash individual and team capability. In those environments, accountability is something that happens to you when things go wrong. And how wrong minded that is! Getting accountability right makes all the difference in the world and is the key to unlocking individual talent and potential.

Throughout my career, I've looked to mentors, role models, and successful leaders to build a set of skills that I could add to my own management tool kit. Making a difference matters . . . and we need more people in business, politics, and service who know how to do it. It begins and ends with people. People who believe in the purpose of the enterprise. People who care about the quality of their work. People who want to deliver the promised result. Building a culture in which people take accountability to deliver on its promises is hard work and can be difficult to accomplish. Only when every person is held accountable to themselves, their peers, and their shared possibility can the impossible become possible.

My personal success with the *Fix It* ideology has led me to take its concepts and models everywhere I go: at home, at work, and in the community. I've repeatedly used this accountability framework to create a Culture of Accountability while running a variety of businesses. I recommend Partners In Leadership's practices to all the CEOs I coach through my consulting business. And I recommend Roger and Tom and their team to any organization that wants to accomplish great things and make a difference in the world.

So do you know how to create accountability for results at every level? Are you skilled in creating a common purpose—describing *WHY* the results matter? Have you built the credibility and the capability to both *give* and *receive* honest feedback so that open and candid conversations keep the organization on track? If you want to get accountability right and build a track record of vibrant, powerful results, read *Fix It: Getting Accountability Right*.

In *Fix It* you will find that the authors have interviewed more than 120 successful executives and conducted more than three years of specific research into workplace accountability practices. It's a one-of-a-kind, page-by-page tool kit that will load you up with what you need to build a Culture of Accountability that delivers exceptional results. You don't want to miss it!

Ginger Graham
Innovative CEO; Harvard Faculty in Entrepreneurship

About This Book

Accountability in business is in crisis today. Our extensive study confirms what many suspect: leaders and managers are not getting accountability right. And that is translating into a big negative impact on desired business results. Other recent studies have shown that there is a massive decline in employee engagement, reflecting an overall lack of commitment on the part of both employees and employers. Our work in the field of workplace accountability for nearly three decades connects the dots between this dearth of employee engagement and the misfire on workplace accountability.

Our message is simple: fixing accountability is key to business success and is the best solution for addressing problems with employee engagement.

As you begin reading *Fix It*, you will immediately discover that it's unlike any book you've ever read. Built on the foundation of our extensive Workplace Accountability Study of more than forty thousand working professionals, the chapters walk you through the 16 Accountability Traits that the most successful individuals, teams, and companies practice every day, traits that have emerged in our work with millions of people worldwide.

This book is designed to do exactly what its title implies: to help you *fix it*: fix accountability, fix ownership, and fix engagement. The read is fast, the chapters targeted and short, the information concrete and usable. Part 1 of the book begins with an assessment that helps you determine where you need to *fix it*. Part 2 introduces you to the 16 Accountability Traits and the results of the Workplace

Accountability Study. Part 3 provides practical, proven solutions to *fix it* for yourself, your team, or your entire organization.

We gleaned the 240 practices in part 3, along with other important insights, from 120 executives who are successful in their own fields:

Gene Abernethy, Chief Human Resources Officer

Otto Aichinger, Strategic Partnership Manager

Jim Arnold, Senior VP

Ian Baines, CEO

Chris Baldwin, President

Mary Bartlett, COO

Bill Becker, COO

Lois Bentler-Lampe, Chief Nursing Officer and VP of Clinical Operations

Jared Bentley, Senior Director of Global Product Management

Boyd Blake, Senior Director, Information Technology

David Bonnette, CEO

Debbie Bowles, General Manager

Lance Boynton, COO and Global Director of Operations

Chris Brickman, CEO

Tony Bridwell, CPO

Matt Broder, VP of Corporate Communications

Jack Butorac, Chairman and CEO

Mario Cajati, Managing Director of Business Development

Lisa Carron, District Manager

David Chapin, CEO

Sheree Chiang, Senior VP of Human Resources

Chris Christensen, President

Matthew Clark, Chief of Police

Carl Coburn, CEO

Loressa Cole, Chief Nursing Officer

Laura Coleman, President

Tom Cromwell, Group President

John Cuomo, General Manager

Lance Davis, CFO

Tom Day, Group VP

Mike Dufresne, Regional VP

Gabriele Eaton, Director of Global Talent Management and Organizational Development

Hugh Ekberg, President

David Ellis, VP of Investigations

Kevin V. Farrow, VP

Stuart Fetzer, CEO

Jamey Fitzpatrick, CEO

Tim Frawley, Manager

Larry Gelwix, CEO

Signe Godfrey, President

Mike Gummeson, President and CEO

Sandi Guy, Partner

Pete Hammett, Managing Director of Talent

Janee Harteau, Chief of Police

Jon Horn, Chief Human Resources Officer

Peter Hotz, Industry Adviser

Steve Jeffrey, VP of Corporate Services

Dave Jennings, Performance Psychologist

Casey Jones, President

Paul C. Kelly, President and CEO

Chuck Knutson, Founder and Partner

Laura Kohler, Senior VP of Human Resources

Karen Korytowski, General Manager of Lean Operations

Mark Landes, Global Director of IT

Nathan Leaman, Human Resources Leader

Brad Lee, President and CEO

Darren Lee, Executive VP

Dr. Bernadette Loftus, Executive Medical Director

Terri Longbella, Senior Director of Worldwide Human Resources

Martin Lowery, President

Jesse Marshall, VP

Robert Martinez, Sales Manager

Hany Massarany, CEO

Sandra Massey, Chancellor

Kim McEachron, CPO

Brad McKain, Refining GM

Mark McNeil, President

Denis Meade, Director of Training and Development

Lisa Miller, VP of Human Resources

Sherry Moore, Human Resources Director

Cinny Murray, President

Mark Neave, Owner

Mike Niblock, Fire Chief

Steven Nickel, VP

Joe Nilson, Director of Business Development

Joseph O'Callahan, Manager of Organizational Development

Doug Omichinski, Project Manager

Ron Pace, Group President

Alan Padlock, Plant Controller

Brad Pelo, Cofounder and CEO

Tim Peoples, Plant Director

Elizabeth Pimper, Director of Learning

Richard Pliler, EVP

Mark Polking, Director of Tax and Internal Audit

Tami Polmanteer, Chief Human Resources Officer

Kim Popovits, CEO

Adam Porter, Senior Director of Human Resources

Suzanne Pottinger, VP of Employee Experience

Johnny Priest, Division President

Nicole Reilly, Director of Talent Management

Cliff Reyle, Chief Human Resources Officer and CIO

Joe Rigby, Chairman, CEO, and President

Tim Robinson, CMO and Managing Director

Craig Roper, SVP and Chief Deposit Officer

Christina Sarabia, Manager of Organizational Development

Jeff Schmitz, EVP

Jason Schubert, Senior Manager

Darryl Shiroma, Assistant VP

Tom Simon, Senior VP of Talent Management

Marty Smuin, CEO

Carlyn Solomon, COO

Krista Stafford, VP of Human Resources

Bryon Stephens, President and COO

Matt Stevens, VP of Sales and Marketing

Rachael Stiles, Organizational Development Consultant

Daniel Swartz, Director of Human Resources

Dave Szczupak, EVP

Alan Taylor, CFO

Elaine Thibodeau, VP of Strategy and Deployment

Kevin Thissen, Design Engineer Manager

Erin Trenbeath-Murray, CEO

Kelli Valade, COO

Dave Valentine, Performance and Development Manager

Barbara Van Dine, Director of Talent Development and Learning

Denise Van Tassell, Training and Talent Development Manager

James Vera, Director of Learning and Development

Don Vinci, Senior VP of Human Resources and Chief Diversity Officer

Paulette Wage, Regional Human Resources Manager

Vincent Weafer, VP

Tiffany Zakszeski, Director of Human Resources

The five authors of this book bring one hundred-plus years of combined Accountability Training and Cultural Transformation training and consulting experience to this book. Their years of teaching and learning, combined with the experiences of these 120 successful executives, have enabled us to assemble a more complete repository of practical ideas for promoting greater positive accountability than you can find anywhere else.

We invite you to take a deep dive into using accountability to get better traction, improve results, and *fix it*!

> —Roger Connors, Tom Smith,
> Craig Hickman, Tracy Skousen,
> and Marcus Nicolls

Introduction

You can imagine that there was a bit of a debate over the title *Fix It.* It's bold, perhaps even a bit assuming. "Fix it" implies that there is something wrong—really wrong—that needs to be addressed. The title is an imperative, one we feel very strongly about, and suggests that something needs to happen now.

In fact, based on our collective one hundred-plus years of experience with thousands of clients, our extensive consulting and coaching experience with managers and leaders in almost every type of company, and our own industry-first Workplace Accountability Study with data from more than forty thousand respondents, we feel confident in suggesting that there is an issue affecting you, your team, and, most likely, your entire organization that you need to fix, and that you need to fix now. It's an issue that stands in the way of your ability to get the real business results that you need to achieve now.

Just what is it that needs to be fixed in organizations today? The readers of our first book, *The Oz Principle,* will know the answer to this question: the way we do accountability. And that includes the way we do it at every level: personally, in our teams, and throughout the organization.

With so much real-world experience under our belts coaching the top business leaders in the world, and working with both the best (and the worst) workplaces around the globe, we remain convinced that accountability is broken and must be fixed in order for people, teams, and organizations to get the results they want. It's a problem that's getting worse in almost every society around the globe. And those societal accountability ills are now bleeding over and bleeding out into the business environment faster than ever before. We started writing about this topic more than twenty-five years ago, and today it is even more relevant. In our view, fixing accountability will be the low-hanging fruit for optimizing performance in business for at least the next decade.

Accountability Is Not Working

When David Bonnette became CEO of Big Machines, he immediately recognized that the organization had problems. Founded ten years earlier, the $32 million cloud-based company had become the market leader in automated configuration, pricing, and quoting (CPQ), to accelerate the conversion of sales opportunities into revenue. But the organization's two hundred people struggled to achieve results, build alignment around priorities, and develop scalable, repeatable processes. Bonnette, a former Oracle executive, had to act quickly—two private equity firms had just recapitalized Big Machines and the clock was ticking. Not only did Bonnette have to preserve the company's eroding market leadership, he had to maximize the company's growth while driving profitability to new heights.

A year after starting as CEO, Bonnette brought in our company, Partners In Leadership (PIL), to help. PIL found that the people at Big Machines were stuck, engaging in victim or blame-game thinking, where the rampant finger-pointing and excuse making made it impossible for them to deliver the results they needed. Drawing upon our model for creating greater accountability for results, Bonnette and his senior team began focusing on how they needed to change—how they needed to think, act, and lead differently to achieve the needed engagement, ownership, and follow-through at every level of the organization.

Their work to create a Culture of Accountability had significant impact. In just three years, the company posted remarkable results: revenues grew by more than 100 percent with profitability increasing more than 250 percent. In November 2013, Big Machines was acquired by Oracle for approximately six times revenue and four times the private equity investment—and a year earlier than expected. Reflecting on the extraordinary turnaround in the spring of 2014, Bonnette, now a serial CEO for Vista Equity Partners, said, referring to the accountability model we present in this book, "I will re-create this same experience everywhere I go. It's that powerful!"

Like David Bonnette, we all seem to know there's a problem, but have been calling it by different names for years: empowerment, trust, execution, personality styles, conversations, habits, etc. All of these have their roots in how accountability is addressed, but few are nailing the real problem: fixing accountability.

As a result, people at every level of their organizations are trying to figure out how to *fix it*: shop supervisors, frontline managers, team members, C-suite executives—everyone. The price paid for getting accountability wrong is huge. Everything becomes an "at risk" endeavor:

- Project goals and objectives
- Execution on strategic initiatives
- Accomplishment of important business results
- Generating creation and innovation
- Employee engagement
- Alignment to key systems and processes
- Individual and team morale

Members of the rising workforce (including millennials) are not taking to traditional management philosophies and methods, and almost every possible indicator is showing that, in general, they don't like the way they are being managed. A Zogby poll reveals the following:

- 25 percent of American workers described their workplace as a dictatorship.
- Barely half of those surveyed said their boss treated subordinates well.
- Only 51 percent said their coworkers often felt motivated or were mostly motivated at work.

To add fuel to the fire, the *State of the American Workplace* report, by Gallup, suggests that nearly 70 percent of American workers are disengaged from their jobs. In other words, only three out of ten workers can be characterized as engaged, or mostly engaged, in the work that they do. Thirty percent! Globally, that number drops to a dismal 13 percent.

Our own three-year Workplace Accountability Study is the most comprehensive of its kind ever conducted, the results of which will be revealed for the first time in this book. It shows that this global accountability problem manifests itself in many dimensions. Sixteen, in fact. The 16 Accountability Traits, as you will come to know them, are where the issues show up the most, and are where there is the greatest opportunity to attack the problem and *fix it*.

You'll notice we said "attack." That's a strong word, but the right one, because complacency abounds. People and organizations today have come to accept the problems that arise in these sixteen areas as "just the way things are in organizations today," and then live with all the grief and performance obstacles they bring, both personally and at the organizational level. Throwing up their arms in frustration, people develop clever work-arounds to get by, thinking these hoped-for fixes are good enough to minimize the crippling impact the real problems impose. The challenge is that these work-arounds often fool everyone into believing they've solved the issues, only to find the same problems coming back again and again.

More Than 120 Top-Level Executives Are Here to Help You *Fix It*!

Now, in *Fix It,* the official sequel to *The Oz Principle,* we will not only provide you with an understanding of what the 16 Accountability Traits are but offer real, practical advice on how to *fix it* for good. On the pages ahead, we've combined our collective experiences as field practitioners over the last thirty years, along with more than 240 notable practices from 120 high-level executives who deal with challenges and obstacles just like you, and who have found real, useful ways to solve problems, *fix it,* and get traction toward real results. Because these proven, boots-on-the-ground "trade secrets" are offered here for the first time, you will come to find this book a vibrant and vital ready reference that you can use time and again to get ideas and suggestions about *fixing it* and getting accountability for results back on track. And even greater news is that we are currently offering an online resource at www.fixit-book.com where you can contribute your own favorite practices to *Fix It*'s original 240. Add your own and while there check out what other fellow readers and executives have contributed to the growing database.

And if you're not an executive yet, you will discover this book equally helpful as you learn how to master the 16 Accountability

Traits and put them to work for you in everything you do. The foundation you are about to receive will not only help you now but prove immensely valuable as you move up to managing your own team, or even someday becoming the CEO of your organization.

In *Fix It,* we are talking about building a vibrant Culture of Accountability that will likely far surpass any working environments you have ever experienced and that will rival the very best teams you have ever enjoyed. Is *"fix it"* too strong a message? Only if you want to keep spending precious time, money, resources, and emotional energy on the things that don't produce real results.

When you get accountability wrong, don't expect anything else to go right in your own job, on your team, or in the organization as a whole. Treating only the symptoms of dysfunction that stem from poor accountability practices will cause you to lose time and miss opportunities to get real traction toward the results you want.

You must fix accountability first, before anything else.

When you get accountability right, everything else will go right as you execute, overcome obstacles, and work to get results.

The Steps To Accountability

We probably should stop here for a moment. You may have been saying to yourself: "This sounds right, but when I think about accountability, I think about people imposing consequences when things go wrong—who needs more of that?"

Our answer: no one!

In our previous books, we describe this "wrong definition of accountability" that operates in organizations today as one that almost always backfires, moving you away from solving real issues and instead wasting time and energy focusing on who's to blame. When accountability is used as a club for beating people over the head with when things go wrong, solutions are easily lost, teams fracture, and members scramble for the safety of defensiveness and self-preservation.

So where does this ineffective view of accountability come from? Try the dictionary. Check this out: "subject to having to report, explain or justify; being responsible; answerable." The accountability described here is something that happens to you when things go wrong. And when they go really wrong, watch out, because the only reasonable response is to stop, drop, and roll, then duck and cover, because anyone who can be made answerable will feel the avalanche of consequences come down all around them. No wonder we're not getting it right in business today.

In our first book, *The Oz Principle: Getting Results Through Individual and Organizational Accountability,* we presented readers with a new view of accountability, one that has become even more relevant than when we originally wrote the book more than twenty years ago.

This new accountability model is captured in the Steps To Accountability Chart. If you are familiar with this chart, then bear with us for a moment. If it's your first time, prepare yourself to become acquainted with a principle that can transform results wherever you go—in business, in your personal life, wherever.

You will note that a line divides the chart in half. Above The Line are the Steps To Accountability—to See It, Own It, Solve It, and Do It. Here, Above The Line, people take accountability for the circumstances they face and ask the question "What else can I do?" Below The Line is where the blame game or victim cycle occurs. Down here is where the traditional dictionary definition of accountability seems to drive people. Nothing good happens Below The

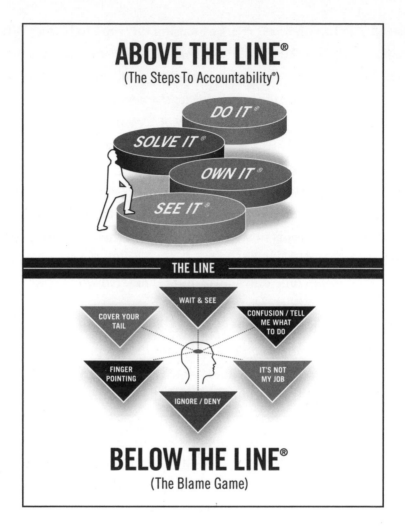

Line, except perhaps a bit of venting. Other than that, when we are Below The Line, we are stuck, feeling like the obstacles that stop us are outside our control and making us victims of our circumstances. When that happens, everyone can see it. We look and feel powerless to change our circumstances. We aren't considered for the best promotions, the best teams, and/or the best performance reviews and pay raises.

It's not wrong to go Below The Line; it's just not effective. It's a natural human reaction to drop Below The Line when we face bad news and difficult obstacles that are seemingly outside our control. But rising Above The Line allows us to attack the problem and get the results we are looking for.

The more time you spend Above The Line, the more effective you, your team, and your entire organization will be.

With this as background, we offer a new definition of accountability, a more positive and powerful one that is: "Accountability is a personal choice to rise above one's circumstances and demonstrate the ownership necessary for achieving Key Results: See It, Own It, Solve It, and Do It." Imagine the impact on someone's personal effectiveness, on the team, and on the entire organization when people adopt this approach to getting things done—truly transformative!

The 16 Accountability Traits

After introducing the four Steps To Accountability in *The Oz Principle* (See It, Own It, Solve It, and Do It), we studied the best practices that individuals, teams, and organizations exhibited when they successfully took those steps. We also studied the common problems organizations and leaders face in creating a Culture of Accountability. In industries ranging from nuclear power to banking to medical devices, every project started with an assessment, including the following questions:

- What's not working in the organization/team today?
- What is the reality we most need to acknowledge as an organization/team?

- What are we pretending not to know?
- What is getting in the way of making progress as an organization/team?

These assessments included online responses, sampling a large population of the organization, as well as directed one-on-one, in-person interviews and focus groups, which included people at all levels of the organization, from the C-suite to frontline workers. Literally, hundreds of these interviews were conducted and thousands of people surveyed. The result: a list of common organizational and team ailments began emerging—pervasive problems in the culture of the organization that were getting in the way of making progress.

The similarity in responses from one organization to the next was astounding and eye-opening. While there were specific similarities within industry groupings, there were also similarities across industries. Again and again we would see common themes emerge.

In the end, the message was clear: there is a certain set of traits that people, teams, and organizations don't do well when struggling to develop a Culture of Accountability. Similarly, there are traits, Accountability Traits, that they do practice well when high levels of positive accountability—the kind of accountability we focus on in this book—are present. These 16 Accountability Traits are presented in the chart opposite, and as you focus your efforts to *fix* them, you will experience the positive power of greater personal and organizational accountability for results.

The 16 Accountability Traits—Above The Line

For more than two decades, millions of people have worked with these 16 Accountability Traits, experiencing better results as individuals, in their teams, and in their organizations. Doing so

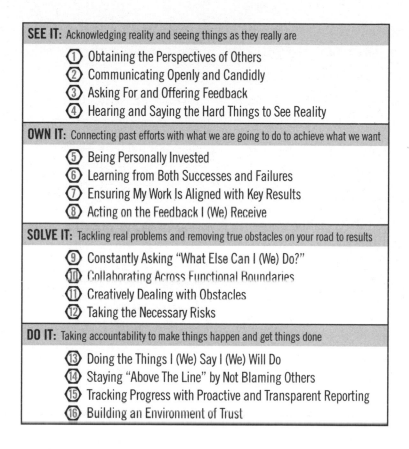

SEE IT: Acknowledging reality and seeing things as they really are
1. Obtaining the Perspectives of Others
2. Communicating Openly and Candidly
3. Asking For and Offering Feedback
4. Hearing and Saying the Hard Things to See Reality

OWN IT: Connecting past efforts with what we are going to do to achieve what we want
5. Being Personally Invested
6. Learning from Both Successes and Failures
7. Ensuring My Work Is Aligned with Key Results
8. Acting on the Feedback I (We) Receive

SOLVE IT: Tackling real problems and removing true obstacles on your road to results
9. Constantly Asking "What Else Can I (We) Do?"
10. Collaborating Across Functional Boundaries
11. Creatively Dealing with Obstacles
12. Taking the Necessary Risks

DO IT: Taking accountability to make things happen and get things done
13. Doing the Things I (We) Say I (We) Will Do
14. Staying "Above The Line" by Not Blaming Others
15. Tracking Progress with Proactive and Transparent Reporting
16. Building an Environment of Trust

guarantees increased profits, better corporate cultures of vigorous problem solving, and hitting targets.

The Workplace Accountability Study

As alluded to earlier, *Fix It* presents the never before published Workplace Accountability Study conducted by our Accountability Training and consulting company, Partners In Leadership. With more than forty thousand respondents, the three-year study involved hundreds of organizations from a wide variety of industries and job titles. Here's a sample of the titles of people who participated in the study:

Account Executive	Head Coach
Battalion Chief	Hotel Manager
Cardiology Clinic Director	IT Director
CEO, COO, CFO, C-suite	Juvenile Probation Officer
Children's Research Manager	Lead Pastor
Convention Services Director	Operational Risk Manager
Criminal Justice Instructor	Plant Manager
Digital / Social Media Manager	President
Dining Room Manager	Professor
Engineering Supervisor	Risk Manager
Events Coordinator	Senior Vice President of Human Resources
Executive Dean of Students	Statistician
Forensic Program Supervisor	
General Plant Manager	Strategic Marketing Director
Global Talent Leader	Talent Development Manager
	Workforce Specialist

The study data was collected via live online polls during webinars hosted by Partners In Leadership. The content of the webinar polls primarily focused on personal and organizational accountability and the impact these principles have on the workplace. The respondents were presented with an understanding of the context of the questions at hand and then asked for their opinions via multiple choice, true/false, and ranking-type questions.

The purpose of our study was to uncover current practices and attitudes about accountability in the workplace and how those practices affect the ability of individuals, teams, and organizations to get results. The study uncovered trends, challenges, and opportunities regarding workplace accountability in a variety of contexts and situations.

As you will come to see, the data reveals important themes

about what is working and not working today with accountability. The conclusions and ideas in *Fix It* are fully supported by the study results, which help to illuminate the opportunities for individuals, teams, and organizations to get accountability right.

How to Read This Book

We designed *Fix It* to get you quickly into the solutions you need for your own daily work, for your work as a team leader, or for the entire organization. While this book can be read cover to cover, it is designed to offer you more flexibility than that. You can make this a customizable read based on your current role and needs, focusing on some chapters and skipping others. This approach also allows you to come back throughout your career and use the book as a ready reference when your role and circumstances change.

Let's take "Adriana," for example, a senior executive in her company who has decided to read this book. Before she jumps into reading about the Accountability Traits, she needs to decide how she wants to read it. That's right—*how* she wants to read it. Does she want to read it to improve herself, her team, or her organization as a whole? After thinking for a moment, she decides that she wants to focus on herself to see what she can learn that will help her in her own daily work, though she admits, "I'll probably come back and go through this another time on behalf of my team."

Knowing that she is initially reading for herself, she will choose Path A when given that option:

PATH **A**: fix it for **Myself**

PATH **B**: fix it on **My Team**

PATH **C**: fix it in **My Organization**

After choosing her path (A, B, or C) to determine how she will read this book, Adriana will follow a simple three-part process:

PART 1: First, Adriana will take a three-minute *Fix It* Assessment that will help her determine areas that are most critical to her (because she chose to follow Path A and is reading for her own personal development). The assessment will help her identify which of the 16 Accountability Traits she does well, doesn't do well, or must fix immediately—which she will put in her Fix It Bucket. Her *Fix It* Bucket List will then provide the guidance she needs for what she should read, and what she can skip, in part 2. Not surprisingly, she is a little excited about the idea that she doesn't have to read the whole book to get the value she's looking for, just the parts that the *Fix It* Assessment shows will be most useful to her.

PART 2: Here, Adriana will learn about the Accountability Traits that her *Fix It* Assessment in part 1 said she needs to focus on the most. At the conclusion of each Accountability Trait, she will then be directed to specific solutions on how to *fix it,* as presented in part 3, based on the path she has chosen. (In her case, Path A, as she is reading for herself.) Adriana realizes that she could read about every Accountability Trait right now if she wanted to. However, she's still stoked about focusing on just a few!

PART 3: Adriana's eyes open wide when she realizes that this part of the book offers specific solutions she can implement to *fix* those Accountability Traits in her Fix It Bucket—incredible solutions and proven ideas from 120 living, breathing successful executives across the globe who agreed to be interviewed exclusively for this book. These are executive-level men and women who were willing to share what they are doing now, today, and what they have seen others do throughout their distinguished careers, things that really work! These notable tips, secrets, and specific practices are like *fix it* gold nuggets just waiting for our fictional Adriana, and the real you, to pick up and put into practice.

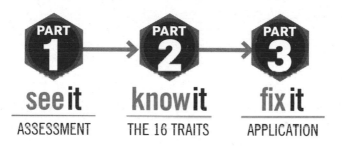

By taking the steps Adriana has taken, you will follow a path through the book that is customized to your current needs and interests. Later, you can return and take a different path to discover solutions for your team or organization.

And remember, if you want to read this book in the conventional cover-to-cover way, you can. Just skip the assessment in part 1 and dig right into parts 2 and 3, reading as you ordinarily would.

Pick Your Path

Let's get started by picking the path you want to take:

Path A: Reading it for yourself
Path B: Reading it with your team in mind
Path C: Reading it with your organization in mind

The path you select will determine how you fill out the assessment and will guide you toward which practices you will read about in part 3. As you decide which path to take, ask yourself the following:

- Where do I most need to focus to ensure results?
- What's keeping me up at night that needs to be addressed?
- What is my primary responsibility today (my individual performance, my team, or my organization)?

Whether you are a member of a team that has to turn in big deliverables, a team leader working to guide a team toward certain objectives, a leader of an organization that has specific results to achieve, or an individual contributor with clear objectives to execute, the right path in *Fix It* will provide practical and tested ideas that you can implement right away.

Once you've picked your path, we recommend checking the box below as a visual reminder.

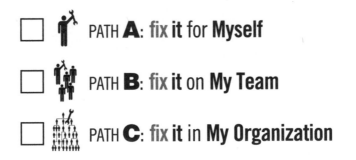

☐ 👤 PATH **A**: fix it for **Myself**

☐ 👥 PATH **B**: fix it on **My Team**

☐ 👪 PATH **C**: fix it in **My Organization**

The next step is to move to part 1 and take the quick *Fix It* Assessment, which will guide you in your journey to *fix it*.

see it

TAKE THE *FIX IT* ASSESSMENT

Take the *Fix It* Assessment

Take the three-minute *Fix It* Assessment for the path you've chosen by recording the trait number below in one of the three buckets on the opposite page that best fits the bucket description.

The fix it Assessment	
My path:　☐ 👤 Self　☐ 👥 Team　☐ 👥👥 Organization	

SEE IT	Obtaining the Perspectives of Others	①
	Communicating Openly and Candidly	②
	Asking For and Offering Feedback	③
	Hearing and Saying the Hard Things to See Reality	④
OWN IT	Being Personally Invested	⑤
	Learning from Both Successes and Failures	⑥
	Ensuring Our Work Is Aligned with Key Results	⑦
	Acting on the Feedback We Receive	⑧
SOLVE IT	Constantly Asking "What Else Can We Do?"	⑨
	Collaborating Across Functional Boundaries	⑩
	Creatively Dealing with Obstacles	⑪
	Taking the Necessary Risks	⑫
DO IT	Doing the Things We Say We Will Do	⑬
	Staying "Above The Line" by Not Blaming Others	⑭
	Tracking Progress with Proactive and Transparent Reporting	⑮
	Building an Environment of Trust	⑯

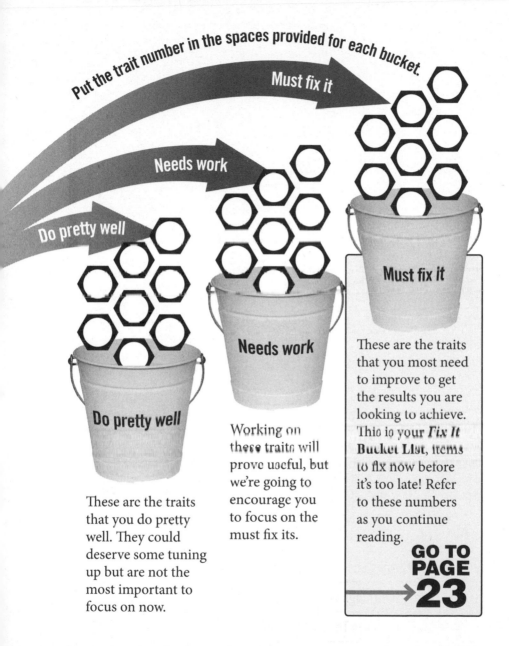

Put the trait number in the spaces provided for each bucket.

Must fix it

Needs work

Do pretty well

Do pretty well

These are the traits that you do pretty well. They could deserve some tuning up but are not the most important to focus on now.

Needs work

Working on these traits will prove useful, but we're going to encourage you to focus on the must fix its.

Must fix it

These are the traits that you most need to improve to get the results you are looking to achieve. This is your *Fix It Bucket List*, items to fix now before it's too late! Refer to these numbers as you continue reading.

GO TO PAGE →23

NOTE: For those of you who may want to come back and read with your focus on a different path, you will find blank *Fix It As-sessments* at the back of the book.

knowit

LEARN ABOUT THE ACCOUNTABILITY TRAITS

Learn About the Accountability Traits

Part 2 is all about the Accountability Traits—what we have learned from our vast experience working with literally thousands of executives over the last twenty-five years, and what we think you would want to know about each trait.

Here's how to read part 2. First, the numbers on your *Fix It* Bucket List from the assessment on page 19 refer to the Accountability Traits that you identified as the *fix it* targets that will most help you get the results you need now. Here, in part 2, you will use your *Fix It* Bucket List to dive into the traits you want to read about. At the end of each trait, you will be directed to the *fix it* solutions that pertain to it in part 3. This format gives you a focused, targeted approach to getting the information you are most interested in right now.

So Adriana, our fictional reader, would put a checkmark on the following page next to each of the trait numbers from her *Fix It* Bucket List (see the page you just came from), which will tell her exactly which pages she should turn to in order to learn about the traits she's interested in. Consider this page your very own Accountability Trait Table of Contents. Pretty cool, don't you think?

At the end of each Accountability Trait section you will be directed to the page in part 3 with the appropriate *fix it* solutions for the path you are on: yourself (A), the team (B), or your organization (C).

Okay, enough explanation, go ahead and choose your first trait and let's get started!

For your reference, you can check the box by the Traits in your *Fix It* Bucket List (from page 19).

			GO TO PAGE
SEE IT	☐ ①	Obtaining the Perspectives of Others	**24**
	☐ ②	Communicating Openly and Candidly	**32**
	☐ ③	Asking for and Offering Feedback	**41**
	☐ ④	Hearing and Saying the Hard Things to See Reality	**49**
OWN IT	☐ ⑤	Being Personally Invested	**57**
	☐ ⑥	Learning from Both Successes and Failures	**65**
	☐ ⑦	Ensuring My Work Is Aligned with Key Results	**72**
	☐ ⑧	Acting on the Feedback I (we) Receive	**80**
SOLVE IT	☐ ⑨	Constantly Asking "What Else Can I (we) Do?"	**88**
	☐ ⑩	Collaborating Across Functional Boundaries	**96**
	☐ ⑪	Creatively Dealing with Obstacles	**105**
	☐ ⑫	Taking the Necessary Risks	**115**
DO IT	☐ ⑬	Doing the Things I (we) Say I (we) Will Do	**123**
	☐ ⑭	Staying "Above The Line" by Not Blaming Others	**131**
	☐ ⑮	Tracking Progress with Proactive and Transparent Reporting	**139**
	☐ ⑯	Building an Environment of Trust	**149**

fix it BUCKET LIST   Must fix it

① ACCOUNTABILITY TRAIT 1
Obtaining the Perspectives of Others

the need to fix it

Is this trait a **clear strength** of people in your organization?

NO **77%**

YES **23%**

Is this trait a **clear strength** in team leaders?

NO **62%**

YES **38%**

Source: Partners In Leadership **Workplace Accountability Study**

The Workplace Accountability Study reveals a startling statistic: most of us get a failing grade when it comes to taking the See It step and finding out what people are really thinking. Uncorrected, this inability to obtain perspective could be a fatal flaw in your efforts to stay Above The Line and take advantage of the power of personal accountability.

Perhaps you've heard the centuries-old story that is said to have originated in India called "The Blind Men and the Elephant." There are many variations, but in the United States John Godfrey Saxe popularized the story in a poem back in the 1800s.

As it goes, six blind men with no knowledge of an elephant find themselves attempting to describe one. Privy to only one piece of the animal, the first blind man feels the elephant's broad and sturdy side, and believes it to be like a wall. The second gets hold of the tusk and instantly thinks it's a spear. The third is no doubt a bit uneasy holding a squirming trunk, thinking it to be a giant snake. The fourth feels the knee and pronounces the animal to be like a tree. The fifth strokes the large flat ear, calling it a fan. Finally, the sixth blind man gets hold of the tough cordlike tail and argues that the animal is none of the above—it's much more like a rope. The blind men are to be commended; each did his job of describing the animal based on his own experience and the limited information he had. The problem, however, is obvious: we all operate on limited information based on where we stand relative to the challenges we face. As a result, we rarely see the whole picture, relying instead on just our own bias and restricted point of view.

Going back to the Workplace Accountability Study, three out of four respondents said that people in their organizations didn't obtain the perspectives of others well enough for it to be considered any kind of a real advantage. Ouch! Clearly, it's hard to see the whole elephant when you're not even looking.

You can greatly enhance your own ability to take the first step Above The Line and See It if you make it a practice to obtain the various, and often conflicting, perspectives of others.

Let People Know You Want It

Marty and Rick Lagina, brothers and owners of Oak Island Tours, both star in the reality-based television show *The Curse of Oak Island*. They're in the business of seeking buried treasure on an island in the North Atlantic known to have been frequented by pirates and rumored to contain hoards of buried treasure. The island has actually been the focus of treasure hunters for more than two hundred years. In one episode the brothers are engaged in a debate about whether to continue digging in a particular area. Rick wants to stay on it, but Marty wants to move to a different spot on the island that he just knows is going to be more productive (this is a business, after all). They disagree, even argue. Marty finally becomes convinced to go with his brother's plan and then says, "When I was young and I was certain about something, I was sure I was correct. Now that I am older, I realize I could be wrong, and you have to listen to other people around the table. . . . Okay, I'm going to listen."

Here's the big takeaway: obtaining the perspectives of others can't be an option; it's an operational necessity. The annals of history, in every discipline from science to business to government to sports, are filled with stories—incredibly disappointing stories—of people who should have obtained the perspectives of others but did not. The result of that lack of perspective can be devastating.

We were recently chatting with the president of a midlevel company whose desk was perpetually drowning in paper. When we asked how effective he was at obtaining the perspectives of others, he laughed and quipped, "No real leader has OTP [obtaining the perspective] time." Many of the leaders we work with often feel the same way. Our reaction: if you're too busy to walk the hallways or plant floor to chat with your people, too busy to let people know you want to know, then you're doing something wrong. This is about letting others know that you value and care about them. That's the first and most important step in ensuring you're getting valuable perspectives.

Take It to the Next Level

Given that *only* 23 percent of our study respondents viewed obtaining perspective as a "clear strength" within their organizations, let's take the following brief quiz to identify how you're doing with obtaining perspective personally. We believe it will help you see that, regardless of how well you're doing now with this, you can reach an even higher level of perspective-gathering efficiency. Everyone can do this better. Apply this quiz to your current level by answering these questions for yourself, your team, or your entire organization. Select the response that best describes your answer (4 = always, 3 = very often, 2 = seldom, 1 = never):

_____ 1. You ask Find Out questions that inform your view of the world with information that you would otherwise not obtain.

_____ 2. You seek the views and opinions of those who don't agree with you.

_____ 3. You build and/or utilize processes and mechanisms that ensure a regular dose of what people think, so that it comes automatically and unprompted.

_____ 4. You effectively use digital means to speed up and broaden the process of getting input and testing opinions.

_____ 5. You build relationships with people and organizations that provide a perspective that you would otherwise not have.

_____ 6. You regularly remind others to ask for input before decisions are made.

_____ 7. You reach out of your normal circle of influence to get opinions and perspectives from people you would not ordinarily consult, people who really know their stuff.

_____ Total

If you scored a 28, you're doing an excellent job of getting input. In view of the fact that everyone is used to you asking for it, you might consider sampling the people you work with to complete this assessment about you, just to see what _they_ think.

A score between 21 and 27 means you are pretty good at reaching out, but getting better at it could pay sizable dividends.

Between 14 and 20 indicates a great opportunity for you to make progress in this area.

Anything below 14 reveals that you most likely work by yourself on projects in dimly lit, even isolated closets.

Obtaining the views, opinions, and input of others provides a steady current of ideas and perspectives that can help you understand problems and shape solutions in new and more effective ways. Can you think of a time in recent weeks when you sought input, gained a new perspective, and used that new view to make a real impact on what you were attempting to do? If you are good at this Accountability Trait, your answer would be yes. If you answered no, then you should work on fixing this trait for better results.

Be Humble

Though you won't find humility on the list of key core competencies of most organizations or leadership development programs, a certain degree of humility is critical to getting accountability right. Humility is a deep, authentic acknowledgment that we can't do it alone, that we should be mindful of the perspectives others bring, and that we can be better and do more with input from others. The notion of humility is emerging in business literature of all types: from *Harvard Business Review* to *Fast Company*. Many are beginning to recognize the need to balance great talent with great character—an essential combination for lasting success.

In our combined experience, we have developed the view that humility is on the list of the most essential leadership attributes because it strengthens one's ability to learn. To be humble means to be teachable. By definition, the very nature of leadership brings opportunity to "go where no one has gone before," to blaze new trails, cut new ground, and try new things. Climbing a steep learning curve quickly requires being willing to risk learning in front of others, hopefully with some grace, the very essence of leadership.

True humility is not just about admitting you can't solve, resolve, or fix every problem on your own. Rather, humility promotes a very personal and real recognition that the experiences and opinions of others matter, and that they can make a difference in your success.

One key: we have found that great leaders who possess this "leadership humility" demonstrate it by asking a lot of relevant questions, questions meant to help them hear what they suspect they are not hearing. That example of asking more probing and relevant questions can go a long way toward influencing others for the good. In fact, our Workplace Study shows that a vast 84 percent cited "the example set by others" as the single biggest factor influencing whether they would adopt new principles taught at work. To be humble is to be teachable, and that begins by having the confidence to ask the right questions, even if, and perhaps especially if, it exposes a lack of knowledge or understanding.

To assist with all this, we recommend asking what we call Find Out questions, which evoke something beyond a simple yes/no response. They require more than a superficial reaction and show how much you really want to know. It's one thing to hear someone's opinion; it's quite another to get their advice. Here are some good and better Find Out questions that we have coached some of the top leaders in the world to ask:

- "Are you on board?" Or better: "What else do you need before getting on board?"
- "Can I help?" Or better: "If there was one thing I could do to help, what would that be?"

- "Can you get it done on time?" Or better: "What is your greatest challenge to getting it done on time?"
- "Do you agree?" Or better: "What are your concerns?"
- "Do you have any questions?" Or better: "What questions should we be asking right now?"

Asking questions like these shows others you are humble and open enough to break out of your own tunnel vision and learn from those around you. So be an outlier and ask people what they think! You may just shock a few into contributing their genius to a project or problem.

Reach Out and Ask Someone

Often people on the front lines who are closest to the problem have a good idea of what needs to be done to move forward, but too often those views never make it up the chain of command. Learning to ask the right people while probing with the right questions that reveal what those people are thinking is essential to avoiding the pitfalls of a solitary vision.

For example, as you've no doubt heard, opening a restaurant is risky. It costs a lot of money. Failure rates are huge. In fact, according to the National Restaurant Association, 30 percent fail in the first year. Another 30 percent collapse within three years. Steep odds.

If you were a budding restaurateur absolutely convinced you were on the cusp of the next successful brand, but had these scary numbers staring you in the face, what could you do to swing the odds?

Brian Bordainick to the rescue. He created the Dinner Lab social dining concept to help chefs do their own market research *before* sticking a sign in the window. His New Orleans–based start-up organizes ad hoc events in various places where chefs can try out new ideas. Basically, Dinner Lab can be hired by budding chefs, who ask diners for feedback on what they're eating. It's a public test kitchen, a place to vet a restaurant's menu, as well as a marketing hook, allowing hopeful restaurateurs to test-drive ideas before dumping big dollars into their dreams.

Bordainick thinks it's crazy to spend a lot of money on something when you have no idea whether it works. And it's not just restaurateurs. Most entrepreneurs don't seek enough input from those who have succeeded and failed, don't listen to the perspectives they can offer, aren't sufficiently humble, or are too easily blinded by passion.

Of course, you should take accountability and passionately move forward and make things happen, but your actions should also be informed by the views and opinions of the people around you who may see things from a perspective that differs from your own. How often do you avoid asking for another person's perspective because you fear they will tell you exactly what you don't want to hear? Not asking can prove a very expensive mistake, whether you're running a restaurant or working in a nuclear power plant!

Learning how to reach out and ask someone is at the heart of this Accountability Trait. When you learn to obtain the perspectives of others and do it well, you enable yourself and others to take that first, important step Above The Line and See It.

Go fix it!

PART 3

PATH **A**: fix it for Myself → PAGE **161**

PATH **B**: fix it on My Team → PAGE **165**

PATH **C**: fix it in My Organization → PAGE **170**

ACCOUNTABILITY TRAIT 2
Communicating Openly and Candidly

---

the need to fix it

Is this trait a **clear strength** of people in your organization?

NO 68%

YES 32%

Is this trait a **clear strength** in team leaders?

NO 60%

YES 40%

Source: Partners In Leadership **Workplace Accountability Study**

It shouldn't surprise anyone that dealing openly and candidly with others is a business necessity and is how a real business pro operates. Being open and candid saves time. It helps everyone see the reality of the situation. It speeds up solutions. It eliminates guesswork and helps people know where they stand. And yet our research clearly shows that only about one in three people believes they or anyone in their company or organization consistently and clearly says what they think.

One of the most successful movie production studios in recent years is Pixar. Beginning with *Toy Story* in 1995, all the films the company has released to date have achieved critical and/or immense financial success, earning the studio nearly $10 billion worldwide and averaging more than $600 million per film. *Finding Nemo* and *Toy Story 3* rank high among the fifty highest-grossing films of all time. The studio has earned twelve Academy Awards, seven Golden Globes, and eleven Grammys . . . and counting. In a business where the vast majority of films flop, how has Pixar scored 100 percent on profitability?

Ed Catmull, cofounder of Pixar, writes in his book *Creativity, Inc.,* "A hallmark of a healthy creative culture is that its people feel free to share ideas, opinions, and criticisms. . . . Candor is the key to collaborating effectively."

Pixar's creative success lies in what they call the Braintrust. According to Catmull, the Braintrust can be as large as twenty people at the table, with fifteen more in chairs around the walls, involving writers, heads of story, directors—those involved in the film and who have a knack for storytelling. "Its premise is simple: Put smart, passionate people in a room together, charge them with identifying and solving problems, and encourage them to be candid." Each participant loads up a plate of food, then sits around a table and digs into lunch, and into the movie in the making.

Michael Arndt (writer for *Toy Story 3* and *The Hunger Games: Catching Fire*) remembers one Braintrust lunch where they were discussing *Toy Story 3.* They were focused on a key moment at the end of the second act when Andrew Stanton (director/writer for *Finding Nemo, WALL-E,* and *Finding Dory*) said, "I don't buy it. These toys aren't stupid. They know Lotso isn't a good guy. . . ." Others chimed in. The back-and-forth give-and-take eventually led the group to a solution each individual never would have found on their own.

Catmull says, "You don't want to be at a company where there is more candor in the hallways than in the rooms where fundamental ideas or policy are being hashed out. Seek out people who are willing to level with you, and . . . hold them close."

Contrast Pixar with one executive's insight into what happened at an early meeting of Google and Motorola soon after Google had purchased the telecom giant. In that first meeting, the Motorola people didn't ask questions, even though the Google employees were firing off tough comments and questions one after another. When the meeting ended, one of the senior execs for Motorola incredulously asked a Google manager about an employee who had asked a particularly tough question, "Are you going to fire that guy?" The Google manager was shocked, explaining, "We'd never fire him. Anybody can ask anything here." Mr. Motorola was stunned.

Pay Attention to *How* You Say What You Say

Sadly, most organizations function far more like Motorola than like Google or Pixar. But big surprise . . . most people would rather work for the latter. This begs the question: If the vast majority of cultures and bottom lines thrive when everyone feels free to open their heads, hearts, and mouths, why, then, don't more companies make a conscious effort to adopt and become proficient at this Accountability Trait?

Maybe we should first ask if people really *do* want to work with, for, or near someone who is open and candid. The answer is a highly scientific "It depends." Albert Mehrabian, best known for his work on the importance of verbal and nonverbal communication, came up with the 7/38/55 rule. By that he meant that meaningful communication is 7 percent verbal, 38 percent tone of voice, and 55 percent body language. In other words: it's not just what you say, it's *how* you say it. That's certainly the conclusion you could draw from our own study, in which nearly 80 percent of respondents said that the "manner" in which they were held accountable had a greater impact on them personally than the "method" that was used to do it.

People prefer open and candid versus the alternative. Wouldn't you rather know what people are thinking, especially when their views may directly influence your success? Wouldn't you want to hear their untainted opinion before it's too late? Don't you think they would prefer to hear the truth directly from you? However, it's a real art to get people in the workplace, or anywhere else, for that matter, to tell you what they *really* think.

The Workplace Study also shows that 87 percent of people would rank improving their ability to hold others accountable as one of their top three development needs. Nearly as many as 88 percent said, "There are people I depend upon today who will cause me to fail in my ability to get results for the organization if they don't do a better job of holding me accountable." Being open and candid with those you work with does factor into the accountability equation in a big way.

Try answering these simple true-or-false questions:

1. Usually, I'm better off knowing what people really think than not knowing.
2. Generally, I like working with people who share what they really think.
3. I don't really like working with people who "go along to get along"—I would rather know where I stand with them.

If you're like most people, your answers probably reflect the view that being open and candid really is the only way to operate.

By *open* we mean "real time." That is, you share your views at the right time with the right people before it's too late. Often we share our views, maybe even at the right time, but with the wrong people: ever had the meeting after the meeting in the hallway, with everyone but the person who could help you solve the problem? You need to take accountability to say what you think in a way that also allows others to chime in; after all, your intention should be to influence the outcome for the good, not to just sound off on your perspective.

Say What You *Really* Think

By *candid* we mean "to say what you really think, to share your untarnished, smartly expressed opinions." In the training and consulting work we do, we refer to *candidness* as being willing to "speak right": speak up at the right time with the right people in the right way.

Let's take a little assessment to determine how you're doing with *open* and *candid*:

	All the time at work, regardless of the circumstance	Most of the time, but very aware of the risks involved	Only in very carefully controlled circumstances at work	Never at work, but often in my personal life	Never in any circumstance
For "candid":					
Forthright					
Straightforward					
Truthful					
Up front					
Telling it like it is					
Authentic					
For "open":					
Accessible					
Clear					
Movable					
Reasonable					
Timely					

Mark an "**x**" in the column that best describes how often you display the attribute listed in each row.

Who can argue with this list? Seems reasonable and appropriate, doesn't it? How did you do? If you're like most of us, you will see room for improvement. You may also be thinking that your ability to be open and candid isn't really a choice but a function of simply interacting with other people and the circumstances in which you happen to find yourself. However, we're going to push you a bit and tell you that you are better than that. Your ability to be open and candid in any circumstance *is* a choice and you can do it successfully in almost any situation. And the payoff? You get things moving and gain the reputation as being authentic, nonpolitical, and effective.

We understand that not everyone will see this list as the right way to operate. Based on past experience, many have learned that the so-called smart way, or "the way things are done around here," is to be cautious and manage any risk that may pop up by closely guarding what you really think. But that's simply not true.

Act Like It's Your Own Company and Speak Up!

This leads on to your other option. *not* being open and candid. We call that closed and stranded. Yes, stranded: helpless to affect an outcome because you are not able to say what you think. Marooned on an island of "If they only knew!" This is even more of a problem when it comes to achieving Key Results. According to our study, 68 percent of respondents said that priorities changed frequently, creating confusion around the Key Results they needed to achieve. That glaring fact makes it all the more essential to have an open dialogue about what is really going on.

Closed and stranded is not better; it's always worse. Consider some antonyms for *candid:* biased, devious, dishonest, prejudiced, artful, deceitful, and lying. And think about the opposite of *open:*

hindered, limited, restricted, concealed, ambiguous, blocked, closed, and vague. Yuck!

Our advice: let go of the false belief that *not* being open and candid is ever an option. Instead, ask yourself, "What would I say if this were my own company, if it were my own money, my own reputation, my own legacy at stake?" That sort of thinking is remarkably freeing and uplifting. When you commit to being completely open and candid, you:

- Create authentic, lasting relationships
- Speed up the ability to solve problems
- Foster a positive, nonpolitical culture
- Establish mutual respect
- Deepen real engagement

Plus your open and candid involvement will contribute to getting real traction, moving things forward, and getting results. In the study, 58 percent of the respondents said yes when asked: "Have you ever seen a problem developing in your organization but did nothing about it?" In other words, nearly six out of ten of those sitting in that meeting with you could have helped out just by saying something. Our recommendation: act like it's your own company and speak up. Of course, if your workplace doesn't value this kind of transparency, then you must find ways to share your views that are strategically smart: right time, right people, right issues. In the end, being open and candid is always better than letting truth languish in the shadows.

Make It Safe and People Will Start Talking

At this point, you might naturally wonder, "How do I mitigate the risks that come with saying what I think? How do I get people, at any level, to truly be interested in what I have to say?" We'd answer that "it's all in the tee up." That is, it all depends on getting people ready and willing to hear what you have to say *before* you say it. In golf, the tee up involves placing the ball on the tee at the appropriate height before hitting the shot. Much of your score depends on that opening shot. Taking the extra step to tee up your views before you share them will speed you toward the results you seek.

Devise your own tee-up questions, something like, "Can I tell you what I really think about this?" or, "Not to slow us down, but I really think there is something we should look further at here." Maybe, "Have you considered another possibility. . . ?" Or, "I want to help you succeed; can I give you some input?"

In the end, building a relationship of trust by offering and seeking open discussion creates a communication path that speeds things up and drives real impact.

The other side of the communication path involves getting other people to be open and candid with you. Most people will do that if they think it's safe, but you should never assume that people will just naturally tell you what they're thinking. Never.

Here are some helpful hints to getting this job done:

- Ask people what they *really* think.
- Don't rely on formal meetings for all your communication; touch base with people informally and privately.
- Check and recheck with people along the way to ensure you feel you are getting the straight scoop.

- Ask someone unrelated to the situation what they are hearing and how they see it.
- Be the last to comment and say what you think.

Armed with a deeper understanding of Accountability Trait 2, you are now ready to jump into your path of choice: either the individual, team leader, or organization. See below for the page number and we'll meet you there.

Go fix it! PART 3

PATH **A**: fix it for Myself → PAGE **174**

PATH **B**: fix it on My Team → PAGE **178**

PATH **C**: fix it in My Organization → PAGE **182**

ACCOUNTABILITY TRAIT 3
Asking For and Offering Feedback

the need to fix it

Is this trait a **clear strength** of people in your organization?

NO **73%**

YES **27%**

Is this trait a **clear strength** in team leaders?

NO **63%**

YES **37%**

Source: Partners In Leadership **Workplace Accountability Study**

Our Workplace Study findings support what most of us experience, that the majority of people in organizations today avoid asking for, or offering, feedback. Why? Because people believe feedback happens only when something has gone wrong, is going wrong, or will soon go wrong. In other words, no feedback means things are flying along just fine. This false belief has led to extremely low levels of feedback in most organizations. In fact, most people say that feedback really happens only during annual performance appraisal time (if it comes at all), when it's often too late to do anything about it.

Feedback does not have to come in person. In fact, our experience has shown that asking for and offering feedback using digital forums can speed up the process of exchanging feedback, creating even greater reach and faster response. You might be surprised to learn that feedback given in a digital way is often more candid and informative. Perhaps that's because people take time to think about it; or they don't feel as intimidated as they often feel in a face-to-face discussion. Whatever the reason, it's important for you to know one thing: if you're not using a digital tool of some kind both to ask for and offer feedback, then you're cutting your chances of benefiting from feedback by at least half.

Get a Coach

Everyone, from great athletes and famous musicians to award-winning actors, bestselling authors, and senior executives, relies on some kind of a coach to help them see what they can't see themselves.

Most athletes striving for great results know that they can't achieve optimal performance at a world-class level without constant feedback from a wise coach. In fact, playing at the highest level demands free-flowing feedback. Feedback is oxygen. It's lifeblood. We can't grow and develop without it. The feedback a coach provides is the key to gaining and sustaining competitive or organizational advantage in any discipline.

Take, for example, November 13, 1875, when Harvard and Yale met to play one of the first ever games of what would become American football. Harvard won (and won't let Yale ever forget it). Soon after, however, Yale employed a coach for their team, who immediately hired several other position coaches to develop players individually by:

- Establishing improvement targets
- Monitoring progress
- Carefully planning for games

Yale had discovered a new approach to sports by adding coaching to the mix.

Harvard, on the other hand, continued the old British approach of training without coaches. Over the next three decades, Harvard beat Yale only four times.

Often the best coach will be someone sitting near you in the office, your workstation, or the lunchroom. These people see what's going on day to day around you; they understand the context of what you're trying to achieve and how well you're doing it.

If you haven't selected a peer coach, then you should give it some serious consideration. Pick someone who can watch you in action and regularly provide a perspective based on direct observation. Let them know you want to be coached, and you want their feedback. Soon after trying this, you will probably be asking yourself why you didn't do it sooner. In our view, if you want to play and perform at the highest level, you will find a peer coach invaluable. All you have to do is ask. Most people will be happy to help you out.

Ask for Feedback or You Won't Get It

You must take accountability to get feedback; it won't just happen. One in five people in our Workplace Accountability Study said that people almost *never* gave feedback to one another. More than half (64 percent) said it happened only when there was a problem. These numbers are a bit surprising when you consider that 86 percent of those surveyed agreed that getting people to exchange feedback freely and effectively on a change effort would definitely help speed up the process.

For more than two decades, working with thousands of organizations and hundreds of thousands of people at every organizational level, we have found one reliable rule: *You probably won't get feedback unless you ask for it.* (Unless something has gone wrong!) Our experience has also taught us some concrete lessons about the extraordinary power associated with giving and receiving feedback. These include:

- Feedback doesn't happen unless you make it happen.
- It's easier to filter feedback out than to accept it.
- Appreciative feedback is one of the most powerful forms of communication you will ever engage in.
- In the end, everyone learns this important lesson: offering feedback can be risky, but not offering feedback is even riskier.
- Almost everyone falls prey to the false idea that if people aren't giving you feedback, that means they don't have any for you and everything is okay.
- You will distinguish yourself in a very positive way if you become good at offering and asking for feedback.

When people regularly ask for and offer feedback with the intent to help others succeed, they not only show genuine respect for others, they almost always succeed themselves. That's the incredible power of feedback.

Use "STP" When Exchanging Feedback

When you exchange feedback, it's best to follow the three key rules that help ensure it's a healthy and effective experience. We call it STP:

- **S—Be Specific.** Feedback works best when it addresses a particular issue. Avoid generalizations: "You're doing well." Make it clearer and more specific: "Your focus on costs has helped to add 5 percent to the bottom line."

- **T—Be Timely.** Real-time feedback is the most effective for all because it's current, making it easy to understand and process, and it's relevant, ensuring that it will positively influence outcomes.

- **P—Be Personable.** Given that people respond better to information presented positively, you should offer feedback as constructively as possible. This does not mean that information should be sugarcoated. It must be accurate, factual, and complete. But you should offer it with the clear intention of helping, not hurting, the recipient. And should always deliver it in a respectful, professional manner.

All three of these rules apply to the two basic types of feedback:

1. **Appreciative feedback.** Everyone craves appreciation for a job well done. When offering feedback, it is essential to reinforce what's working and what we want to see happen even more.

2. **Constructive feedback.** At the same time, we can all benefit from hearing about things we could do better, could do more effectively, or could stop doing. This is the scary type of feedback, especially if done poorly.

Not every feedback exchange must include both types, but every relationship does. If the feedback is always just one type or the other, trust and credibility will erode. Everyone feels that they are doing something that deserves praise and appreciation, and everyone also knows, in their hearts, that they can do some things even better. If, over time, your feedback does not match with this self-view, then people will question the authenticity of your motivations.

It's the rare organization where offering constructive feedback to the boss seems like the smart thing to do. Not surprisingly, the lack of healthy feedback about strategy between people at different levels has often been described as one of the greatest "silent killers" of organizational alignment and commitment to the company's vision.

We will never forget the case of a major Fortune 500 client who hired us to help them get their culture aligned with their strategy. When we asked people what was important to the organization, they all said pretty much the same thing. They also *didn't* say pretty much the same thing. In fact, almost to the person, after explaining their understanding of the strategy, they joked about their CEO's "pet project." As we learned in our later discussions with management, the so-called pet project was, in fact, the organization's key strategy! We were stunned by this huge disconnect. No one bought into, understood, or even took the strategy seriously. No one was telling management; and it appeared that management wasn't asking. Eighteen months later, this pet project became the key driver of the organization's turnaround efforts. The trigger that made this happen was some straight feedback regarding where people were in their heads and what needed to be done to *fix it*.

You might benefit from asking yourself a few good yes/no questions about your current level of feedback competence and commitment:

1. Do you ask for feedback regularly?
2. When you ask for feedback, do you *really* intend to get it?
3. Do people often offer you feedback?

4. Do you frequently offer feedback to others?

5. When you do offer feedback, is it candid and open?

6. Do you consider the feedback you get from others to be a gift that will potentially help you, rather than a criticism that could hurt you?

7. Do the people who work with you expect to receive feedback regularly from you?

If you answered yes to four or more of these questions, you are probably on the right path. More than four and you are a real feedback pro!

Unfortunately, real feedback pros are not easy to find in the business world. Of the forty thousand-plus respondents in our Workplace Accountability Study, only 27 percent said they belonged to organizations that effectively sought and offered feedback. That means the remaining 73 percent were failing to take advantage of the power of feedback. This negative perception of feedback— *something that happens when things go wrong*—has led to work en vironments where people are failing or refusing to see and address the real issues that exist.

To *fix it*: engage in feedback by deliberately and regularly asking for and offering it.

Offer Feedback and Show You Care—About Results and People

We have found that most people agree that honest feedback, received and given, both appreciative and constructive, is something they want. When we don't give it, it means we don't care enough, either about the outcome the feedback is targeted toward or about the person who needs it. Feedback done properly is one of the highest forms of mutual respect one can express in a professional setting. It says, "I've got your back," "I trust you enough to receive this," "You're a pro, so I know you will want to hear this," and "I know we all want to get the result, so here's one way I can help."

This is *really* important. Your belief system needs to include the idea that feedback from others should not be feared but desired. There is an old Swedish proverb that goes "With the eating comes the appetite." If you can take that first feedback bite and taste the valuable input that comes with it, then you will desire more. It won't take long for you to realize that operating without feedback is like flying without radar: risky, dangerous, and even life threatening! *Fix it* today by asking for feedback.

(4)

ACCOUNTABILITY TRAIT 4
Hearing and Saying the Hard Things to See Reality

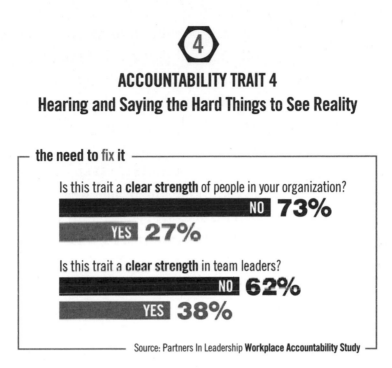

the need to fix it

Is this trait a **clear strength** of people in your organization?

NO **73%**

YES **27%**

Is this trait a **clear strength** in team leaders?

NO **62%**

YES **38%**

Source: Partners In Leadership **Workplace Accountability Study**

Why are hearing and saying the hard things so darn hard? For many, saying them can be just as hard as hearing them. The plight of one senior leader, "Bill Sherman," who works for a multinational tech company, illustrates this point. A series of 360-degree feedback assessments revealed, with almost 100 percent alignment, that Bill had a tough time listening (which is something he had heard many times before). Whenever anyone came close to questioning his decisions, it appeared that he would immediately play the higher-authority card.

At one point, we were sitting with this tough CEO in a room filled with more than fifty of his top executives when this issue came up. After a few minutes, Bill grew visibly flustered and, much to his credit, admitted, "I'm wrestling with this whole thing. Should I be taking this feedback personally?" More than half the room showed support and sympathy for their boss by chiming in with an emphatic and supportive "No!" Only one problem, however: those who said, "No, don't take it personally," were dead wrong.

The feedback *was* personal. After all, it was about Bill's style and how he approached collaboration and alignment. For years, Bill had been damaging the performance of others, squelching productivity, and, as a consequence, eroding the business's bottom line. We were actually stunned to see people urging Bill to embrace a reality they knew was wrong, and that was, in fact, harmful. Why did they encourage the boss to ignore the feedback that *they* had given him? Was it due to loyalty? Fear? The setting?

Using Occam's razor, which states that the simplest explanation is often the best, we would chalk it up to the basic fact that it's difficult to say the hard things people need to hear, even when they know they would be better off hearing them. It's even harder to say them when that person occupies a very high position in the organization or displays a personality that can be threatening. Mark Twain may have said it best: "It ain't what you don't know that gets you into trouble. It's what you know for sure that just ain't so."

Recognize a "Hard Thing"

At the outset, let's be clear by what we mean when we use the word *hard*. One use refers to something that is "solid, firm, and resistant to pressure; not easily broken, bent or pierced (the ground is frozen hard as a rock)." What may make a conversation hard in this sense is people's natural resistance to seeing the reality of their situation. Another use of the word implies "done with a great deal of force or strength (as in a hard blow to the head)." When it comes to *hard things,* then, perhaps we fear that we will be on the receiving end of something that's going to hurt to hear!

Saying or hearing the hard things sounds like hard work, doesn't it? Maybe that's why 73 percent of survey respondents said they belonged to organizations that were failing to benefit from this trait.

However, the dictionary definition we think most appropriate in this case is "potent, powerful or intense (that hard cider was really strong)." The hard things people need to say and hear are those things that can do the most to help them see the reality of a situation, a reality that can make all the difference between success and failure. That's the prize. It's not about the hard things *hurting* you; it's about the hard things *helping* you see a reality that will move you to a better place to get the results you want.

Now let's get back to Bill, the CEO in our opening story. The next step for him was to acknowledge the experiences of others and how they were feeling. Whether or not he thought their conclusions valid, it was essential that he understand them. We asked him one simple question: "Is this the belief you want people to hold?"— referring to the idea that he did not listen and would not collaborate. Of course he didn't. But it didn't matter if people's impressions were right or wrong; it mattered only that it was *what* they were actually thinking. We also helped him see that the hard things people were telling him were not meant in a mean-spirited way, but in a sincere effort to be helpful, for everyone's sake. As a result, Bill began to shift his view of his behavior and expand his understanding of reality. And that shift in leadership style brought some very good results.

The team's reaction to their experience with Bill is consistent with our study, which shows that almost half of the people surveyed acknowledged that they were not effectively engaging people who currently were critical to a project's success, and who might have been jeopardizing their ability to get the desired result. That hesitation is clearly linked to the ability or inability to hear and say things that may be hard to hear or say.

Consider these keys to saying the hard things to others in an effort to help them see the reality of their situation:

- Ask for permission to go there: help them invite it.
- Provide a short tee up: frame what you are going to say within the right context.
- Go right at the topic: don't sugarcoat it or beat around the bush. No coddling.
- Keep the discussion on point: don't yield to the temptation to make them feel better in a way that causes them to miss the point.
- Be their friend in the foxhole: say the hard things with a strong dose of empathy.
- Be respectful: be polite, be calm.
- Focus on the prize: always tie your comments back to the desired results.

A lesson learned long ago: if you do it right the first time, you won't have to do it again. Treat the wound, stop the bleeding, rip off the Band-Aid. Just get it over with. But do it right the first time. Otherwise, you will find yourself back in the same position, only it will likely be doubly hard to *fix*.

See the Full Reality of the Situation

Over our years working with more than a million people in many of the world's most successful companies, we have seen firsthand how difficult it is to capture a view of "full reality" that is complete enough, unbiased enough, objective enough, and candid enough to allow for a new way of thinking—usually the essential step toward making true progress.

What do we mean by seeing the full reality? Reality is defined as "the state of things as they actually exist, rather than as they appear or might be imagined." That's a tough view to obtain, particularly when reality consists of several differing perspectives. It's probably best to assume that you should always be adding to your view of how things really are, keeping it updated and unbiased. Not an easy thing to do.

Mull over these five clues for determining whether you possess a fairly accurate view of reality:

1. You can effectively state the case of those who do not agree with you.
2. You have spoken with the person who you know will most likely disagree with you.
3. You have gone out of your way to seek the views of people whom you ordinarily would not speak to, but who might offer some insight into the situation.
4. You have confided in the person(s) you most trust and have convinced them that you really want to know what they think.
5. You have confided in the person(s) you most trust and have convinced them that you really want to know what they are hearing.

Human beings don't live in a static world. In fact, things change so quickly from day to day, it's impossible for anyone to claim that they have a total handle on all the realities they face. The best solution is to be constantly checking and rechecking to stay current and up to speed on how things really are. In the end, you should always be scanning the world around you to add to your view of reality, as it's always changing.

They're Telling Everyone but You the Hard Things

How do you know if you are someone to whom it is difficult to say the hard things? The problem is, if you're in that camp, no one will ever tell you *that* hard thing! At least, it won't come easily. On this point, it's important to remember that a lack of feedback doesn't mean there isn't any, it may just mean that they're talking to everyone but you.

We suggest you conduct this little survey with four people you work with routinely. Take a minute to tee it up and explain that you want to know what they *really* think:

1. Do I have a reputation for being willing to hear the hard things? On a scale from 1 to 10, how well do you feel I am doing with respect to hearing the hard things in our communication?
   Note: Remember, it doesn't matter if your reputation is justified, what matters is that you are able to create an experience for others that suggests you are willing to hear the hard things.
2. When is the last time you recall my being told something that you would consider a hard thing from anyone in the organization? How well do you feel I handled it?
   Note: If they can't recall one, it doesn't mean that it hasn't happened. However, it might suggest that you need to try a little harder.
3. What's a hard thing you think people would tell me today?
   Note: If you're surprised by what they say, you may want to spend more time exploring reality with others.
4. What else do you think I need to do to ensure I am hearing the hard things in order to see reality today?
   Note: Probe to identify the "what" and the "who" of the situation.

If people see you as someone who won't consistently hear the hard things, then they are most likely sharing the feedback they have for you with everyone else but you. To this point, almost 60 percent of respondents in the study said that, based upon their experiences, they believed that people do not want to be held accountable for their results, a perspective that underscores a general unwillingness to ask for feedback and a universal loss of appetite to hear the hard things. Bottom line: you have to do more than invite the kind of feedback you need; you have to go looking for it. At the end of the day, it's not about being wrong, it's about getting it right.

Go Ahead and Say It!

Netflix has a number of highly publicized cultural behaviors and skills they expect all employees to share. Among them is honesty. Here's how they actually describe the skills they expect to see:

"You are known for candor and directness."

"You are nonpolitical when you disagree with others."

"You only say things about fellow employees that you would say to their faces."

"You are quick to admit mistakes."

Netflix understands that staying competitive in a fast-moving world requires a culture of straight talk where people are expected to say what they think. Anything less is considered unprofessional and countercultural.

Our advice: speak up, say what you think, and be authentic in your views and expressions. Develop a reputation as someone who says what you think, who is willing to say the hard things, but who also maintains a sense of alignment and the ability to support the team once you have said what you need to say.

We coach a lot of senior-level executives and have found that, from a coaching perspective, Netflix has it right: it's important to go right at a person, not to beat around the bush. Bottom line: tell it like you see it. High-level leaders have learned how to give tough feedback, and how to receive it. They tend to respect those who provide it.

Perhaps when it comes to saying the "hard things," we should reframe it as saying the "really useful, relevant, and powerful things" that can help individuals, teams, and organizations make good decisions and get results.

Go fix it! PART 3

PATH **A**: fix it for **Myself** → PAGE **200**

PATH **B**: fix it on **My Team** → PAGE **204**

PATH **C**: fix it in **My Organization** → PAGE **209**

ACCOUNTABILITY TRAIT 5
Being Personally Invested

```
┌─ the need to fix it ──────────────────────────────────┐
│                                                        │
│   Is this trait a clear strength of people in your organization?  │
│   ████████████████████████ NO  62%                     │
│   ████████████ YES  38%                                │
│                                                        │
│   Is this trait a clear strength in team leaders?      │
│   ██████████████████████ NO  54%                       │
│   ████████████████ YES  46%                            │
│                                                        │
│        Source: Partners In Leadership Workplace Accountability Study │
└────────────────────────────────────────────────────────┘
```

Here is the first of the Own It traits: Being Personally Invested. The study reveals that it's the strongest of all the Accountability Traits, yet when asked how well people in their organizations Owned It, 62 percent of respondents said that achieving their desired organizational results was currently in jeopardy due to a lack of engagement and ownership within the organization. An additional 8 percent actually said they *would not* achieve their key organizational results for that same reason. That's a full 70 percent who said that not being personally invested was an issue that would affect organizational success in a major way.

This important finding is supported by Gallup's study of engagement, which reports that only 31.5 percent of American workers are actually invested, up a bit less than 2 percentage points from the year before. Even more shocking is the finding that only 13 percent of employees worldwide qualify as engaged. That means just one in eight workers globally and one in three in the United States are committed to their jobs and making real contributions. Just one in three in the United States! That's sad. And costly.

How do you know if someone, including yourself, is personally invested? Here are some questions you should consider: First, how inventive, creative, imaginative, and resourceful are they in their job? And second, do they leave their fingerprints on everything they do? By this, we don't mean whether they look for ways to take credit, but do they personalize their work, their reports, their desk, and their approach to making work better, to making the workplace "theirs"?

Be Invested by Being Inventive

Inventiveness doesn't just mean generating new ideas about doing things better, it also means being creative in getting your work done, owning it so much that you won't take no for an answer. Consider the following experience with frontline engagement that one of the authors of this book, Roger Connors, experienced while shopping for a pair of walking shoes:

"I went out to look for a pair of walking shoes, when I found myself in a big box retail store. I made it to the shoe department and found an associate working there stocking an end cap. I was in a bit of a hurry, and not wanting to get slowed down by explaining what I needed to an associate, I responded to his query of 'Can I help you?' with a 'No, I'm good,' and headed off down an aisle hunting for what I was after.

"At this point in my life, I had never bought a walking shoe and had only heard about them. As I was trying to figure out exactly what and where they were, this same associate shouted down the aisle, 'What are you looking for?' I responded, 'Walking shoes.' He pointed and said, 'They're over there.' I soon found myself standing in front of this huge bank of shelves, floor to ceiling, wall to wall, with fifty or so different pairs of walking shoes. Immediate confusion took over, and I began wondering how badly I really wanted to walk in the first place!

"The associate could smell my confusion from thirty feet away, so he walked over and said, 'You're looking for walking shoes?' I replied, 'Yep!' He reached over, pulled a shoe off the shelf, and said, 'This is the best one.' I looked at it, and since it was in the price range I wanted, I said, 'Thank you, I can take it from here.' He backed off, sensing that I still wanted to go it alone, and watched as I fumbled around trying to find the right size. He reappeared, asked for my size, and then disappeared. He came back in what seemed like seconds with two pairs of the shoes I was looking for in my size.

"Before I knew it, he had me sitting down ready to try on the shoes. Surprisingly, he managed to slide some type of gel insole into the shoe. When I tried them on, my feet immediately felt like they were in shoe heaven! I let him know that I would take two pairs with the gel insoles. Before I could get up, he reached into his back pocket and pulled out a brochure; it was a three-year service contract for shoes! Who'd ever heard of such a thing? While the concept piqued my curiosity and I admired his courage, I passed on the contract and headed off to check out.

"As I walked away, my consultant instincts kicked in, making me realize that I had just experienced a marvelous thing: *an engaged frontline employee creating the ideal customer/brand experience.* He really owned it. He wasn't just complying; he was totally invested and committed to getting the result. He could have given up on any of four different occasions, but he chose not to. It was awesome!"

Personally invested is always awesome, and it always yields great results.

Measure Your Own Investment

It's not too difficult to read the signs in others. Most people have a sense of when someone is truly invested. The problem is that personal investment is often easier to observe in others than it is in yourself. Let's dive a little deeper now, and have you take a quick four-question Being Personally Invested evaluation. This simple diagnostic will help you calibrate ownership (check the answer that best applies to you):

1. For you, being personally invested in your job is?
 _____ a. A clear strength
 _____ b. A strength, but not an advantage
 _____ c. A weakness, but not a detriment
 _____ d. A clear weakness

2. Have you ever felt totally powerless, with no control over your circumstances or situation?
 _____ a. Yes
 _____ b. No

3. In an average day, would you say that you simply go through the motions?
 _____ a. Never
 _____ b. 30% or more of the time
 _____ c. 20% of the time
 _____ d. 10% of the time

4. In an average day, would you say that your coworkers go through the motions?

_____ a. Never

_____ b. 30% or more of the time

_____ c. 20% of the time

_____ d. 10% of the time

The questions you just answered are identical to questions we asked those participating in our Workplace Accountability Study. You might find it illuminating to compare your answers with the scores from thousands of respondents below:

1. Being personally invested in your job is:	2. Ever felt totally powerless?
38% Clear strength	**85%** Yes
36% Strength, not an advantage	**15%** No
15% Weakness, not a detriment	
11% Clear weakness	

3. Go through the motions?	4. Coworkers go through the motions?
13% Never	**3%** Never
17% 30%+	**42%** 30%+
26% 20%+	**33%** 20%+
43% 10%+	**21%** 10%+

Source: Partners In Leadership **Workplace Accountability Study**

Some of these numbers may make you feel a little better about yourself, confirming you're not alone. Most of the numbers are probably a bit shocking. Whatever the case, at this point you might be asking yourself, "How do I solve this, especially if I need others to be personally invested in what I am trying to get done?" The answer yields real progress and movement.

Understand and Teach the "Why" Behind the "What"

There are many carrot-and-stick techniques people use to drive personal investment, but increasingly, and especially with millennials, the older management styles are going the way of the dodo. Tyrannical bosses, threats of firing, demeaning and demoralizing call-on-the-carpet speeches—all of these old-school hard-line techniques don't work anymore and will drive people away from your organization. So it's vital that you understand what positive approaches motivate people in today's workplace.

There are plenty of healthy examples of impressive organizational cultures out there. You've undoubtedly heard about a lot of them, from Apple and Amazon to Google and Zappos. There's also a nearly infinite number of articles debating the benefits of such techniques as flex hours, remote worker programs, workout rooms, and in-cubicle catering (okay, we embellished a bit with the last one, but give it time). These programs are essentially engagement entitlements. But as nice as all these programs can be, they aren't lasting and are not what really makes a difference.

Peter Hotz, industry adviser for Vynamic, a prominent healthcare industry management consultant firm, told us, "All those programs are really only buying a little time." He went on to say, "What drives engagement today is having a mission that people believe in, and a leadership team that people want to be part of." In other words, as wonderful as programs and gimmicky work entitlements are, after their fifteen minutes in the sun they burn off, unless founded on the bedrock key to engagement.

Krista Stafford, vice president of human resources for KLX Aerospace Solutions, a full-service aerospace industry provider, believes the key to achieving this personal investment, even from your outliers, is an organization-wide focus on Key Results and the business case behind them. Your organization's desired results are the "why" behind the "what." Defining and getting clear on a few Key Results becomes a powerful tool to help generate personal investment and engagement.

Without this Key Results foundation, leaders are left with the traditional, old-school approaches to managing people, which really work only if you're after compliance, not true buy-in and investment. We mean *real* investment. Imagine the questions you need answered before you put your hard-earned savings into a financial investment: What are the downside risks? What are the upside potentials? What will this require of me? In much the same way, for the people you work with to become personally invested in work initiatives, they need a lot of the same information. Communicate the "why" to get the heart and head involved, because that's where investment, and reinvestment, really kicks in.

Accelerate Buy-in with Team Discussions

When Steven Nickel was vice president of the Sony VAIO service organization, he learned just how powerful it is to get people personally invested when chasing an important result. His team had set an ambitious goal to improve customer satisfaction scores by 15 percent over the prior year. Although they had talked about the goal over and over in meetings, it wasn't until they got everyone on the team together and held an exhaustive discussion about (1) what the goal really meant and (2) what would be required to achieve it, that everyone fully bought into just what it would take to get there. However, because everyone knew the specific desired target and could focus on it, it soon became easier to make real progress. Their weekly key performance indicators (KPI) meetings came to life.

Many who had never spoken up in meetings before now shared ideas and took ownership around how to make things happen.

Nickel said, "I learned the equivalent of several volumes of business books from this experience. At the top of the list was that getting aligned around the result across the entire organization brings ownership. This doesn't come from slide shows or speeches. It comes from engaging everyone on the team to get clear on what success looks like and what we need to do to achieve it." For their outstanding performance, the VAIO service team was awarded the Chief Operating Officer Award from Sony Electronics that year.

Without personal investment and engagement, people tend to focus on their immediate task list, often to the detriment of the broader Key Results the team or organization is trying to deliver. Personal investment comes as people take time to poke at it, discuss it, and test it, particularly when that chance occurs in a team setting with those they must work with to carry out the task. When done properly, there is great value in the team discussion process that can accelerate individual buy-in and ownership. In fact, there really is no other way to get there.

Go fix it! PART 3

PATH **A**: fix it for **Myself** → PAGE **213**

PATH **B**: fix it on **My Team** → PAGE **218**

PATH **C**: fix it in **My Organization** → PAGE **222**

ACCOUNTABILITY TRAIT 6
Learning from Both Successes and Failures

┌─ **the need to fix it** ─────────────────────────────────┐

Is this trait a **clear strength** of people in your organization?

NO 68%

YES 32%

Is this trait a **clear strength** in team leaders?

NO 62%

YES 38%

Source: Partners In Leadership **Workplace Accountability Study**

Brian Herbert, son of the author of the popular science fiction novel *Dune,* writes in *House Harkonnen,* the second book of the prequel trilogy to *Dune,* "The capacity to learn is a gift; The ability to learn is a skill; The willingness to learn is a choice." From our vantage point, the very best and most successful leaders have harnessed the ability to learn quickly and deeply whatever they most need to master in order to achieve personal and organizational success. We also think that it is virtually impossible to sustain the journey Above The Line without making the conscious choice to learn in every situation. Shockingly, when it comes to learning from both success and failure, more than two thirds of respondents in our Workplace Accountability Study said that people in their organizations weren't doing it very well.

Otto Aichinger, strategic partnership manager for industry-leading mortgage lenders, told us, "More can be learned from failure than from success. Whenever I've been trampled by failure, I've learned, survived, come out the other side better for it, and moved on—hopefully never to be trampled by that same failure again." Conversely, in a recent *New York Times* article, Kat Cole, president of Cinnabon said, "I've learned to question success a lot more than failure. I'll ask more questions when sales are up than I do when they're down. I ask more questions when things seem to be moving smoothly, because I'm thinking: 'There's got to be something I don't know.'"

Success or failure? Yeah, both matter.

For example, at one point in World War II a significant effort was made to limit bomber losses. The problem was turned over to researchers from the Center for Naval Analyses, who carefully studied the planes that survived their bombing runs. They observed that the fuselage was taking more hits than the engine or cockpit. From this the researchers concluded that additional armor plating should be placed where the most damage had been done to the plane.

However, statistician Abraham Wald recognized a fatal flaw in their learning process. Turns out the naval scientists were studying only the planes that survived their bombing runs, not the failures, the planes that did not make it back. Wald recommended that the armor be placed in the areas where the returning aircraft had not been hit, as those were likely the fatal areas and the reason some planes never safely returned. Seems obvious when we talk about it this way now, but not so much at the time.

The logical error of learning only through your successes is called survivorship bias, and is a mistake that is easy for any of us to make. For that reason, looking at both success *and* failure can engender a lot of learning, something that allows you to stay Above The Line and solve the right problems.

Learn How to Learn

Learning doesn't necessarily come easy for many people. In fact, 50 percent of respondents to the Workplace Study admitted that the single biggest reason they found it hard to hold others accountable was that they simply didn't know how to do it: they weren't sure how to do it in a way that yielded positive results. The study also shows that 82 percent said they either avoided holding others accountable, didn't do it very often, or tried to do it but didn't get the results they wanted. These numbers are a bit jarring and speak to the learning gap that exists when it comes to getting accountability right.

In a world of big data, faster bit speeds, greater bandwidth, and more efficient and competitive markets, everyone, no matter how much experience they have, must stay in a learning mode. And many of us are promoted up to our "highest level of incompetence," meaning that we will be constantly asked to do things we have never done before. Better be a good learner in that environment.

One of the authors, while attending a senior-level executive meeting, watched as a CEO jumped up from his chair three times in the first twenty minutes, waving his hand in the face of his fellow leaders, fingers spread, shouting, "I got your point! I got your point!" We eventually pulled this successful CEO aside and gently suggested, "Mr. CEO, you have to stop this. You're looking down on your team. You're beating them up publicly and overstating your authority to the point where they are unable to contribute."

Much to his credit, our excitable CEO chose humility and quickly resolved, "I get it, I'm going to change the way I act."

Flash forward a year. This same CEO was standing before a

room full of his senior leaders when the head of HR asked, "How has the last year impacted your life?" The CEO became surprisingly emotional and told the story about how the feedback Partners In Leadership gave him a year earlier had caused him to realize that his acidic style was not only poisoning the halls of his company but also damaging the walls of his home, marriage, and relationship with his daughter. He shared through tears how he had changed and how his relationship with his daughter had improved dramatically in the last year. Of course, his coworkers also loved what he had learned and were inspired to make similar changes in their own lives.

Learn from Success

The key to learning from success is to pause and take the time to understand what's working. In fact, you should periodically conduct a What's Working Inventory. Set aside a time to meet with all relevant parties and analyze your successes in order to understand what's working and why, so that you can replicate that success in the future. You might be surprised at the differing opinions that pop up when you actually start digging. Moving beyond a hunch to factual data and analysis can be enlightening and empowering.

Learning from success takes a strong dose of humility. We made a big point about humility in Accountability Trait 1: Obtaining the Perspectives of Others, but it bears repeating here. Personal humility lies at the core of learning, not only acknowledging that we don't know everything, but remaining willing to learn and be taught. To inform your What's Working Inventory and gain some personal insight, think about your answers to the following short humility quiz. For the best results, set it in the context of your work, home, or community:

1. Have you asked a "How do you do that?" question lately?
2. How long has it been since you said, "I don't know"?
3. Do people see you as interested in understanding the details behind what they do?
4. Can you honestly say that you see how the contribution of others has made a difference in your success?
5. Would others consider you a mentor or a boss? A student or a numb employee?
6. What new skill have you gained in the last twelve months?
7. When something goes wrong, are you quick to point out what you could have done better?

Your What's Working Inventory will work best if you keep an open mind and maintain a willingness to learn what is really behind a success. Most important, make sure the inventory is not just about proving your own point of view on things.

Learn from Failure

Ian Raman, CEO of the popular family-style restaurant chain Cheddar's Scratch Kitchen, relayed to us that when he first became COO of another popular restaurant chain in Canada, he felt the COO title meant that he needed all the answers. That he needed to appear as if he had gone beyond learning. Then came a time when the company needed to make dramatic changes to a menu. He procrastinated, stalled, and brought it up in three successive board meetings. Finally one board member flatly asked, "When are you going to quit talking about it and just *do* something?" The board member recommended the following steps: first, stop solely owning whatever impending failure you feel is coming; second, share accountability for success *and* failure with others; and third, recognize that any so-called failure would offer a good learning opportunity.

This rattled Ian's mind enough that it forced him to make decisions and get on with it. Guess what. The changes to the menu worked! It turned out fine. Better than fine. Just as humility offers a key to learning from success, it plays a huge role in learning from failure. You need to be comfortable with the fact that taking risks to achieve greater results will inevitably bring about some failure. Understand that. Accept it. Plan on it. Then, when it happens, use that failure to learn the needed lessons so that it doesn't happen again.

Professionals and performers make mistakes all the time. Singers miss notes. Actors forget lines. Olympians fall. Million-dollar ballplayers drop the ball. But the great ones learn from every error. The key to learning from failure is remembering the real objective, the higher purpose: the Grammy, the Oscar, the gold medal, the championship. You may lose the battle, so focus on winning the war. Failure is seldom a permanent condition, just a temporary circumstance. This view empowers you to fail fast, learn quickly, shed any baggage of Below The Line thinking, and then get Above The Line to try again and get the result you are looking for.

Let the Learning Sink In to Ensure Improvement

Gene Abernethy, chief human resources officer for Progrexion, a market leader in credit repair, told us, "You must learn from your failures and your successes. But especially from your failures, or else you'll be throttled by repetition, creating unnecessary work for yourself and whatever cause you're a part of." In our experience we've found that there are biases that can hamper one's ability to let any learning that could guarantee progress sink in. Be aware of your biases, and you will enhance your ability to learn.

Topping our list is "ego bias," which involves a death grip on preserving your self-image, instead of revealing that you are vulnerable and willing to learn. To *fix it*, we refer you to our seven-question humility quiz above. Next is "experience bias," a common tendency to rely almost solely on your own personal experience. To *fix* this, remember to obtain the perspectives of others. Then there's "Belief Bias," the natural human propensity to validate your current view of the world, your current beliefs, which usually involves ignoring any evidence suggesting the need for anything new and different. To *fix it*, try to disprove the hypothesis that you are right.

Setting aside biases will improve your ability to learn and will help you tap into the power of positive accountability as you operate Above The Line to get the results you want.

Go **fix** it!
PART 3

PATH **A**: fix it for **Myself** → PAGE **227**

PATH **B**: fix it on **My Team** → PAGE **231**

PATH **C**: fix it in **My Organization** → PAGE **235**

ACCOUNTABILITY TRAIT 7
Ensuring My Work Is Aligned with Key Results

┌─ **the need to fix it** ────────────────────────────────┐

Is this trait a **clear strength** of people in your organization?

NO 73%

YES 27%

Is this trait a **clear strength** in team leaders?

NO 67%

YES 33%

Source: Partners In Leadership **Workplace Accountability Study**

└──┘

Are the above numbers hard to believe? Unimaginable? Even shocking? How can it be that so few people align their daily work with the Key Results the organization needs to achieve? If they aren't working on tasks that lead to the most important results, then what are they working on? A good question. Accountability begins by clearly defining results. If the results are not clear, then accountability will break down, resulting in lower morale and misaligned work, a problem the Workplace Study made abundantly clear.

For example, Brinker International was looking at an economy that had nearly collapsed, with the company's casual dining business sector experiencing one of the sharpest downturns on record. Brinker's thirty-five-year-old organizational culture had slipped into the blame game, where no one would take responsibility.

Finger-pointing, confusion, cover your tail, and a host of Below The Line excuses were not just common but cultural.

It should come as no surprise to hear that, given all this, profits were down and shareholders were abandoning ship, with company stock hitting an all-time low of $3.99 a share. Employee engagement plummeted to below 50 percent, while turnover had risen to 110 percent annually. What was going on?

The diagnosis was clear: it had to do with Brinker's forty-plus key performance indicators that were inadvertently being used as Key Results. While a big number like forty would not surprise most people with any corporate experience, it turned out that nobody could keep track of so many. Confusion reigned around what to measure, and just what anyone was accountable to do. "Brinker as usual" could not continue. What could hold true for most organizations today was very true for Brinker back then:

1. There was a real hunger among leaders for more conversations about how their job titles, responsibilities, teams, projects, and priorities could better fit with what everybody was trying to accomplish.
2. They were not yet narrowing the most important results they needed to achieve down to the top three or four, even though they wanted to.
3. Leaders and managers were not accustomed to discussing the organization's Key Results but were clearly willing to begin doing so.

Tony Bridwell, chief people officer for Brinker International, the company behind Chili's and Maggiano's Little Italy restaurants, said: "While at first we were chided for an oversimplistic version of our Key Results, this approach has rocked our world. Since beginning this exercise, we have returned more than 200 percent total return to our shareholders as of this writing." He added, "Turnover has dropped and engagement scores have risen."

In the years since redefining accountability they have narrowed their Key Results from forty down to four, namely, (1) engage team members, (2) bring back guests, (3) grow sales, and (4) increase profits. This narrowed focus has helped Brinker hit record milestones in revenue growth, profitability, guest satisfaction, and team member engagement, with company stock producing a nearly 30 percent annualized return. At the foundation of this success is their clarity around the most important results and a strong Culture of Accountability, where people take accountability to ensure that their daily work aligns with those objectives.

Identify Your Top 3 or 4 Key Results

Most companies talk seriously about their Key Results only during annual planning. Because those objectives don't receive the needed focus and effort throughout the year, many organizations never actually achieve complete alignment and engagement among their people, not to mention any real ownership around these top priorities.

In order to ensure that people's work is aligned with your company's Key Results, everyone needs to know what those results are. Obvious, right? But the big reveal from our Workplace Study is that the vast majority of workers don't know. Most don't really understand what their companies are chasing. Believe it or not, most C-suite teams would find it hard to describe their most important results in a clear and consistent way. Our study glaringly revealed the fact that 85 percent of employees believed their companies either failed or could improve at defining results.

Consider these stats gleaned from our research:

- Only 48 percent of respondents said that it was true that the Key Results were clearly defined and understood throughout the organization, 76 percent said they needed improvement in this area, and only 15 percent said results were sufficiently defined for the organization.
- A full 75 percent of respondents said that people at every level could not make the link between what they did on a daily basis and the Key Results.
- Only 7 percent said that people in the organization effectively aligned their work with the Key Results.
- More than 68 percent said that priorities changed frequently, creating confusion around the organization's Key Results.
- 66 percent-plus said that their performance management was not making an effective tie between daily work and organizational priorities.
- 64 percent said that the front line did not understand the top priorities the organization needed to achieve, although 98 percent said that they should.

What does all this mean and how does it tie to your company's success? To us it means that a Culture of Accountability is sadly beyond the reach of those organizations that have not effectively defined the Key Results they need to achieve. Without clearly defined results, confusion takes center stage, and the curtain rises on poor execution and ineffective action. Employee engagement suffers, and goals are missed because they are unclear or untracked. Along with that, momentum dies because no one feels confident about which direction to move, or worse, if what they're doing every day even matters. All of this gives people permission to maintain the status quo and dismiss their own accountability, leading to missed results and poor performance.

Communicate Your Key Results

True accountability calls for a clear focus on well-articulated, measurable Key Results and encourages people to look at what they can personally do to improve company performance and deliver on those results. Defining Key Results in a meaningful, measurable, and memorable way can give everyone in the organization the benefit of knowing exactly what they are accountable to do and By When. For those who possess a crystal-clear understanding of their organization's Key Results, their actions suddenly matter, and they consistently demonstrate higher levels of ownership, motivation, and engagement.

Of course, the communication of all top organizational priorities should be accompanied by a compelling business case that explains why those results are strategically more important than others, and why they are important to the success of the organization. Then you need to repeat that communication at every opportunity.

Dieter Uchtdorf, former chief pilot for Lufthansa airlines, said the airline had to teach new safety procedures to their crews seven times, seven different ways, before they got it right—and that's with people whose lives depended on getting it right! Repetition is key to communicating Key Results. Once driven home with multiple messages, the Key Results keep everyone pointed to true north, keeping their daily work connected to the organization's most important organizational imperatives.

Own Your Organization's Key Results

In our view, every member of the organization, regardless of position, has an ethical responsibility to understand and take ownership for achieving its mission and Key Results. It's an essential part of the worker-employer contract. They hire you, pay you, and then you sign up to support what everyone should focus on accomplishing. Of course, the organization has accountability for defining and communicating those results so that people will understand them. To facilitate this, leaders should provide a process that allows people to engage in the sorts of dialogue, debate, and discussion that allow them to achieve real alignment.

When this happens, it becomes everyone's job to ensure that their daily work remains aligned with the Key Results. Creating a Culture of Accountability where people ensure this happens *will* have a huge impact on performance.

Ask yourself these questions, which will help you check your own alignment with your organization's mission and Key Results:

1. What would I put on the "stop doing list" to align my daily work even more fully with the mission and Key Results?
2. Where do I feel like I am going through the motions, getting work done, but not seeing it make any real difference?
3. What would I put on the "start doing list" to get real traction in my daily work and make even more of a contribution to achieving the mission and Key Results?
4. If it were totally up to me, what changes would I make in my job duties to bring even more real impact to get the results we need?

No one is in a better position than you to determine what else you can do to align your daily work with the Key Results. When everyone in the organization makes that personal choice to take accountability to create even greater alignment in their daily work, performance will improve.

Have an Own It Conversation to Ensure Alignment

Ultimately, what we call alignment is a personal choice that reflects a sense of commitment to the direction in which the organization is headed. Because that commitment lies at the heart of alignment, everyone in the organization must be accountable to both working toward creating it and then maintaining it. However, getting everyone moving in the same direction often represents the greatest challenge to getting results.

And while alignment doesn't mean you need to agree with every decision, it does mean you'll agree to grab an oar and help keep the boat moving in the same direction once a decision has been made. The power that comes from everyone energetically rowing in the same direction cannot be underestimated. Getting and staying aligned depends on holding what we call the Own It Conversation. With an Own It Conversation you engage the needed conversations for people to buy in and invest on deliverables and deadlines related to delivering the Key Results. Here's some Q&A on the concept:

Who is accountable to have the Own It Conversation?
You are. No one is in a better position than you to know when you need a dialogue around getting your daily work aligned with the Key Results.
When should the Own It Conversation happen?

Whenever you sense your daily work is not aligned. The four questions we presented above should help you determine that.

What makes a good Own It Conversation?

Open, candid dialogue about what's really going on.

How do you measure the effectiveness of an Own It Conversation?

You put things on the "stop doing list" and the "start doing list." You optimize your daily work and *fix it*!

In order to adjust any misalignment, ask and answer the central Own It question:

How am I contributing to the problem and/or solution?

By asking this question with the Key Results in mind, you will do a lot to get and stay aligned.

In a Culture of Accountability, people at every level of the organization feel personally committed to achieving the Key Results, and everyone buys in to them. No one ever waits to be asked for a progress report or a follow-up plan. They engage in Own It Conversations constantly. They report proactively and follow up consistently. They diligently measure their own progress because they are committed to achieving results with everyone around them.

PATH **A**: fix it for Myself → **PAGE 239**

PATH **B**: fix it on My Team → **PAGE 243**

PATH **C**: fix it in My Organization → **PAGE 248**

Go fix it!

PART 3

ACCOUNTABILITY TRAIT 8
Acting on the Feedback I (We) Receive

---

the need to fix it ──────────────────────────────

Is this trait a **clear strength** of people in your organization?

NO **71%**

YES **29%**

Is this trait a **clear strength** in team leaders?

NO **68%**

YES **32%**

Source: Partners In Leadership **Workplace Accountability Study**

If feedback is "the breakfast of champions," then, according to our study, a whole lot of people are going hungry. Our experience consulting and training leaders, teams, and organizations over the last three decades bears this out; and while this is perhaps the single most important Accountability Trait, it's often the most intimidating and the one done the least well. Acting on the feedback you receive can often make the difference between success and failure, and that can be a *really* big difference.

Jason Schubert, senior manager at the Kohler Learning Academy for the Kohler Co. family of companies, acknowledged that acting on feedback is hard for most, often because it's hard for people to process the feedback effectively to begin with. "Unless the feedback is 100 percent positive, most people quickly defend themselves and begin rationalizing or justifying their actions or behaviors to lessen the impact or explain it away." Jason offered one story where an associate was nervous about sharing an idea with an executive, even though the executive was happy to listen. As the idea was shared, the leader quickly determined that it was probably a bad idea.

How would you encourage a continued effort to share feedback while not validating the idea? In this case, the executive simply responded, "Thank you for sharing that with me," and left it at that. The person went away feeling engaged and motivated.

In the days that followed, the executive returned to close the loop with the employee and said, "You know, I had time to think about your idea, and I wanted to share my thoughts with you. . . ." This action alone was engaging, as the associate was reminded that not only did the executive listen to the idea but thought about it after. However, the person stopped the executive after only a few moments and said, "Oh, that's not what I meant, I must have misspoke. What I meant was . . ." The executive was surprised. In the end, the idea was a good one and the leader admitted that once he judged the idea to be bad, he had stopped listening. If the executive had immediately responded by telling the associate why the idea was bad or wrong, the feedback channel would have shut down, likely for good.

As Jason pointed out to us, "Your first reaction should be one of gratitude; you can always circle back later once any tension has been reduced. So remember to always ensure that you understand the feedback, to make sure you got it right. This will allow you to act on it in a way that actually achieves the impact you want."

Acting on any feedback you receive will create the experience for others that you really do want feedback, and that you will consume it in a way that makes taking the risk to offer it worthwhile.

Filter to Act, Not to React

We all do it; we just don't want to admit it. Negatively reacting to feedback is a perfectly human thing to do. And that reaction usually leads to filtering, often in a major way. By filtering, we mean screening input so finely that very little gets through.

One of the authors related how his wife came to him early in their marriage and said, "You don't listen to me." His immediate reply was, "What are you talking about, of course I listen to you." He followed that with how he'd been told many times at work that he was a great listener. And if that wasn't enough, he then started offering examples to back up his argument. Her response? "See, you're *still* not listening." Talk about filtering!

Actually looking for feedback to act on is an entirely different way to filter feedback, one that is empowering and brings big impact. Rather than screening for what's not correct about the feedback, consciously look for what you can do with what you're hearing. When you make acting on as much feedback as you possibly can a common practice, it sends the message to the people around you that you want to Own It and drive results. It's that propensity to action that will ring the bell of results.

Just fewer than half of those surveyed said they knew who the people were who might let them down but were not engaging them effectively to *fix it*. When asked about the impact this was having on results, a full 70 percent said that their desired results might be in jeopardy because they were not effectively engaging these folks. Two thirds also said that they might not turn in the expected result because they were not effectively holding those they depended upon accountable. This data clearly supports the business case for prioritizing the need to get and act on feedback related to holding others accountable. Otherwise, you might not get important stuff done.

Try this little test: keep a record of how much feedback you act on in a given week, then track those actions over time. Personally commit to improving that score by 10 percent a week. We feel certain that the ability to act on the feedback you receive will move you rapidly into the top 5 percent of professionals who can produce results anytime, anywhere.

Do Just One Thing Differently

A giant step toward getting accountability right is to act on the feedback you receive so that others observe you taking the Own It step Above The Line. When that happens, you signal to everyone that accountability starts with you, and in that way you become a model for what they need to do.

Our tip is to listen to feedback and try doing just one thing differently. As you gather feedback, make a prioritized list of what you can do to respond, and then circle the top one and act on it. As people see you acting on the feedback you receive, it will entice them to give you even more, often when you most need it, and probably when they would feel least inclined to provide it.

When Chris Brickman was hired as the new CEO at Sally Beauty Holdings, it didn't take him long to realize that a common practice within the organization needed to change. No one went into the executive offices without an invite. In fact, the practice was assured by lock and key. One of the first things Chris did was to remove the door, tear down a wall, and create a twelve-foot opening. That sent a clear message: "Anyone is welcome to visit the executive offices to talk with me at any time."

Chris acted on the feedback he received as a new CEO and did something demonstrably different, taking one very clear action. No one could miss that he was listening and was willing to act. Consider the "walls" you need to tear down in order for people to see you doing something different as you act on the feedback you receive.

Be Courageous and Act

Andrew Grove, former CEO of Intel, observed, "Every company faces a critical point when it must change dramatically to rise to the next level of performance. If the company fails to see and seize that moment it will start to decline. The key is courage." We would add that not only do all companies face such a moment, every individual does, too.

A divisional vice president for a well-known top corporation we worked with recently shared that he and a few peers got together to offer up some specific feedback to their CEO. When they sat down to discuss the items with him, they had only lightly touched on two bullet points into a lengthy list when the CEO said, "Wait, why are we doing this? I don't have time for this." With that he got up and left the meeting.

This CEO allowed the discomfort of hearing what he didn't want to hear prevent him from hearing what he needed to hear. If this leader had understood the power of feedback, he would have known that he couldn't afford *not* to listen and act on the items his team wanted to share.

Contrast this with Tony Bridwell, chief people officer for Brinker, who we met earlier. Tony told us that when he first joined Brinker he was inundated with requests to overhaul their process for annual reviews. As he and his team dug into the feedback, they discovered that Brinker was burning more than eighty-eight hundred work hours every year to execute the process.

To make it worse, because of the way their fiscal year was set up, these reviews happened in July and August, during peak family vacation time. One director-level team member reported that for the last five years he was forced to spend the first half of his vacation sitting with his laptop while watching his wife and children play without him.

Tony came to believe that if the company used feedback correctly, there would be nothing revealed in a review that wouldn't come out naturally during the quarterly check-ins throughout the year. So he suggested they toss them. Annual reviews, gone. He and his team had listened to the feedback and acted. The result? A thunderous roar went up company-wide across Brinker's some sixty thousand team members. Tony's e-mail box became flooded with "I can't believe I have my summers back! Thank you, thank you!" Not only did the action affect Brinker's people on a personal and emotional level, it stopped them from wasting those eighty-eight hundred hours, time and money that contributed significantly to their best reporting period in six years.

Close the Loop: Get Feedback on How You Act on Feedback

The best test for determining how well you act on feedback is to simply ask others if they think you do it well. You may have to convince them you really want to know, but try asking people these two questions:

1. Do you think I have a reputation as one who acts on the feedback I receive? Do I have that reputation with you?
2. Is there feedback that you have given me that I haven't acted on, but that you wish I had?

Closing the loop on how well you get and act on feedback can help you tune up the way you practice this Accountability Trait, and thus perfect your ability to operate Above The Line.

Brad Lee, president and CEO of Breg, Inc., a large medical device manufacturer, shared with us one important caution: "It's important to realize what a gift feedback is and treat it like that. I never, ever blow anyone up for telling me truly bad news. I try to categorize bad news and good news as 'just news,' and never, ever shoot the messenger. This attitude keeps the feedback channels open and the information flowing."

By now you can probably guess that if you don't *own* feedback, it's worthless. If you don't acknowledge and act on what you're hearing, what good is it? If you don't close the loop on how well you encourage and act on feedback, you won't do well.

To help you *fix it,* remember these four tips for acting on feedback:

1. **Filter to act.** Consider some recent feedback, re-create it in writing, then decide how you should act on it.
2. **Do one thing.** Don't plan to do five things. Pick one and do it.
3. **Be courageous.** Go to those who gave you the feedback and say, "Here's what I heard, and here's what I'm planning to do with it. What do you think?"
4. **Close the loop.** Check in with those who gave you the feedback to ensure alignment so that they know you acted on it one way or another.

Acting on the feedback you receive lets others know that you appreciate the gift; and that gift may just be what's missing to help you take the next step to better results.

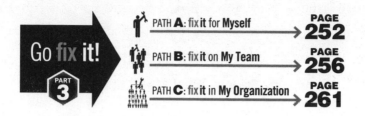

PATH **A**: fix it for **Myself**   **PAGE 252**

PATH **B**: fix it on **My Team**   **PAGE 256**

PATH **C**: fix it in **My Organization**   **PAGE 261**

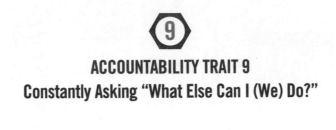

ACCOUNTABILITY TRAIT 9
Constantly Asking "What Else Can I (We) Do?"

the need to fix it

Is this trait a **clear strength** of people in your organization?

NO **74%**

YES **26%**

Is this trait a **clear strength** in team leaders?

NO **70%**

YES **30%**

Source: Partners In Leadership **Workplace Accountability Study**

What else can I do? are perhaps the five most powerful words anyone can say when it comes to operating Above The Line to get results. In fact, just repeating these very words can move someone from Below The Line to Above The Line and set them on the best path to Solve It!

In our training workshops, we run a Solve It brainstorming activity that we call the Million Dollar Exercise. Team members use a small Hacky Sack–type Solve It ball, which they toss around in order to identify who needs to offer up a new idea. It's a bit like passing a hot potato, except here, the person holding the ball must provide an idea that could help solve whatever problem the team has selected. On more than one occasion, this little exercise has produced solutions that have netted more than $1 million in returns to the client. The game proves that solutions to any problem exist; you just need to uncover them.

Jesse Marshall, a vice president at Native Foods Café, was gearing up for a "Special meal limited-time offer" at their Denver, Colorado, location—the company's first café in the region. Then Jesse got word at his Chicago office that a shipment of specialty vegan hamburger buns wouldn't arrive on time due to bad weather delaying a delivery truck. The team was expecting more than five hundred hungry customers to show up, and these buns were an essential part of a premier menu item.

At first, Jesse and his team on the ground in Colorado were disappointed and even a bit angry. How were they going to tell customers they couldn't order the item? They began to discuss how they could communicate it to their guests, how they could work with marketing on a sign to tell customers that they would not have this item available—never an experience you want your guests to have.

Understanding his people's concerns in Colorado, Jesse stepped back and started asking, "What else can I do?" There still had to be a way to make this happen. As he and his team mulled over solutions, it suddenly dawned on them that they were just forty-five minutes away from one of their Chicago cafés. After he got the manager on the phone, Jesse asked if they could spare some of the needed vegan buns. They could. Again asking, "What else can I do?" Jesse booked a last-minute flight to Denver. Before racing to the airport, he picked up two cases of the specialty buns. Running late, there was no time to check his luggage or his packages, so again, asking, "What else can I do?" he took the buns as carry-on baggage, of course! He personally escorted the buns through security, through the terminal, and eventually loaded them in the plane's overhead bins.

We are happy to report that he did make it on time, Native Foods Café had their specialty buns for the signature menu item, and the Denver location's special promotion was a great success, all due to Jesse and his team asking, "What else can I do?"

"What else can I do?" or "we" in the case of a team, begins as a personal question that tests your resolve against taking no for an answer and for finding a way to get it done regardless. There will always be something hindering your progress and dragging you Below The Line. Constantly asking the Solve It question will create a steady stream of solutions.

Hurdle Boundaries, Both Real and Self-Imposed

Asking "What else can I do?" will bring you face-to-face with many boundaries and barriers that you must overcome to get the results you want. You know you are doing a good job in the Solve It department when you are blasting through boundaries, both real and imagined. In most cases, only by pushing the boundaries can you redefine the problem in a way that makes it solvable. That's also usually the only way you can tell a real boundary from a toothless imaginary one, by testing it and seeing what happens. Remember, a boundary is a condition or rule that limits you in some way, something that lies beyond your control. A real boundary will reveal itself with a loud shout: "You don't have the personnel for this!" or, "You need upper-level buy-in to get that approved!" An imagined boundary will quietly fade away, as though it never existed: "We've never done that before," or, "We thought we couldn't do that."

Removing barriers that block performance, creativity, communication, or problem solving is crucial to success in business today, but it often happens too slowly or not often enough. To help you understand this concept a bit more, here's a short Boundaries and

Barriers Self-Test. Consider a challenging problem you're facing and ask these questions about any boundaries and barriers you see in your way:

1. If your efforts to find solutions were being hindered by a single boundary, what would that be?
2. How can you test that boundary to determine if it is real or self-imposed?
3. What would you include on a complete list of all the boundaries or barriers you think you're facing? In other words, list everything that seems to lie beyond your control.
4. If you had the power to remove any boundary or barrier you are currently facing, what would that be?
5. What else can you do to remove/adjust that boundary to enable you to move forward unhindered?

Whether you're facing real or imagined boundaries, the Solve It attitude almost always requires testing them and pushing the limits. Redefining boundaries puts you back in control and allows you to solve problems that would go unsolved.

Learn That "What Else" Often Means "Think Differently," Not "Do More"

Denise Van Tassell, training and talent development manager at the network communication services company Spirent, told us that she helps her people understand that the *else* in the question often means "something different," not just "do more," as in more hours in the office or more weekends at work. "What else . . . ?" shouldn't be a guilt trip. She went on to say, "Asking the question helps when you're banging your head against the wall. By asking, 'What else . . . ?' you will eventually find a way under, around, or through to a different way. If the new way is less work with better results, then more power to you."

The problem, however, is that it's easy to get stuck in that "banging your head against the wall" mode, despite all the headaches it causes. It's also easy to coast when things are going well, lulling yourself into accepting the tried and true when you should be exploring the new and improved. Asking, "What else can I/we do?" cures both.

The popularity of this "stuck in the rut" thinking shows up in another data point from our study. When looking at something as simple as "by-when's," 62 percent of respondents said that people often failed to stick to established deadlines, viewing them as general guidelines rather than must-do organizational mandates. This casual, or even lazy, way of thinking and acting puts a stranglehold on asking "What else . . . ?" and kills any "under, around, or through" thinking.

It's good to remember that there are many problems you can't solve on your own. You need help and help can come from surprising, and unexpected, sources. This is where "What else . . . ?" can reveal a new way of thinking. We see it happen all the time. Call it karma, positive energy, good vibes, or heavenly help. Whatever label you use, not giving up and continuing to operate Above The Line with a Solve It attitude can almost magically invite an unexpected and desperately needed solution.

Case in point: When Michigan resident James Robinson's car broke down, he couldn't afford to *fix it*. So every day for more than ten years he walked twenty-one miles round-trip to work and back! Leaving home at eight A.M. for his two P.M. shift, he would finish his work by ten P.M. and make it back home by four A.M. Rain. Shine. Snow. Sleet. Wind. He was more dependable than the U.S. post office.

As it turns out, after his years of hoofing it, others finally got wind of his story and came to the rescue by demonstrating the power of "What else can I do?" After a *Detroit Free Press* reporter wrote an article spotlighting Robinson's story, a university student read it and launched a GoFundMe campaign. A local car dealer offered a new car. Others chipped in, and eventually thousands of people donated more than $250,000 to assist Mr. Robinson. You can bet he no longer walks to work!

When you're doing all you can and "what more?" seems an impossible task, try thinking differently, step outside your box, and open your mind to solutions that were there all the time. Solutions you just couldn't see.

Act as If Your Life Depends on It

Salem, Oregon, fire chief Mike Niblock and his team of fire captains ιι ι ιι Ιΐ τι μ Ρι ιιαιΐτ ιτι ιι Ιιΐααυα ιΐιυ Ιιιμΐιυυι ααναιαξ ξαλι ιαιι ιιι ιιι nation—an ambitious goal. At the time, a fire department in Seattle held the nation's highest rate at 63 percent. Salem's sat at a mere 41.2 percent. With a severe lack of funds and emergency calls increasing, the Salem Fire Department was tapped out, overworked, and lacking resources. Mike and his team could easily have thrown up their hands and said, "Oh, well, forty-one's the best we got." Or they could ask a truly life-and-death question, "What else can we do?"

By asking the question over a period of weeks, the team eventually concluded that to increase the cardiac save rate they needed quicker CPR and earlier defibrillation. That led them to realize the need for more automated external defibrillators (AEDs) in the city. Their goal: an AED in each cop car. But there were no public tax dollars for that.

Asking the Solve It question once again led them to set up the Salem Fire Foundation. People throughout the city became engaged in the new foundation's quest. After all, who doesn't want to save lives? When naysayers asked why the foundation was raising money to buy equipment for the police instead of the fire department, Mike just said that they were raising money to save people, and that the police often got there first.

Asking "What else can I do?" yet again led Mike and his people to pitch the Salem Fire Foundation in public forums. Cardiologists and other doctors saw the good and got in on it, adding credibility and making it possible to raise thousands of dollars. In a little under a year the foundation has raised nearly $220,000 dollars, allowing the purchase of sixty-four AEDs for the police cars and an additional fifty AEDs to be placed in the community. The foundation has also provided the funding to teach forty-five hundred local eighth graders CPR and AED skills each year. Mike reported, "We've already shaved three seconds off our response time, and that translates into saving more lives. We won't stop asking, 'What else can we do?' until we have the highest save rate in the country. In fact, we won't stop asking that question ever!"

Taking an "if my life depended on it" view will help you ask the Solve It question the right way, with the right urgency and determination.

Whatever You Do, Tie It to Results!

Asking, "What else can we do?" is vital to seeing, owning, and solving, but the question needs the proper context to be most effective.

"What else can we do to achieve desired results?" provides that context.

We've already discussed Key Results at length back in Trait 7, but it's healthy to remember that most respondents to our survey felt that their organizations did not define their Key Results clearly enough. Additionally, when we asked if people throughout their organizations aligned their work with Key Results, 32 percent answered true, while 68 percent answered false. Clearly, you need to know the results you wish to achieve; otherwise, you won't be able to align your Solve It efforts with results.

Finally, Chris Baldwin, president of Kohler Co.'s faucets business, reminded us not to mistake motion and activity for results: "Make sure you're getting points on the board. Don't just keep engaging in activities that fail to advance your strategies. Tie your efforts to results and look for where your efforts can produce points."

Once you learn to constantly ask, "What else can I/we do to achieve the desired result?" you open the door to new solutions and breakthrough performance.

Go fix it! PART 3

PATH **A**: fix it for **Myself** → PAGE **265**

PATH **B**: fix it on **My Team** → PAGE **269**

PATH **C**: fix it in **My Organization** → PAGE **273**

ACCOUNTABILITY TRAIT 10
Collaborating Across Functional Boundaries

---

the need to fix it

Is this trait a **clear strength** of people in your organization?

NO **73%**

YES **27%**

Is this trait a **clear strength** in team leaders?

NO **68%**

YES **32%**

Source: Partners In Leadership **Workplace Accountability Study**

Imagine your preschool-aged son or daughter coming to you and asking, "Mommy, where do silos come from?" Recognizing that as a really smart question, particularly given the challenges in breaking down silos at work and getting people to work well across functional boundaries, you respond, "Well, everyone knows they come from elephants, dear." Surprised? That image came to us when we recalled the words of Creighton Abrams Jr., Chief of Staff of the United States Army, when he proposed that *the way you eat an elephant is one bite at a time*! Silos in organizations are big and complex, like elephants, and the only way to attack them is to divide and conquer, taking one bite at a time.

People need structure, and that structure ultimately shapes how they think. In our view, the only real solution for breaking down silos and getting people to collaborate is culture. A Culture of

Accountability overcomes structural silos and opens the door to taking the Solve It step in effective and powerful ways.

Consider the story of when Tim Peoples, new plant director for Ocean Spray's Kenosha plant, along with his boss, the vice president of operations, held an ominous early-morning meeting on the warehouse floor. The VP had launched into a severe scolding, calling out the employees for being the highest cost producers while racking up the worst safety record, the worst material loss, the poorest employee morale and engagement scores, on and on. He wrapped up by showing everyone a picture of how Ocean Spray's senior leadership viewed their plant: a broken-down, rusted-out, dead Volkswagen Beetle. The COO's parting words: "You're broken, Kenosha."

Tim heard the message loud and clear, and he knew they needed to make some big changes that would demand a new kind of teamwork across the organization. "We could no longer be stuck in our individual silos. We had to collaborate. To be willing to reach across boundaries and embrace labor and management coming together."

After that early-morning wake-up call, Tim enlarged the picture of the VW into a four by five-foot poster and hung it on a wall in the cafeteria. He then had a picture of a new Porsche cut into puzzle pieces, representing the kind of change they needed to achieve—the "new Kenosha." Over time, as Kenosha's people made progress, the Porsche puzzle pieces were placed over the broken-down VW poster. The incomplete Porsche picture that emerged provided a daily reminder of the need to work together differently to finish the job and turn the plant around. One piece at a time, the VW disappeared, while the high-performing, turbocharged Porsche took its place.

Tim reported that his plant ultimately delivered the lowest costs in its forty-five-year history, drove millions of dollars in expenses out of their budget, accrued more than 600,000 aggregate plant work hours (450 days) without a lost-time injury, and saw employee engagement jump. To top it off, hourly employees nominated the plant as the best place to work in the area through the local chamber of commerce.

Collaborate

What did Tim Peoples and his management team in the plant do to get these results? They trained everyone, all the way down to the frontline workers, to understand that they all had joint accountability to fix organizational problems. They were in it together, and they could complete the puzzle only with everyone's help.

Management went onto the plant floor to engage with anyone and everyone, knocking down boundaries and collaborating in a way they had not experienced before. Plant employees eventually came to expect their leaders to be there, engaging them in conversation, helping to solve problems, and offering support to the team. Departments came together to power through problems and find solutions.

To us, the word *collaborate* means to "co-labor" for a common purpose. The fruit of that effort is always creative problem solving. If you're not getting a creative charge, that's a sign that you're not achieving cross-functional collaboration. We saw this happen in a big way at Cardiac Pacemakers, Inc. (CPI). The transition the organization finally experienced was significant, moving from a collection of silo groups, all competing for resources and influence, to a single team, with everyone focused on the same result: *to develop and launch new products successfully.* Initially, people said that CPI could not "develop their way out of a paper bag." Ultimately, however, they produced fourteen new products in fourteen months and became the leader in their industry.

But those results came only after something important happened: people began to collaborate. They shared resources, lent people to other departments when necessary, cared enough about how things were going to give one another important feedback, offered up budget dollars for the good of the whole team, and assigned their most creative people to the heavyweight dedicated product development teams.

When Cardiac Pacemakers co-labored for a common goal, they harvested the fruit of that labor in the form of the world's first pacemaker with a lithium anode and a lithium-iodide electrolyte solid state battery, a product that became the industry standard for pacemakers worldwide.

Create a Common Purpose with Key Results

Most of you know the game of American football. If you do, here's a good question for you: Whose job is it to jump on a fumble? Is there a designated "fumble jumper" who comes off the bench as soon as the ball touches turf? Of course not. When a ball is knocked loose, it's instant pandemonium. A fumble triggers instinct. Bodies pile. Why? Because the common goal across all positions is to win the game. Make the play-offs. Win the Super Bowl. A recovered fumble can change the game. Even though each player has a clearly defined role, they all know none of that matters if a ball gets loose. When that happens, everyone's a fumble jumper!

Fumbles happen in business, too. But why do so many people avoid jumping on a fumble, refusing to take ownership, as though the entire game didn't depend on it? We think, in part, it's because the business has not clearly defined what *winning* means.

According to our Workplace Study, only 57 percent of employees said their organizations had identified three to four Key Results that everyone rallied around. That means nearly half (43 percent) didn't know or understand the importance of why jumping on the ball even matters. Although 57 percent might sound acceptable, when you combine that with the fact that almost 68 percent of respondents thought people in their organizations did not properly align their work with the Key Results, it suggests a problem with shifting priorities, poorly defined Key Results, and misaligned job roles.

When we asked Dave Szczupak, executive vice president of global product organization at Whirlpool, about the concept of team collaboration and alignment around Key Results, he told us that he's heard employees watching others in tough spots actually say, "Well, sorry for you, but there's no hole in *my* end of the boat." This silo view can sink the ship. Dave continued, "What people don't realize is that nobody in business is alone in their own boat anymore, it's always a company boat now, and even though there may not be a perceived hole from their perspective, there's generally a leak somewhere."

To plug those holes we recommend that you:

- Clarify three to four organization-wide Key Results.
- Make those Key Results meaningful, measurable, and memorable.
- Ensure that each functional leader understands, aligns with, and promotes these enterprise-wide Key Results.
- Align every group's goals with Key Results.

It's the lack of alignment around a clear set of meaningful organizational priorities that allows people on teams, and teams within the organization, to remain fractured and combative. Only common results can pull people together across the great functional divides and get them solving problems together.

Make Time to Collaborate

The kind of collaboration that leads to creative solutions doesn't just happen in the normal course of business. Someone, somewhere, must take steps to get the right people talking about the right things in the right way.

Vincent Weafer, vice president at Intel Security Group, McAfee Labs, a cyber security thought leadership company, openly admitted to us that they have struggled to get cross functional teams all pointed in the same direction. Vincent said that a few years ago they needed to get two dysfunctional groups working better together. But planning meetings and team-building workshops were just not getting the job done.

Then one day someone suggested everyone drop what they were doing and jump on a bus for a little Wednesday evening bowling. On the shuttle to and from the bowling alley, they started talking. Barriers miraculously crumbled. Vincent said, "Of the forty people on the bus, twenty must have been interacting, laughing, strategizing, talking shop. 'Maybe we can do it this way?' 'No, not that way, but maybe this way?'" Such a strong camaraderie had developed among the team that when the bus drew near the office at the end of the night, they told the driver to just keep driving around.

Although Vincent's group had tried to crack the collaboration code for weeks and weeks, they didn't make much progress until this bus ride. When they finally loosened up, all the pieces started coming together. There's no way to reproduce the energy of a bowling bus trip with phone calls, e-mails, texts, or WebEx conferences. It's taking the time, often outside the office, to stir up the needed chemistry for true collaboration to take place.

This brief yes/no assessment should help you pinpoint what you can do to speed up collaboration:

Have you introduced a set of Key Results for your organization and asked functional leaders to connect what they do to those results?
_____ Yes/No

Have you scheduled time for cross-functional team building (a little bowling, for example)?
_____ Yes/No

Have you set aside time for an exchange of cross-functional feedback to facilitate open, real-time communication?
_____ Yes/No

Have you allowed time for cross-functional problem solving around the Key Results: "What else can we do to ensure we achieve these results?"
_____ Yes/No

Have you asked functional leaders to meet one-on-one to coordinate their working relationships and lead the collaboration effort?
_____ Yes/No

If you want to infuse greater collaboration and joint accountability among teams, departments, functions, divisions, or peers, start with a set of clearly defined results that everyone can share.

See the Big Picture

In the Workplace Accountability Study, when asked how well people worked together in their organizations to find solutions, 46 percent of respondents said that people "tend to get stuck quickly on problems and obstacles they face." Another 27 percent said people didn't even try, expecting others to solve problems for them. These are pretty alarming numbers that reflect a Below The Line approach that leads to less collaboration and more cross-functional finger-pointing company wide.

Just how do employees become so blind to their own lack of collaboration? It often comes from a focus on protecting their own turf, even at the risk of not getting results. Hard to believe, but it happens every day. Turf and territorialism must be traded for teamwork and trust. To do that, try a few of our favorite turf blasters, techniques guaranteed to help people become less preoccupied with their own territory in order to become more cross-functionally savvy:

1. Invite a leader from another function to attend an occasional staff meeting and exchange input and feedback with your staff.
2. Get a "collaboration coach" from another team or division to facilitate greater teamwork between functions. Treat the goal of greater collaboration as seriously as any business result you need to achieve.
3. Solicit feedback from members of another team to tell you where you or your team's actions help or hurt their efforts.
4. Insist on a collaborative approach during your one-on-one conversations.

5. When asked, "What do you think?" or, "What do you want to do?" ensure that your views are informed by the collaboration of others.

6. Declare that the collaborative model across functional boundaries is the way you want to operate.

Collaboration is about breaking down boundaries and generating ideas that solve problems and get results. As you achieve this, you will find new success in working across what was once a great divide.

Go fix it!   PART 3

PATH **A**: fix it for Myself → **PAGE 278**

PATH **B**: fix it on My Team → **PAGE 282**

PATH **C**: fix it in My Organization → **PAGE 286**

ACCOUNTABILITY TRAIT 11
Creatively Dealing with Obstacles

┌─ **the need to fix it** ─────────────────────────────────┐

Is this trait a **clear strength** of people in your organization?

NO 71%

YES 29%

Is this trait a **clear strength** in team leaders?

NO 68%

YES 32%

Source: Partners In Leadership **Workplace Accountability Study**

└──┘

J. K. Rowling's life is a rags-to-riches story that evokes the best of the Solve It mentality. Seven years after being rejected by Oxford University, Rowling found herself jobless, with a dependent child and a failed marriage. Seeing herself as a failure, she suffered from depression and even contemplated suicide. Subsisting on government welfare, she described herself as "poor as it is possible to be in modern Britain, without being homeless."

In spite of these challenges, she somehow persisted and ultimately penned the bestselling Harry Potter series. The journey to getting her story published wasn't an easy one. She wrote the drafts for her books in cafés while tending to her baby daughter, scribbling notes on napkins, and eventually finished her first manuscript on an old manual typewriter. No fewer than twelve publishing houses rejected the manuscript of her first book. The one that did finally accept it advised Rowling to get a day job because she had "little chance of making money in children's books." Ultimately, J. K. Rowling's Harry Potter books would become the best-selling book series in history.

Forbes identified Rowling as the first person to become a billionaire by writing books, and during her heyday she was considered the second-richest female "entertainer" in the world. She achieved all this despite her difficult childhood. In her own words she said, "There is an expiry date for blaming your parents for steering you in the wrong direction. The moment you are old enough to take the wheel, responsibility lies with you." Rowling's story shows how embracing accountability to creatively deal with the obstacles you face leads to success.

Janee Harteau, police chief of the Minneapolis Police Department, is one of only a few female police chiefs in the country. Like Rowling, Harteau also attributes her success to a strong sense of accountability. "Obstacles are just something you must deal with and move on. You can't dwell on them, or they will keep you from getting where you want to go. It's all about a focus on the goals—without that focus you get lost in the weeds. So stop saying can't and start asking how you can."

We assume that you too want to *fix it* badly enough to muster the energy to do what it takes to break through whatever blocks your path to results. According to our Workplace Accountability Study, when we posed the statement "I can readily and clearly identify that there is something that I really want to achieve—a clear result in my life or work that I really want to get," we found that 83 percent said yes and only 17 percent said no. Clearly, for most people, motivation isn't the problem, it's the hard work it takes to conquer the obstacles.

Think Outside the Box

Of course, this kind of creativity does not always involve coming up with something new; it may just be a new way of attacking existing problems. The nine-dots puzzle makes this point. Take a shot at it:

1. Connect all nine dots using only four straight lines.
2. Never go through any dot twice.
3. Don't lift your pen or pencil from the page.

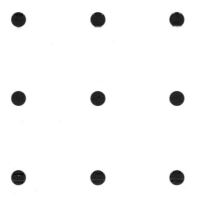

How'd you do? In our experience only about 10 percent of first-timers will figure it out. For those who have seen it before and forgotten its solution, the odds are still only one in four that they will solve it. It's tougher than it looks. We've put the solution at the end of the chapter, but a big clue for you here is that most people restrict their thinking with boundaries, building a fence around the dots and making a solution impossible.

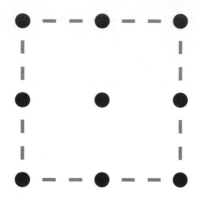

The answer actually demands that you jump the self-imposed fence and get outside the box to find the solutions. We realize, however, that getting outside the box isn't easy.

"Necessity is the mother of invention." That's why you should see obstacles not as problems but as opportunities for out-of-the-box thinking. Back in 1888, an undertaker named Almon Strowger suspected that the local telephone switchboard operator, who was the wife of a competitor, was sending all the calls for burial services to her husband. Faced with a problem seemingly outside his control, Strowger eventually invented the automatic telephone exchange that allowed for direct dialing of numbers. Talk about getting outside the box! Adopting a Solve It mind-set sits at the heart of what it means to operate Above The Line, a mind-set driven by the question "What else can I do?"

Free Your Imagination

You likely don't know the name Jeff Hawkins, but he's been dubbed "the father of handheld computing." Back in 1989, many experts considered his GRiDPad invention "an engineering marvel." So why did it bomb? *Obstacles.* Most potential users thought it too clunky to carry around. That forced Jeff to reevaluate, reimagine, and reinvent, eventually coming up with a device that would fit in a shirt pocket. As the story goes, he went to his garage and cut a block of wood into a slice not much bigger than a deck of playing cards. He printed various "screens" on paper simulating buttons and icons, and then glued them to the small block. People thought Jeff was crazy when he would pull the wood block from his shirt pocket in meetings and pretend to use it to check his calendar, schedule appointments, write memos, and jot notes. He eventually added a chopstick as a stylus he pretended to use to write messages.

The first product based on his wood-block design came out in 1992. Called the Zoomer, it failed due to poor and unproven emerging technology. *More obstacles.* More reimagining and more reinventing. A product called Graffiti came next. *Again more obstacles.* That version also failed. Again, reinvention. Reimagining. With new and improved partners and ideas, a few years later Jeff Hawkins finally released the Palm Pilot in 1997. Success! The Handspring Visor followed in 1999. Another success, and the handheld computer, precursor to the smartphone, was born.

When it comes to imagination and reimagination, to invention and reinvention, the Palm Pilot story suggests some crucial questions you should ask as you move forward along your own GRiDPad–Zoomer–Graffiti–Palm Pilot–Handspring Visor path. Consider these questions (and recommendations) in light of any obstacles currently blocking your path:

How would I grade my level of creativity on a scale from 1 to 10?
Force yourself to come up with three new ideas before dinner.
Who is the most creative person I know?
Give them a call and brainstorm solutions with them.

Who else has faced this challenge, and what did they do?
Find out.
If my life depended upon it, what else could I do?
Consider everything, and make a list.
How much research/reading have I done on the topic?
Study and learn as much as you can about what others have done or recommended.

In today's tech-savvy world, you must realize that "I don't know" doesn't cut it anymore. If you need to know the current temperature in Bora Bora or estimate the number of ants alive on planet Earth at any given moment, you can ask Google or Siri and find either answer in under half a second. It's amazing. In today's innovative marketplace, creativity and invention are necessities, not luxuries, particularly when working to overcome tough obstacles. (Incidentally, it's currently 82 degrees in Bora Bora, and the world's ant population hovers at 321,035,624,829,901,000 . . . and counting.)

Collaborate to Be Creative

One key to any creative problem-solving dilemma is recognizing that you don't have to go it alone. There are others you can and should seek out and partner with. Often the key to creative code cracking is collaboration. This means involving the right people at the right time in order to help you discover creative solutions for moving forward and overcoming the obstacles you face. Consider your own potential team of problem-solving advisers by identifying people in your life who you could plug into the specific and necessary roles described below. Ask them to consult with and advise you on what else you can do.

1. **The Professor.** This person should be really good at thinking critically, possessing strong analytical skills and maintaining a

strong bias toward data. They may be an engineer, mathematician, doctor, lawyer, or anyone who is academically successful. They may not be able to generate ideas, like the Ideator described below, but they should be the type of person who can help you break down the problem and think about it differently.

2. **The Problem Solver.** This person should be someone with a proven track record for solving their own problems in the real world. Most likely, they will bring a fresh view to ways you might attack the challenges you are facing. They will likely have been an entrepreneur themselves and no stranger to problem solving. They display a bit of a MacGyver instinct, and the ability to make lemonade out of lemons.

3. **The Ideator.** This person should be a deep thinker who can help you generate ideas that you have not yet considered. This should be someone with a reputation for being creative, a real "idea guy/gal." Invite them to brainstorm solutions with you. Don't filter them in any way; just let them run wild with ideas.

4. **The Questioner.** This person should help you test-drive and prove your ideas, looking for the risks and downsides involved. They should show a talent for seeing and raising the concerns that you might overlook, a skill for playing the devil's advocate.

5. **The Veteran.** This is someone who has done it before, one who knows the ropes and has probably stood in your shoes. Their past experience will prove invaluable as you strive to find solutions.

You most likely know the people you could cast into one or more of the categories above. Build your network and develop these relationships so that you collect a solid group of core individuals you can turn to when faced with difficult obstacles. They may or may not be people you work with regularly or who are even in your organization. You may find their advice, counsel, input, and ideas key to the breakthrough you've been looking for.

Believe That All Obstacles Can Be Overcome

Bobby Jones, the most successful amateur golfer in history, once said, "Competitive golf is played mainly on a five-and-a-half-inch course, the space between your ears." That seems exactly right to us. When it comes to Solving It, it's all in your head. Everyone faces tough obstacles they must overcome. In the Workplace Study, we asked respondents to consider: "I am currently facing difficult circumstances that stand in the way of the result I want to get . . ." The chart below shows how they responded.

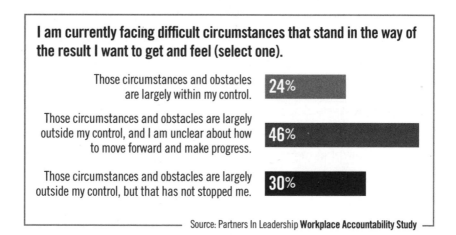

I am currently facing difficult circumstances that stand in the way of the result I want to get and feel (select one).

Those circumstances and obstacles are largely within my control.	24%
Those circumstances and obstacles are largely outside my control, and I am unclear about how to move forward and make progress.	46%
Those circumstances and obstacles are largely outside my control, but that has not stopped me.	30%

Source: Partners In Leadership **Workplace Accountability Study**

Almost half of those surveyed indicated that they faced obstacles that were largely outside their control, meaning that the respondents were unable to move forward and believed that solutions would come only from somewhere else.

If you want to ramp up your ability to Solve It, then consider every obstacle as a solvable problem. When you approach problem solving in this way, you keep searching for solutions and avoid the trap of getting stuck Below The Line, where you will find only frustration and stagnation. Considering every problem as solvable doesn't mean you have to solve them all by yourself, but it does mean that only you can drive the discovery process for finding solutions.

This Solve It mentality will pay off big-time as you discover the extra determination and motivation to find answers that allow you to overcome obstacles and get the result you want.

The Nine-Dots Solution

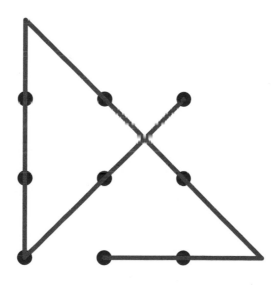

The answer to the nine-dots puzzle shows how the key to creatively overcoming obstacles lies outside the box, outside the lines, outside your normal way of thinking. We encourage you to break out of the box and try something new: intentionally collaborate, believe you can overcome, find your imaginative resources or those of others on your team, learn what worked and what didn't. New experiences in these areas will create new beliefs around your confidence and capability and improve results for everyone.

PATH **A**: fix it for Myself → PAGE **291**

PATH **B**: fix it on My Team → PAGE **295**

PATH **C**: fix it in My Organization → PAGE **299**

ACCOUNTABILITY TRAIT 12
Taking the Necessary Risks

— **the need to fix it** ———————————————————

Is this trait a **clear strength** of people in your organization?

NO **80%**

YES **20%**

Is this trait a **clear strength** in team leaders?

NO **73%**

YES **27%**

———————— Source: Partners In Leadership **Workplace Accountability Study** —

An accountable person working Above The Line who practices the 16 Accountability Traits disrupts the norm of how things are done. By being disruptive, we mean they are rocking the boat, shaking things up, or taking a break from the way people are used to doing things. In fact, the very act of Solving It implies that someone is inventive, creative, thinking out of the box, and taking the necessary risks to overcome challenges and make things happen.

Of course, the objective isn't just to take risks, it's to get results; but that often can't happen unless you are willing to place your bets on different strategies and tactics, understanding that the chance of failure is always present. Risk taking should remain true to the one real purpose in business: achieving results in light of both the obstacles and the potential. That often means trying something that might fail in order to bring about a highly desirable result you could

obtain no other way. We have found that every breakthrough requires a "break with" something. A *break from* the norm. *A break
from* the way you've always done things, from familiar patterns and
systems, in order to try something untried, untested, or unproven.

It's easy to see this in entrepreneurs who disrupt entire market-
places. Take Oakley, Inc., founded by Jim Jannard with just three
hundred dollars. He is known today in his organization as someone
who is "disruptive by design." Though at the time he launched his
business many manufacturers were serving the motorcycle-
motocross circuit, Jim Jannard took a risk and turned the market
upside down with an innovative idea. Jim had noticed a feature on
the typical motorcycle that most overlooked: the handgrip. In his
home garage lab, the budding entrepreneur invented his first disruptive product, an out-of-the-box bike handgrip made from a new
material with a distinctive shape and feel. Soon after, he began sell-
ing his revolutionary handgrips from his car trunk at motocross
events. The pros quickly took notice, and Oakley was born.

Jim's next "break with" arrived in the form of the O-Frame gog-
gle. Sunglasses have been around since the caveman, so why bother
to think differently about them? Jim's answer: give riders clearer
lenses and a wider peripheral view. Oakley's Eyeshades started a rev-
olution in eyewear, moving sunglasses from a mere afterthought ac-
cessory to a piece of equipment every biker suddenly seemed to need.

The reward for all the risk and disruption? To date, Oakley has
won more than one thousand design and utility patents worldwide,
and the company has become a household name, with its sunglasses
worn by celebrities and the world's greatest athletes (and likely even
by you). To top it off, Oakley was acquired by Luxottica in 2007 for
more than $2 billion, all made possible by a risk-taking, disruptive
guy who started a business in his garage.

Take a Risk, Be Disruptive

Of course, we like to think of risk taking and disruption as outcomes of accountable behavior. The Solve It question "What else can I do to achieve results?" captures the mind-set that is essential to this kind of progress. This mind-set causes you to question boundaries and potentially rewrite some of the rules.

In the Star Trek movie *The Wrath of Khan,* Captain-in-training Kirk solves the unsolvable-by-design Kobayashi Maru, a war simulation test. After struggling three different times to find a solution to the no-win scenario, Kirk takes a risk, sneaking into Starfleet Academy headquarters and reprogramming the simulation in order to beat it. When confronted by an academy colleague for cheating, Kirk replies, "I don't believe in no-win scenarios." For him to win, it turned out, he had to think differently and rewrite the rules.

In their bestselling book *First, Break All the Rules,* authors Marcus Buckingham and Curt Coffman came to the same conclusion as Captain Kirk. Based on Gallup interviews of eighty thousand managers over the last twenty-five years, the best managers operate contrary to the standard guidelines for managing and retaining talented people. For example, the authors found that the best managers don't try to fix people (the default mode for all too many managers), but focus instead on people's innate strengths and existing talent. Disrupting the old way of managing people by emphasizing strengths rather than weaknesses has gone a long way toward rewriting the rules of "best" management practices.

Searching for new and different ways to approach problems is essential to the Solve It step. In our study, almost half of the respondents said that they were facing difficult circumstances that largely fell outside their control and that they felt unsure about how to move forward and make progress. Only 27 percent believed circumstances and obstacles were within their control. Another 33 percent said that while certain circumstances were outside their control, that did not stop them from moving forward.

One fact that has become clear from our research and work with leaders from all over the world is that the Solve It mentality requires that you take the necessary risks and embrace disruption in order to solve the tough challenges people face in business today. When it comes to business success on both the personal and organizational levels, disruption is the new normal.

Disrupt Purposefully

Taking the Solve It step means that you are intentional and deliberate in your efforts to solve problems and overcome obstacles. This makes risk taking strategic and targeted. Personal disruption should be thoughtful, leading to a reimagination of the rules that will inspire a breakthrough in both thinking and actions. Asking yourself these five disruption questions will help to ensure you are on the right track to purposeful disruption:

1. Am I transparent with everyone about the risks that I am taking?
Working in secret or hiding information will only work against you.

2. Are my suggestions self-serving, or do they clearly benefit the team and the organization?
If your efforts will benefit only yourself, then you should carefully evaluate the course you are taking.

3. Am I asking for input and advice?
Open communication helps to ensure necessary risk taking.

4. Am I spending too much time planning for failure?

If you find yourself overly consumed with what could happen and who to blame if things go wrong, then this may be the wrong risk to be taking.

5. Can you make a clear case for the benefit this risk will create?

If that case does not convince others, you should carefully reconsider pursuing the risk.

Taking steps to disrupt with purpose is what we call accountable risk taking. That sort of risk taking is entirely necessary when it comes to solving really tough and challenging problems and it always comes with moving Above The Line. To assist you in your journey, here are a few additional tips for doing this well:

- Focus on the outcome.

    Get very clear on what you're doing, and for whom you're doing it (customers, employees, families, communities, the planet, yourself, etc.).

- Know that complexity affects transparency.

    Make each step simple and clear.

- Anticipate pushback.

    Remember what Einstein said: "Great spirits have always encountered violent opposition from mediocre minds."

- Fail. Fail again. Fail faster: the more cycles, the faster you arrive at a solution.

    Thomas Edison not only failed his way to success, he insisted, "When you have exhausted all possibilities, remember this: you haven't."

When you disrupt purposefully, you move beyond "what is" to "what if." You push to discover the possibilities, which often requires some questioning of the probabilities and inviting the risk of the unknown.

Use Disruption to Speed Things Up

Joe Nilson, director of business development for Tolero Pharmaceuticals, a pharmaceutical innovator, and a weekend car-racing enthusiast, described the mind-set behind what he has learned about driving a race car. "When you're driving a car at 150-plus miles per hour, you need to be looking up and ahead, far ahead, not right in front of you. The rule for moving that fast is: 'Look ahead! Look ahead! Look ahead!'" He told us that the car will basically drive itself with just a little direction, but warned, "If you aren't looking ahead, you'll be going too slow or end up wrapped around the axle of the guy in front of you."

In our fast-paced, digitally driven world, business leaders need to adopt race-car-driver vision. They must harness disruption to accelerate the problem-solving process with a clear focus on the needed outcome, and they must adopt a Solve It quick pedal-to-the-metal mentality. That's accomplished by looking ahead, in most cases, well beyond the present situation to some clear objective far up the road.

However, it's hard to look ahead if you're stuck Below The Line. Our study also showed that 84 percent of respondents experienced at least one excursion Below The Line in the previous two weeks! Operating Above The Line allows you to speed things up and avoid the time and energy wasted playing the blame game and languishing in the victim cycle.

Ultimately, many solutions will benefit from faster cycle time. "How can we do this differently to create a more direct path to the problem?" is a good question to ask on more than one occasion and in more than one way.

Find the Courage to Be Disruptive

Which concerns you more, the risk imposed by change and innovation or the risk inherent in hunkering down, doing nothing, and playing it safe? In our study, we asked: "Once someone has decided to change, the biggest problem is . . . ?"

- 81 percent said they didn't follow through on the change.
- 19 percent said they resisted other people changing.

Why don't people follow through? Why do they resist change in others?

It's usually a lack of confidence or loss of nerve. Taking the necessary risks requires courage. Courage comes from believing that you are right. Being effective at disruption likewise takes believing that you are right. So why don't people follow through with changes they already decided to make? Either they don't believe that the change is really right, or they lack the courage to face the challenges that will come with the change as they work to make it happen. That's a perfectly normal human response, but one that every risk taker and disruptor must overcome.

What does taking the necessary risk look like for you personally? What would it look like for you at your next meeting? At your company, do you fear you're taking a risk when you speak your mind in an Above The Line way? Would others support you? And what about the values of your organization? Most organizational values include some form of honesty, integrity, and focus on the customer. But does your company say one thing and support another? We often hear people say something like, "Yeah, it says that on the wall, but that's not how it works around here." Do you feel it's too risky to stand up for a corporate objective or value in the face of daily experiences that say otherwise? If so, where do you get the courage?

We all know that for a company to stay in business, taking risks is necessary. But when it's *my* risk, *my* job, or *my* reputation, it can be intimidating, even immobilizing. We love these insightful words that are often attributed in one form or another to one of America's most quoted writers of inspirational maxims, William Arthur Ward: *"risks must be taken . . . the person who risks nothing, does nothing, has nothing, and is nothing . . . he cannot learn, feel, change, grow or live. . . . / only a person who risks is free."*

Taking the necessary risk is an essential part of operating Above The Line. It's inescapable. At some point, the accountable person will feel compelled to step out, be disruptive, and put it all on the line in order to get results.

PATH **A**: fix it for **Myself** → PAGE **303**

PATH **B**: fix it on **My Team** → PAGE **307**

PATH **C**: fix it in **My Organization** → PAGE **311**

ACCOUNTABILITY TRAIT 13
Doing the Things I (We) Say I (We) Will Do

┌─ **the need to fix it** ─────────────────────────────┐

Is this trait a **clear strength** of people in your organization?

NO 63%

YES 37%

Is this trait a **clear strength** in team leaders?

NO 69%

YES 31%

Source: Partners In Leadership **Workplace Accountability Study**

When was the last time you heard someone in your organization say something like, "Nobody does what they say they'll do"; "People promise me a response by the end of the day, but don't do it"; "They won't return my e-mail or calls"; "Why must I chase everything down to get people to follow through?"; "It seems like every time someone sets a deadline, they miss it"? In fact, when was the last time *you* said something like this?

A major key to maintaining a Culture of Accountability is people faithfully doing what they say they will do. Only then can they help themselves, their teams, and their organizations execute on initiatives and efforts in a way that produces desired results. In our view the very essence of personal accountability lies in people doing the things they say they will do.

Laura Coleman, president of Bay College in Escanaba, Michigan, faced the challenge of convincing employees to jump into the school's transformational change effort. The professors and staff needed to take the Do It step and think and act differently about (1) improving student retention and success, (2) increasing employee engagement and satisfaction, and (3) building stronger community and employer relations.

After going through our Culture Track training to identify these changes, they discovered a major challenge, one we all face from time to time: the fear of change itself. People were afraid of change and what it might mean for them personally and professionally. Even some members of Laura's own senior team weren't doing what they said they would do. To achieve major improvements in the three areas Laura identified that needed change, everyone at Bay College would have to fully commit. And Laura knew she had to lead the way.

To do that, she remained unwavering in her commitment to provide the best example of personal change by overcoming her own fears and doing the things she said she would do as their leader. She worked tirelessly with the reluctant members of her team. She modified meeting agendas, held weekly Focused Feedback sessions with every senior team member to lead by example, identified employees outside of senior leadership as "Leadership Mentors" to receive the hard feedback she might not have otherwise heard, and concentrated on improving her leadership and communication skills with a personal coach and mentor. As a model of "I Am Change," she inspired several members of her senior team to do the same.

It worked. The Bay College culture moved to a new and better future as the team itself changed and energized around a Culture of Accountability, most notably by everyone doing what they said they would do.

Deliver on What You Promise

When people intentionally set out to make good on their promises, amazing things can happen. The CEO of a hospital service provider and one of our clients (who will remain anonymous to ensure confidentiality with its client) used our Methodology for Changing Beliefs to create a new experience for one of his key customers. This leader we'll call "Chad" approached the disgruntled customer with a simple message: "I know you've developed some rather negative beliefs about us over the past few months, and I'm here to find out exactly what those beliefs are, so we can change them."

After the surprised customer picked herself up off the floor, she offered a detailed description of where she was coming from, how promises made were not kept, and how expectations weren't realized. She warned that this provider's reputation for not doing what they said they would do was becoming firmly entrenched with her employees. Chad surprised her again by saying, "These are not the beliefs we want you to have, so we're going to create a whole new set of experiences for you that will change your negative beliefs about us." For the next several minutes Chad then laid out what his firm planned to do, emphasizing the new experiences that he and his organization planned to create.

What happened over the weeks that followed was a dramatic and positive turnaround in how Chad's organization delivered on what they promised to their customer, and in what the customer had come to expect from them. Experience after experience, Chad's team was racking up points in the win column as they made sure they delivered on everything they promised. The impact was tremendous. Finally, the happy customer now held the belief this CEO wanted them to hold about his organization: that "we deliver on our promises."

Chad's experience illustrates an important point: people want you to deliver on what you promise. It's that simple. To be accountable means to do what you say you will do. That's the baseline for building performance as an individual, as a team, and as an entire organization. Just Do It.

Be True to Yourself

Consistently delivering on what you say you will do takes more than just checking items off a list. It needs to form the very core of who you are. It's called integrity, and everyone needs more of it. Integrity drives you to go beyond the "to do" list, not only doing what you say you will do but doing the things people hope you will do.

Consider this case in point. DeMarcus Smith worked as a janitor for a hospital under the Hospital Corporation of America's (HCA) umbrella of facilities. Among other tasks, he cleaned rooms before, during, and after a patient's stay. One day while tidying up a room, DeMarcus overheard a family encouraging a family member who was a patient to eat. She hadn't eaten for a while, and a nurse and doctor had joined the concerned family in the room to discuss the problem. The next day, when DeMarcus returned to clean the room, he noticed that the patient had once again not touched her food. "Do you need help eating?" he asked. The patient replied with a weak and pleading "Yes." DeMarcus put down his cleaning supplies and helped her eat.

By doing this, he exhibited the values and qualities that HCA hoped every employee would demonstrate: a firm commitment to the care and improvement of human life. With this act of service, his integrity and commitment went way beyond his job description, to the very mission of the organization: to truly "care" for the patient.

There's more to the story, though. Later, as he was on his way home, DeMarcus couldn't stop thinking about the patient and whether she was going to be able to eat her dinner. What would you do? What would you want your employees to do? DeMarcus went home, changed his clothes, and came back while off the clock to feed her dinner. Amazing! What's even more amazing is that De-Marcus continued feeding her for three more days—without telling anyone what he was doing. The patient regained her strength and was later discharged.

Hospital leadership acknowledged this employee as an example of what it means to practice integrity in harmony with the mission of the organization. DeMarcus stayed true to himself and his employer with his purpose-driven action. Doing the things you say you will do can also mean "doing the things you would intend to do, or what everyone would hope you would do, if you were fully aligned with the purpose of what we are all trying to accomplish." When people think and act in this manner, they create a Culture of Accountability that is truly unstoppable, producing consistently amazing results.

Mean What You Say

When asked "When I hold others accountable I generally mean . . . ?," 72 percent of respondents said, "getting people to do what they say they will do." Our Workplace Study reveals that many people lack confidence in their ability to execute on what they say they will do, due to workplace stress and workload pressures: 78 percent of respondents anticipated missed deadlines, 85 percent felt overwhelmed with the amount of work on their plate, and 71 percent thought they could not succeed because of the workload.

Consider these findings from the study:

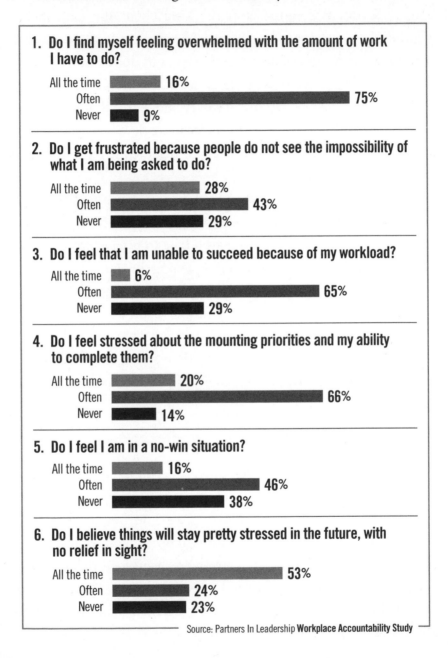

1. **Do I find myself feeling overwhelmed with the amount of work I have to do?**

   All the time — 16%
   Often — 75%
   Never — 9%

2. **Do I get frustrated because people do not see the impossibility of what I am being asked to do?**

   All the time — 28%
   Often — 43%
   Never — 29%

3. **Do I feel that I am unable to succeed because of my workload?**

   All the time — 6%
   Often — 65%
   Never — 29%

4. **Do I feel stressed about the mounting priorities and my ability to complete them?**

   All the time — 20%
   Often — 66%
   Never — 14%

5. **Do I feel I am in a no-win situation?**

   All the time — 16%
   Often — 46%
   Never — 38%

6. **Do I believe things will stay pretty stressed in the future, with no relief in sight?**

   All the time — 53%
   Often — 24%
   Never — 23%

Source: Partners In Leadership **Workplace Accountability Study**

Bottom line, a lot of people around you feel overwhelmed with their workload, frustrated with seemingly impossible tasks, uncertain they can succeed, and quite possibly stuck in a no-win situation, all with no relief in sight. Does this reduce their ability to do what they say they will do? Of course. An overstressed and unrealistic environment will torpedo anyone's ability to take the Do It step and operate Above The Line.

So . . . how do you *fix it*? You start by creating a "mean what you say" culture that enables people to do what they say they will do. Management must not overstress the organization with unrealistic priorities. They need to encourage a reality-based "mean what you say" dialogue that centers on setting achievable deadlines, conducting ongoing conversations about changing priorities, and engaging in straight talk about the trade-offs. When people can say yes to a deadline and mean it, they are liberated to get results. No longer will they just go through the motions.

Make Your Reputation Everything

Henry Ford got it right. "You can't build a reputation on what you are going to do." It's all about what you have done and what you are doing. When people know that you are a go-to, make-it-happen person who gets results, they will seek you out and rely on you. Bigtime. How do you get there? It starts by making an all-out commitment to follow through on everything you say you will do. Check how well you do this with three basic questions:

- Ask your five closest colleagues: "On a scale from one to ten, how well do I do everything I say I will do?"
- Ask your boss: "On a scale from one to ten, what's my reputation for making things happen?"

- Ask your spouse/partner/significant other: "On a scale from one to ten, how often do I do what I say I will do?"

When you honestly and regularly consider these questions, and the accompanying feedback, you launch a *fix it* process that leads to change and an improved reputation for doing everything you say you will do, the keystone of a Culture of Accountability.

Go fix it!

PART 3

PATH **A**: fix it for **Myself** → PAGE **315**

PATH **B**: fix it on **My Team** → PAGE **319**

PATH **C**: fix it in **My Organization** → PAGE **323**

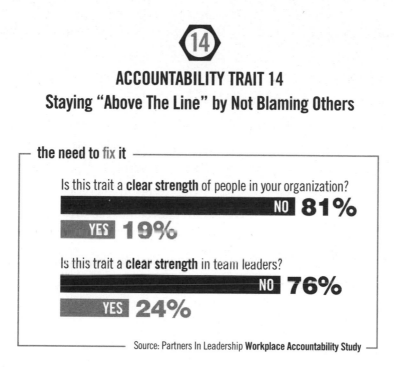

(14)

ACCOUNTABILITY TRAIT 14
Staying "Above The Line" by Not Blaming Others

┌─ **the need to fix it** ─────────────────

Is this trait a **clear strength** of people in your organization?

NO 81%

YES 19%

Is this trait a **clear strength** in team leaders?

NO 76%

YES 24%

Source: Partners In Leadership **Workplace Accountability Study**

You've come a long way on your journey to greater accountability by arriving at this final Above The Line Do It step. One important rule for the Do It journey to be successful, stay Above The Line by not blaming others. This Do It step depends on executing your plans and solutions without getting distracted and dragged back Below The Line. It means putting it all together and making *it* happen, whatever *it* happens to be.

At the manufacturing plant of a well-known food products brand, a union worker at the plant we will call "Ted" applied for a new position, but didn't get it because he didn't pass the required test. Ted, beyond upset, filed a grievance and publicly humiliated the manager of the plant, "Jim," who he claimed rigged the test so he wouldn't get the job. After all, Ted knew he was a solid contributor in the plant and could do the job well, so why shouldn't he get the position?

Both Ted and Jim needed to find a way to stay Above The Line by not blaming others. Both could easily drop Below The Line. Ted because he felt he had been intentionally passed up, and Jim because he had been falsely accused. Each faced a choice. Could they turn this challenge into an opportunity for growth?

Jim made the first move, inviting Ted into his office and asking him, "What do you need from me to succeed?" Ted, drop jawed and in shock that Jim was even talking to him, wasn't sure how to respond. Jim then asked, "Do you know what part of the test you failed?" Turns out Ted had failed the grammar portion. Jim asked Ted if he would like help. Ted took the next step, choosing to open up to Jim and accept his help.

Three months later, the same position opened up again. The same test stood in the way. Thanks to all of Jim's help, however, Ted passed the test, grammar and all, and won the job. If you were to talk to Ted today, which we did, you would not find a more passionate advocate for Jim as the leader of the plant.

Operating Above The Line is a choice, maybe the most important choice you will ever make. Bad things happen, and when they do, your ability to stay Above The Line and focus on what you can do instead of blaming others will lead to better results and, in the end, less stress and frustration.

Resist the Constant Force Dragging You Below The Line

It's difficult to avoid Below The Line thinking and behavior when your best plans encounter the worst obstacles. There is a strong gravitational force constantly tugging at you, dragging you Below The Line. This force originates from all of the legitimate, real issues that seemingly lie outside your control. Problems you don't believe you can solve, people you don't think you can influence, and resources you lack the power to allocate. These and other real issues almost legitimize the "fact" that you can't move forward until someone or something else solves the problems for you.

Have you ever experienced this kind of downward spiral, where it felt as if some outside force or person has created a problem just for you? The Workplace Accountability Study shows that "When it comes to the way other people hold you accountable":

- Only 29 percent said it was done "in a positive way that motivated them to do their best."
- 12 percent stated that it was completely demotivating.
- 59 percent claimed it was mixed, some positive, some negative.

Here's another data point. When we asked respondents to select their greatest concern about the way others held them accountable, they said:

Select the greatest concern you have about the way people currently hold you accountable:

They don't ever listen. **9%**

They are too abrupt and confrontational. **7%**

They hold me more accountable than they do others. **14%**

They are unrealistic. **18%**

They are not consistent in their approach and expectations. **52%**

Source: Partners In Leadership **Workplace Accountability Study**

When you hold people accountable the wrong way (i.e., you use accountability as a threat to punish people for making mistakes), you end up driving them further Below The Line.

So how do you resist this kind of gravity? In high school physics you probably learned that the force of gravity is proportional to the mass that originates it. The bigger the mass, the greater the gravitational force. The key, then, lies in how you see the problems you face. With bigger issues, you feel less in control and an increased gravitational force tugging you Below The Line. But when you focus on the things you can control or influence, the issues and the opposing forces shrink.

Focusing on what you can control, and implementing influencing strategies on the people and issues you thought you could not control, will free you from the force of gravity and energize you to move forward and make progress.

Recognize When You Are Below The Line

In order to stay Above The Line and Do It, you must recognize when you have, in fact, fallen Below The Line. Take "Ron," for example. When he's trying to solve a problem, he likes to tune everything out to "be in his own world," and take a walk, often up and down the hallways and common areas in his office building. Not surprisingly, his team had been interpreting Ron pacing past them without offering so much as a hello as a sign that he didn't like them.

Hard feelings and judgments about Ron's leadership style grew. They were raw and real, yet none of it was being talked about, at least not with Ron, though he knew something was going on. Still, Ron kept choosing to ignore the impact his oblivious strolling was having and how it was hurting morale. He was stuck Below The Line, but didn't recognize he was there.

All of this came to a head during one of our workshops, when the group openly acknowledged the impact of what he had been doing. Finally, Ron realized that his behavior was hurting his team. Much to his credit, Ron took a big step Above The Line when he chose to exchange feedback with the person who had most vocally criticized his leadership style. He received some valuable feedback that helped him see how nearly every day he was creating a Below The Line experience for his team, albeit unintentionally. Implementing the Above The Line feedback took a commitment to making things better and some courage to share honest opinions, but it gave Ron ideas on how he could change: simply acknowledge people when you run into them in the hallways.

As it turns out, the feedback skills you learned about in the See It portion of this book offer the key to helping you see when you're Below The Line. To further assist you, take this short self-test. Your yes or no answers to these questions will help you recognize whether you're Below The Line *right now,* so that you can do something about it.

1. Am I spending time developing my story to cover my tail, in case anything goes wrong?
2. Am I stuck in wait-and-see mode regarding any of the tough challenges that I am facing right now?
3. Did I play the "I'm confused" card recently, asking someone else to tell me what to do?
4. Have I told someone lately, "It's not my job"?
5. Am I ignoring or denying the fact that there is a problem that I need to face?
6. Am I engaging in finger-pointing in any measurable way?

Positive responses to three or more of these questions almost undoubtedly indicate that you are Below The Line. If you are, you're not alone. According to our study, 76 percent of the respondents admitted to saying "Just tell me what you want me to do, and I'll do it." It's so easy to fall Below The Line. The world today is filled with cynicism, blame, and victimization. To combat this you must first recognize that you are Below The Line. Only then can you move to a *better* place.

Choose to Move Above The Line

The most accountable people recognize that the air is better Above The Line. You breathe easier, feel more energy, and stay more focused. When you leave all that Below The Line baggage behind, you shed all the frustration, depression, and disappointment that come with it. The great challenge you face when you make that transition is learning to think differently about the obstacles you face.

Adopting an Above The Line mind-set is a liberating choice. Daniel Swartz, director of human resources for Align Technology, makers of Invisalign and the iTero 3-D digital scanning system, told us that earlier in his career he encountered one senior executive who seemed to dislike him from the start. During an early meeting, the exec was disengaged, constantly looking at his watch, browsing Yahoo! and checking his e-mail. If you found yourself in a meeting with this executive, what would you do? Remember, he's a senior executive. Most of us might walk away quietly, resenting that we're forced to work with the guy. Rather than get stuck Below The Line, however, Daniel chose instead to move up and speak up: "Excuse me, am I doing something that's offending you?"

This frank question shocked the executive. It turned out that he wasn't trying to offend Daniel and he didn't dislike him. He said,

"I'll be honest. I've had five HR business partners in two years. They come and go. I just don't want to waste any more of my time." Daniel could have given in to frustration and shut down when he heard that, but instead he chose to discover why the executive held negative beliefs about HR. Then Daniel set new expectations: "HR delivers and cares about you and your team."

When Daniel refused to go Below The Line, he forever altered this senior executive's opinion and experience with HR, not only initiating a positive working relationship but making some vibrant Above The Line changes within the organization's culture.

Rely on It Both at Work and at Home

Here's what we've learned over the last twenty-seven years of working with these concepts: when you get accountability right, everything else will more likely go right. The payoffs can be huge, both at work and at home.

Take the case of Troy Hawkshead, plant manager for Hormel Foods in Knoxville. After getting home from work one day, Troy was immediately greeted by his daughter, her face wrenched with disappointment and even a little fear. "Dad, I have something to tell you." *This wasn't good.* His daughter said, "Mom asked me to go get ice cream and said I could use your truck." *Gulp, here it comes.* "On the way home, the ice cream started to fall over, and when I tried to stop it, I swerved and messed up your truck." (Troy's truck was his baby. But so was his seventeen-year-old daughter.)

Flash back a few days, when Troy had gone through *The Oz Principle* Accountability Training, where we talked about making the intentional choice to be Above The Line despite challenges. Troy repeated to himself, *"Be intentional, be intentional."* Ordinarily, he told us later, he would have gone to a place of blame and frustration, but not today. Somehow, today he chose to be calm, deliberate, and Above The Line. His daughter was stunned. In fact, beyond stunned.

The next day Troy was sitting in his office when he got a call from her. "Dad, what are you doing after work today?" He said, "Well, I was thinking of going fishing." *Pause.* "I want to go with you." *But she's never wanted to fish. Ever.* Troy was choking up, realizing that because of the way he responded the day before, he had created a chance to get even closer to his daughter, to spend time together that never would have happened otherwise.

Choosing to stay Above The Line by not blaming others can make a huge difference everywhere you go and with every challenge you face. There's definitely an upside to avoiding the downside of Below The Line. The power of staying Above The Line is real and measurable, from the bottom lines of business to the halls of your own home.

Go fix it! PART 3

PATH **A**: fix it for Myself → PAGE **327**

PATH **B**: fix it on My Team → PAGE **331**

PATH **C**: fix it in My Organization → PAGE **335**

ACCOUNTABILITY TRAIT 15
Tracking Progress with Proactive and Transparent Reporting

┌─ **the need to fix it** ──────────────────────────

Is this trait a **clear strength** of people in your organization?

`NO` **80%**

`YES` **20%**

Is this trait a **clear strength** in team leaders?

`NO` **78%**

`YES` **22%**

Source: Partners In Leadership **Workplace Accountability Study** ─┘

An accomplished man we deeply respect, Thomas Monson, hit the nail on the head regarding this Accountability Trait when he said, "Where performance is measured, performance improves. Where performance is measured and reported, the rate of improvement accelerates." What you pay attention to grows. When it comes to following through to Do It, we've learned that the best results come when tracking progress with proactive and transparent reporting.

Commander Jim "Huck" Harris served as a navy fighter pilot and a Top Gun instructor and flying ace, completing more than four hundred missions during his career. He was so good at what he did that he was chosen as the American pilot to fly against a world-renowned Israeli ace in some ally-friendly war games. With those credentials in mind, he told us that one of the most dangerous things you can do in the navy is to land a jet on an aircraft carrier at night. No autopilot, entirely manual. He would hit the deck at 150 miles per hour, ready to slam the throttle back to full takeoff power, just in case the tail hook didn't grab the catch wire.

A landing like that required full concentration as Jim managed to line up the plane in total darkness while dealing with the ship's movement in three directions—up and down, side to side, and forward—not to mention whatever wind speed was screaming across the deck. He described such a landing as a "controlled crash," difficult for even the most experienced pilots.

Each landing presented a life-or-death situation that required the best efforts of all involved. The stakes were too high. The pilot and flight deck personnel's safety, the then $32 million plane, and, of course, the safety of the entire ship and crew were all at stake. The challenge: how do you get everyone to follow through and Do It with all the needed procedures for a safe landing when it had to be done quickly and repetitively? His answer: every landing was graded, posted, and discussed regardless of rank—from the most senior wing commander to the most junior pilot in every squadron. This is transparent reporting at its best.

Because it was so important to get it right the first time, grades were posted in the ready room for everyone to see. Every landing was debriefed as a group following a mission. There were no secrets. Information was open, accessible, and used to keep a keen sense of accountability to stay safe. We think this kind of reporting and transparency is always required in order to get it right the first time, whatever *it* might be.

Make It Transparent by Going Public

Have you ever told someone close to you about your plan to lose weight? What a mistake that was, right? Every time you saw them, they asked how it was going, and what progress you were making. Or they simply sized you up and gave you an unintended look of disapproval, thinking, *I didn't think you'd do it!* (Or at least that's what you thought they were thinking.)

When you "go public" with your intention to Do It, you close the door to backsliding and weak commitments. This level of transparency actually helps you take accountability for getting things done. Going public is like getting your hair wet when you get in the pool—it's the last thing that happens because it takes a total commitment.

The word *transparency* means "easy to perceive or detect; to be open to scrutiny." The more accountable you are, the easier transparency will be for you. Why? Because transparency means you have nothing to hide. It means you're going to be authentic and genuine in what you report, or people will know it's not right.

A lack of transparency almost always indicates that accountability is inadequate or missing. One large-scale change project we worked on involved a company that was facing serious product development issues. Research and Development (R&D) had been behind schedule on a new product platform for more than two years and things were about to get worse. During an annual conference with the company's top one hundred leaders, the CEO confirmed the latest launch date for the new product platform. A week later, in an interview we conducted with the R&D vice president, he revealed that there would be another twelve-month delay in the launch of the new product platform. When the word got out, everyone was shocked—particularly the CEO. No one had seen it coming.

In the aftermath, the R&D VP acknowledged that he'd never taken ownership of the date. And since he did not feel accountable for it, he offered no transparency regarding it; in fact, he sought the opposite, ambiguity and detachment. Hiding the facts in this silo-oriented company was far too easy. But it was a part of their culture they chose to ignore at their peril.

Whenever you witness transparency, it's a sure sign that someone is a champion of accountability in their business or personal life, the kind of accountability that will produce results. When transparency is missing, you would be well served to ask the question, "What are you (we) (they) pretending not to know?"

Real accountability produces transparency; transparency produces accountability. You can't have one without the other.

Track Your Progress

Here's what we believe: If you can't measure it, you can't move it. Whatever it is you are trying to do, make it measurable. Even the most subjective things can be measured in objective ways. One favorite question we routinely ask here at Partners In Leadership: "On a scale from 1 to 10, rank the progress you feel you've made to date." Then we compare the rankings over time. Everything can be measured. Everything.

We learned early on in our consulting experience that every process needs a process control. A process control is the practice engineers use to ensure a consistent, predictable, and stable output from a specific process. In physics, the Second Law of Thermodynamics proposes that all things tend to decay over time. That's called entropy. Your life's experience probably validates this idea that whenever you establish a practice, a pattern, or a process, it will *always* break down quickly over time.

Working with manufacturing organizations of every type, it

became clear that quality, safety, and volume would be accomplished only if they used a solid process and an even better process control.

The right process controls will help you consistently employ the Do It step and make things happen the way you want them to happen. The wrong ones may backfire, causing even less accountability on the part of everyone involved.

A glaring example of the wrong process control involved an associate of ours whom we'll call "Kelly." At one time Kelly worked for a company where her boss insisted on being copied on every e-mail sent. Every one. It was stifling, creating anxiety and insecurity and eventually hampering her ability to express herself. She eventually reached a point where she didn't even know if she was writing e-mails in her voice or that of her boss. Kelly told us that on average she would send maybe five hundred e-mails a year. At a breaking point she left and went to work for another firm in essentially the same role, but with a lot more autonomy to do her job. With the wrong process control finally removed, Kelly sent more than thirty-five hundred e-mails in her first year, found her own voice again, and has never been happier or more productive.

As you look for the right process controls to track, borrow a page from the performance management concepts of leading and lagging indicators. A leading indicator is an early-warning signal that tells you, before it's too late, that the process is at risk for not producing the desired output. A lagging indicator tells you the outcome and that something might have gone wrong after the fact.

Let's imagine you are a pharmaceutical rep given a quota for getting a doctor to write a desired number of prescriptions for the drug you sell. The actual number of prescriptions the doctor writes would be your lagging indicator. Your leading indicator would be the number of patients who could use that drug who visit the doctor's office each week. If that number goes down, you could predict your sales would go down. If the number goes up, then you can anticipate more sales of that drug. Leading and lagging indicators can help you track your progress. It's not rocket science, but it is the discipline of rocket scientists.

Tracking your progress is not optional; it's a necessity. Being transparent by going public with it will serve to help ensure that progress is made.

Take Accountability to Self-Report

When we talk about reporting, most people immediately think it's something that happens to you, something you are required to do. However, we have found that the accountable person looks for every opportunity to self-report. They are eager to review progress; they aren't afraid of it.

Before going further we should comment on how to improve the reporting process in general. Most likely you ask others to report, or will do so in the future. When our study asked, "Which has the greater impact on your ability to hold others accountable successfully, 'manner' or 'method'?"

- 56 percent said "manner"
- 44 percent said "method"

The majority of study respondents acknowledged that, regardless of the method, the *manner* in which you hold others accountable makes all the difference. In our book *How Did That Happen? Holding People Accountable for Results the Positive, Principled Way,* we identify two basic Accountability Styles: Coerce & Compel and Wait & See. Everyone falls into one of these two styles. (By the way, we gave the styles these names to emphasize weaknesses inherent to the style, to enhance learning, and to remind you what to look out for.)

Which style do you think best describes the way you hold others accountable and ask them to report, even if not an exact match?

- Coerce & Compel
- Wait & See

Interestingly, 36 percent of the respondents in our study identified with the Coerce & Compel Accountability Style, while 64 percent identified with the Wait & See approach. When it came to how they viewed others in the organization, 41 percent believed others were Coerce & Compel, and 59 percent Wait & See—a pretty similar split.

Neither style is right or wrong, they both offer enviable strengths and challenging weaknesses. The key is to understand your style and to lead with your strengths while remaining conscious of the impact of your weaknesses on others. Bottom line: when you seek reports from others, understand what to watch out for in the way you go about doing it. That will make all the difference.

When it comes to self-reporting, take the opportunity to offer information that will help others see progress, or the lack of it. Your transparency in proactively reporting will do a lot to engender trust and create the conversations that need to take place in order to make progress. However, you should guard against letting the report deteriorate into an attempt to excuse performance or to throw the problem over the wall to someone else. Self-reporting should be accompanied by recommendations, plans, and ideas for how to ensure progress and overcome challenges.

Close Accountability Gaps

If you discover performance issues related to your Key Results (the top three or four results you wish to achieve), then you've got what we call an Accountability Gap. It's the difference between what you intend to happen and what is actually occurring.

Everyone faces Accountability Gaps from time to time. You're probably facing a few right now. What causes Accountability Gaps? Often it's something as simple as a person's fear of holding others accountable. When we asked our study respondents to do the following: "Select the most descriptive reason for why you find holding other people accountable difficult," the results revealed a lot:

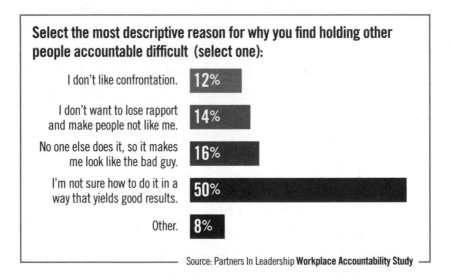

Select the most descriptive reason for why you find holding other people accountable difficult (select one):

I don't like confrontation.	12%
I don't want to lose rapport and make people not like me.	14%
No one else does it, so it makes me look like the bad guy.	16%
I'm not sure how to do it in a way that yields good results.	50%
Other.	8%

Source: Partners In Leadership **Workplace Accountability Study**

We also asked what their hesitation level for holding people accountable in general was on a scale of 1 to 10 (1 being entirely hesitant, 10 not at all):

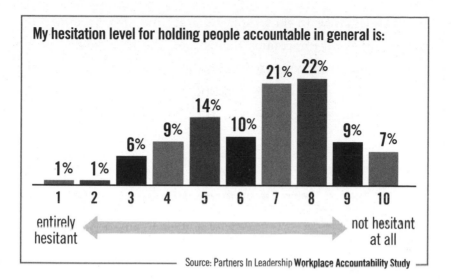

My hesitation level for holding people accountable in general is:

Source: Partners In Leadership **Workplace Accountability Study**

Clearly, people are willing to jump into the accountability pool, but aren't quite sure how to swim once there, at least in a way that gets them to the other side of the pool without embarrassing themselves.

To help close Accountability Gaps, you should conduct a regular Accountability Gap Analysis to determine where the gaps are, how big they are, and which ones you should close first. Here are the four questions we teach clients to use to apply the Steps To Accountability and close Accountability Gaps:

1. See It: What is the reality I (we) most need to acknowledge?
2. Own It: How am I (are we) contributing to the problem and/or solution?
3. Solve It: What else can I (we) do?
4. Do It: What am I (are we) accountable to do, By When?

This last question is a vital one. It helps form the plan you will make public, the plan you will track with proactive and transparent reporting.

When you have to get it right the first time, this Accountability Trait becomes all-important. Remember, the accountable person wants to report and make an accounting for who they are and what they do; they know it's key to operating Above The Line and making things happen.

Go fix it!

PART 3

PATH **A**: fix it for Myself → PAGE **340**

PATH **B**: fix it on My Team → PAGE **344**

PATH **C**: fix it in My Organization → PAGE **348**

ACCOUNTABILITY TRAIT 16
Building an Environment of Trust

---

the need to fix it

Is this trait a **clear strength** of people in your organization?

NO 75%

YES 25%

Is this trait a **clear strength** in team leaders?

NO 76%

YES 24%

Source: Partners In Leadership **Workplace Accountability Study**

This is the last of the Accountability Traits in our Do It step, and the last of the sixteen traits revealed in *Fix It: Getting Accountability Right*. We've chosen Building an Environment of Trust as Trait 16 for a reason, not because it's a new idea by any means but because greater trust is the direct outcome of getting accountability right.

So what is new regarding trust? The low employee engagement scores being reported by all the credible workplace research firms. Some show that barely 10 percent of employees worldwide are actively engaged in their work, though the numbers "soar" to 20 to 30 percent for the United States. Our own study shows that when challenges arise, only 11 percent of respondents said people "stay focused on following through and executing the organization's priorities," while only 28 percent said "people are creative and fully engaged in solving the problems they face at work."

There is a clear connection between engagement and trust. But we think there is an even more significant tie between employee engagement, trust, and the powerful concept of workplace accountability.

As we said, trust is an outcome of how we go about holding people accountable. Done the wrong way, negative accountability can crush any semblance of trust between people, teams, and entire employee populations, infecting the organization they work for. However, done correctly, positive accountability can engender high levels of trust at every level. The way we go about doing accountability (agreeing to deadlines, following up on commitments, prioritizing and reprioritizing work, divvying up responsibilities) largely determines the amount of trust that will exist in any relationship or organization and how we build an environment that sustains it.

Use Positive Accountability to Create Trust

Bottom line: the shortest path to greater trust is through positive accountability, the kind of accountability we talk about in this book and in our original work, *The Oz Principle: Getting Results Through Individual and Organizational Accountability.* In the Workplace Study, 42 percent admitted they "hesitate having an Accountability Conversation," while 58 percent said that they "proactively engage in the conversation as soon as they sense there is a need." These are low numbers, especially considering that a full 94 percent believed "improving the ability to hold others accountable in an effective way is one of the top leadership development needs of the organization."

Adopting *The Oz Principle* definition of *accountability* will produce the right approach to creating greater accountability, an approach that will build trust and ensure that you can successfully take the Do It step and operate Above The Line.

Trust grows when people focus less on the consequences of accountability related to holding others accountable for their actions, and turn their attention instead to the more positive side of accountability. This is an approach that has everything to do with taking personal accountability to overcome obstacles and make things happen.

Operating Above The Line brings out the very best in you as you work to employ all sixteen of the Accountability Traits. Let's summarize just how good this really looks. A person operating Above The Line with a *fix it* mentality will:

1. Obtain the perspectives of others
2. Communicate openly and candidly
3. Ask for and offer feedback
4. Hear and say the hard things to see reality
5. Be personally invested
6. Learn from both successes and failures
7. Ensure work is aligned with Key Results
8. Act on feedback
9. Constantly ask, "What else can I do?"
10. Collaborate across functional boundaries
11. Creatively deal with obstacles
12. Take the necessary risks
13. Do the things they say they will do
14. Stay Above The Line by not blaming others
15. Track progress with proactive and transparent reporting
16. Build an environment of trust

Adopting these Accountability Traits will build trust between individuals, within teams, and across entire organizations. Guaranteed. Trust *is* the outcome of getting accountability right, and becoming an accountable person.

Make the Choice That Builds Trust

When Martin Lowery was senior vice president of leadership and organization development for Sony Pictures Entertainment, he told us that in his two and a half decades working with executives and teams, "Many have written on the value of trust, but it's the absence of trust or breach of trust that seems to be the causal element of almost any team that's not working well." And it starts with leadership. "If you look at leaders with high emotional intelligence, one of the things they do well is trust, which allows them to be trusted in return."

This view squares nicely with our belief that trust is a choice. You choose who you give trust to, and who not to give it to. It may take time and experience for you to be ready to make the choice to trust. And it can be lost in a flash when you think someone has betrayed you. But in the end, it's still a choice.

However, building a culture of trust doesn't just hinge on the choice to trust someone, it's also a choice to start doing things differently so that others can better trust you. Identifying the Accountability Trait you most need to improve is the best place to start. In short, demonstrably working to improve that area will send a clear signal that you care, and can go a long way to building mutual trust.

Laura Kohler, senior vice president of human resources and stewardship for Kohler Co., decided to build trust by being authentic and vulnerable, and demonstrating a willingness to field any question, an approach that combines all four of the See It Accountability

Traits. She said, "The harder questions come from the Gen Ys, the millennials." They often want to know why she's been in the position so long, and how she stays fresh and challenged. Her answer is "to continuously learn." She strives to know what's going on, telling them, "I need your ideas, what's working and not working, inside Kohler and out." Reverse mentoring, asking for help, listening, staying flexible and sensitive—all of these steps are a sure path to building trust.

Be Authentic

To be authentic means to be genuine. It means no hidden agendas. We've always felt that one of the nicest compliments someone could give us at Partners In Leadership is that we come across as *authentic*. Authenticity and trust track together. You can't have one without the other.

Mark McNeil, president of juice bottler Lassonde Pappas and Company, worked for Pietro Satriano back when Pietro was transforming US Foods. McNeil remembers one meeting where Pietro asked his senior leaders to share a major career accomplishment. They went around the room sharing. Mark had just come off running a successful bakery business in Canada, so he shared how he had convinced a large customer to give him four feet of space for packaged bread in all of their supercenters. A real win. Mark was feeling pretty good about himself until Pietro shared his biggest win: "There are several people who used to work for me who have gone on to significant executive leadership positions, including four active CEOs." Mark remembers wanting to crawl under the table, not because he was wrong or had done anything inappropriate but because Pietro's response was all about developing people and valuing their achievements above his own. Pietro's success was grounded in people, a lesson Mark took to heart. "Yes, results are certainly important, but you should be more proud when folks who worked for you go on to succeed beyond you. That's your badge of honor."

Let us help you evaluate your own authenticity and trustworthiness by answering the following questions, so you'll be more effective at the Do It step:

1. When was the last time you admitted to others a misinterpretation, miscommunication, or mistake?
   _____ a. Today or yesterday
   _____ b. This week
   _____ c. Last month
   _____ d. Last year
   _____ e. Never

2. When was the last time you said you were sorry at work?
   _____ a. Today or yesterday
   _____ b. This week
   _____ c. Last month
   _____ d. Last year
   _____ e. Never

3. When was the last time someone gave you feedback that you are genuine in your dealings with others?
   _____ a. Today or yesterday
   _____ b. This week
   _____ c. Last month
   _____ d. Last year
   _____ e. Never

4. When was the last time someone accused you of being too po-
litical in your effort to get something done?

_____ a. Today or yesterday

_____ b. This week

_____ c. Last month

_____ d. Last year

_____ e. Never

5. When was the last time you were told that people trust you in
your role?

_____ a. Today or yesterday

_____ b. This week

_____ c. Last month

_____ d. Last year

_____ e. Never

If you circled *d* or *e* as a response to any of these questions, then
you may want to work on your authenticity—it will be a clear path
to building greater trust.

Manage the Contradictions

Walt Whitman, the respected American poet, wrote, "Do I contradict myself? / Very well then I contradict myself, / (I am large, I
contain multitudes.)" All of us are full of contradictions, intentional
and unintentional. This is the dilemma we must effectively learn to
manage if we want to earn and extend trust and master this Accountability Trait.

For example, let's take a final look at our study, and the simple
task of hitting deadlines. Most people would say that they are

committed to hitting their deadlines, yet when we asked, "How often do people miss timelines/deadlines?" 41 percent said that it happened, and it happened a lot. Compounding this is the contradiction that what organizations most want—people getting things done on time—often isn't what they create accountability for, with 59 percent of respondents saying that people in the organization viewed "Missing your timelines/deadlines . . ." as simply "unfortunate, but not career limiting." Another 12 percent said it was "not really a problem."

When your actions demonstrate something different from your promises, then you have a contradiction that must be managed. Managing this gap doesn't mean "spinning it." It means resolving the contradiction by being honest about what happened, humble about why it happened, and hopeful about what will be different in the future.

Here's a short list of beliefs about people and trust, gleaned from some of our executive contributors, that will help you eliminate your own contradictions, both the intentional and unintentional:

"People work for others, but work hardest for people they trust. It's never about the company, it's always about the individual."

—Mark McNeil, president, Lassonde Pappas and Company

"When someone is proposing something you don't agree with, speak up. If you wait, everything disintegrates into backbiting and gossiping. It takes trust to be able to say 'I disagree' to someone's face."

—Vincent Weafer, VP, Intel Security Group, McAfee Labs

"Create a vision for what you want to be, then get someone in your corner to help you make it happen through mutual respect, shared trust, and a lot of hard work."

—Krista Stafford, VP, HR, KLX Aerospace Solutions

"You can't do any of the 16 Accountability Traits without trust and the proper culture. It begins there. If your people don't feel comfortable speaking up, then what you get will be filtered and you won't learn what you need to know."

—Mike Dufresne, regional VP, LKQ Corporation

"To reach our goals, I need to demonstrate I'm listening. Trust is the biggest thing. My people must trust me and our company. I don't want them to tell me what I want to hear, I want them to tell me what I need to know."

—Jack Butorac, CEO/chairman, Marco's Pizza

"It's important I be very honest with myself, with the talents and capabilities I have versus the talents and abilities I need. That kind of honesty builds trust and makes everyone more effective."

—Brad Lee, president and CEO, Breg, Inc.

"I don't have all the answers, and I don't try to defend it and pretend I do. It's so easy to get defensive. Just build relationships of trust and you'll all move forward together."

—Suzanne Pottinger, VP, Employee Experience, The Original Cakerie

One final note on this topic and one that probably goes without saying but can't be said enough: Be trustworthy. Be worthy of the trust of others. Don't do anything that would violate any trust people place in you. If that happens, then *fix it* quickly by managing the contradictions in the manner we've suggested.

As we conclude our discussion of this final Accountability Trait, we acknowledge that no one will be perfect at living the accountable life. It's a career-long, dare we say lifelong quest to stay Above The Line. However, while the price may be a little vulnerability amid the ups and downs that come with learning new skills and behaviors, the payoffs are huge: better results, better relationships, better outcomes, more fulfilled promises, more opportunities, and more rewards. Your decision to *fix it* and get accountability right as an individual, on your team, and in your organization may be the most important decision you will ever make. Your efforts to be an accountable person will be noticed by everyone with whom you come in contact, both at work and at home. So, what are you waiting for?

Let's *fix it!*

Go **fix it!** PART 3

PATH **A**: fix it for **Myself** → PAGE **353**

PATH **B**: fix it on **My Team** → PAGE **357**

PATH **C**: fix it in **My Organization** → PAGE **361**

fix it

PUT THE ACCOUNTABILITY
TRAITS INTO ACTION

Put the Accountability Traits into Action

Part 3 is all about how to *fix it,* leveraging 120 successful executives who allowed us to pick their brains, pulling back the curtain on their lives and management techniques, to reveal their own personal practices that they actually use for their own development, for leading teams, and for influencing entire companies. Studying and "borrowing" these practices will make you and those you work with far more effective and successful.

Remember Adriana, the fictional executive we met back at the beginning of part 2? At the end of each trait she chose to read about in part 2, she was directed to go to the *fix it* solutions presented here in part 3—specifically to the solutions related to the path she chose to follow at the beginning of the book.

PATH **A**: fix it for **Myself**

PATH **B**: fix it on **My Team**

PATH **C**: fix it in **My Organization**

Like Adriana, we encourage you now to follow your path in part 3 and discover specific solutions to *fix it* so you can enjoy the benefits and payoffs of the personal power of greater accountability and see the impact on the results you need.

And for ongoing support and ideas, check out www.fixit-book .com, where you can add your own accountability practices to the 240 you will read about here and see what other fellow readers and executives have contributed to the growing database.

PATH **A**
fix it for **Myself**

ACCOUNTABILITY TRAIT 1
Obtaining the Perspectives of Others

To *fix it* for yourself when it comes to Obtaining the Perspectives of Others, you can implement some simple, engaging tactics. Remember, the objective here is to find out what people are thinking and why they are thinking it. Becoming proficient at this Accountability Trait will empower you to take the first step Above The Line to acknowledge reality and See It, not just your reality but the composite view of what's really going on, an essential ingredient to creating a Culture of Accountability in your life and in the lives of those around you.

Wear the Uniform

Paulette Wage, regional human resources manager at McDonald's Hawaii, will often wear the McDonald's uniform while shopping, commuting to work, or just running random errands. The uniform solicits comments and gets people talking. She'll show up at any of the thirty-eight McDonald's she manages in Hawaii, Guam, and a few South Pacific islands, working behind the counter just like any frontline entry-level employee. Paulette wants to feel what her employees feel—to experience how her employees are treated. Wearing the uniform and getting in the trenches gives her compassion (and passion), and motivates her to work harder for her people. As a consequence, her people are thrilled that she's willing to be one of them and feel as if they can tell her anything. Paulette has some advice on gaining a little individual perspective: wear your uniform, whether literal or metaphoric; interact, interface, be one of the people who actually work with the customer, and you'll be amazed at what you learn.

Get in the Bucket

Johnny Priest, division president for energy producer-distributor Willbros' Utility Transmission & Distribution, told us, "There's an old saying that a possum and a bear look the same from twenty thousand feet. But there's a huge difference up close. One is very docile and usually plays dead when confronted, the other is going to eat you." According to Johnny, you need to make a conscious personal decision to leave the office and go to where your people are. Johnny will meet them on the street, in the parking lot, at their cubicle, in the cafeteria, on the job site, just about anywhere they happen to be. In fact, he still "gets in the bucket" in order to find out what people really think. He's in his sixties, but continues to crawl into a bucket truck in order to work alongside his people. As he put it to us, "There's nothing like the conversation you can have in a lineman bucket a hundred feet in the air. Up there it's somehow easier to talk about what the person is struggling with or what's on their mind." The next time you want to tap into a little honest perspective, try stepping into "the bucket" with your people, whether that metaphoric bucket is a cubicle, an assembly line, or a scaffold one hundred feet in the air.

Take a Walking Meeting

Illustrating the theme of getting out where people feel more comfortable opening up, Martin Lowery, past senior vice president of leadership and organization development at Sony Pictures Entertainment, and now president of OpusVertex International LLC, a provider of facilitation and leadership consulting services, told us that he values what others think so much that he likes to break with routine and uses what he calls "walking one-on-one meetings." Martin believes people talk more freely when walking side by side than when sitting across a desk. So he makes a point to get out and go for a walk with his people. "There's a different energy while walking; it clears the head and gets people talking." Body language changes. Engagement improves. Intimidation melts. You get down to what people are really thinking and feeling. This means achieving a deeper level of understanding and dialogue that comes only when you can convince people you honestly and earnestly want to know; and that can happen whether it's once around the Sony lot, through your warehouse, or up a city street.

Double Jack the Phone

Gene Abernethy, chief human resources officer for Progrexion, a technology-based consumer credit repair business, said that the first thing he did after being hired was to "double jack" their customer sales and service calls (that is, to hook up an additional headset and listen in on phone conversations). "I wanted to hear what the reps who were dealing with our customers were hearing, so I would plug into their phones and just listen, learning about how the systems worked for the customer and how we explained things." Gene stressed that this wasn't about making his employees nervous, so he would just tell them, "I'm not here to critique what you're doing, I'm just here to learn." By double jacking, or in other ways plugging directly in to what people are experiencing, you not only benefit from the perspectives that can come only from firsthand experience but avoid many of the filters that "dumb down" the information you typically get about what really matters.

Lunch and Learn

Performance psychologist in leadership development Dave Jennings is a solo act who understands the highs and lows of working as a lone wolf sole proprietor. One of Dave's particular skills is soliciting the kind of perspective that helps him See It. He told us that years ago he committed to taking a friend or business client to lunch at least once a week for a Lunch and Learn. At the lunch meeting he floats new ideas, shares passages of upcoming blogs or books, and gets advice. He said that on numerous occasions his casual lunches have stimulated ideas that went on to make him thousands: "Well worth the twenty dollars I spend on lunch." Coincidentally, we were lunching with Dave when he shared this idea, and we assured him that the twenty dollars we were spending on him at the time was worth it.

Go back to **Page 23**
PART **2**

Now go to your *Fix It* **Bucket List** and select the next Accountability Trait that you want to learn about.

PATH **B**
fix it on **My Team**

ACCOUNTABILITY TRAIT 1
Obtaining the Perspectives of Others

To *fix it* for your team and See It as a team leader, you will need to hone your own ability to obtain the perspectives of others, as well as instill that ability within your team. Remember, the emphasis is on *obtaining* perspectives beyond your own. You're after those views and opinions that will allow you to ignite your team's Above The Line approach to making things happen and getting things done.

Take Every Meeting

Brad Lee, president and CEO of Breg, Inc., a large Southern California medical device manufacturer, told us that he is driven by his own sense of personal humility, something that prompts him to take every meeting that people request of him. That's right, the president of Breg meets with *everyone* who wants some of his time. This "take every meeting" philosophy sounds a bit unbelievable in today's hectic, high-demand business environment, but Brad believes he can learn something from everyone. "I always take meeting requests from people who want to spend time with me." He happened to have held one such meeting just before our interview for this book, so we put him on the spot and asked if he learned anything from the person who had asked for his time. Turns out the fellow had developed an acronym using five or six letters that formed a memory trigger to capture his current focus, and this inspired Brad to create his own motivating acronyms, easily memorable mantras he repeats to himself to keep on track and Above The Line. Open yourself up to a bit more perspective by making time to meet with people who reach out to you, especially those who might offer some unexpected genius.

Hold an Innovation Day

Marty Smuin, CEO of a leading high-performance cloud orchestration platform, Adaptive Computing, said that twice a month anyone in the organization, regardless of their title or role, can pitch their thoughts on improving the organization to a lunchtime group hungry for new ideas. It's not an off-the-cuff thing, you need to get on the agenda and prepare a presentation. At the meeting, people present new ideas and get instant impressions and perspectives. Marty said, as a new CEO, "I know that my people know what the problems are and how to fix them. They just need a forum for bypassing the red tape and imagined boundaries to bring it forward." By way of example, Marty told us that for more than six months they had exhausted all efforts trying to overcome a database limitation issue, something that was preventing them from running more workload and applications through their platform. Then they conducted an "Innovation Day." Someone presented a thought. Other people and teams volleyed back with their own, and four people came together on a possible solution. In just four days, they were able to solve the problem that had gone unsolved for months. The idea exponentially expanded the company's capacity internally, and gave it a new software solution for external sales. As Marty put it to us, even beyond the ideas themselves, "It's the fact that we are gathering for a candid exchange of thoughts, a give-and-take, an open forum where people realize that management is actually listening." If you're hitting roadblocks and dead ends, hold your own Innovation Day and see just how much it can spark creativity at every level of your organization.

Convene a Breakfast Q&A

Mark McNeil, president of Lassonde Pappas and Company, a large juice bottler-distributor, told us that every other Friday he conducts a breakfast meeting with a different department, just him and them. The Friday we spoke, he had just met with his sixteen-person IT team for one hour. He buys the team breakfast and presides over a roundtable where every person is expected to ask exactly two questions: a personal one, and a business-related one. According to Mark, "When you force people to ask only questions about business, they get flustered, they feel tested, and there's less substance there." Instead, he starts with such personal items as, "Hey, Mark, what's your favorite car?" Or, "Where did you go on vacation last summer?" The personal questions coming first make everything more casual, loosen people up, encourage honest sharing, and make the team more trusting. Try scheduling your own breakfast and watch the perspectives fly.

Give Them the First 15

Casey Jones, president of a leading national equipment service specialist, Altaquip, has developed his own brand of perspective gathering. In his biweekly thirty-minute one-on-ones with direct reports, Casey always gives his people the first fifteen minutes. The last fifteen minutes are his, but in those first fifteen, "they know they can and should talk about anything: family, work, interoffice issues, anything . . ." and he'll just listen. As Casey said, "I may be the boss, but that doesn't mean I'm always the smartest guy in the room. . . . I need to learn." By establishing this First 15 rule, he lets his people know it's up to them to occupy the start of the meeting, so they come prepared to open up. Plan time for people to share in a way that honors the spirit of the First 15, and in time, people will learn to bring to the surface what might not otherwise arise in a formal business discussion.

Walk the Floor

Laura Kohler believes it's tough to pull honest perspectives from people if there's any kind of leadership intimidation going on. Knowing that, she makes it a priority to do her best to dismantle the inherent intimidation that comes with her role as senior vice president of human resources for Kohler Co. while being a fourth-generation Kohler. Offering advice to other organizations, Laura shared how she makes a point to regularly visit all of Kohler Co.'s larger manufacturing locations just to "walk the floor." She talks to as many frontline workers as she can. While traveling to the forty-eight manufacturing sites around the world, she has a lot of informal and revealing discussions she otherwise would never have. "Being local and on the floor, meeting those who actually make the products, it creates a whole new energy, new environment, a whole new perception around who we are and what we are trying to be as a company." When she's with Kohler teams, she asks, "What are your challenges?" or, "How can I help with that?" This breaks down any executive leadership barriers and promotes her as someone who is real and accessible. Honest information flows to people like Laura because she's local and on the floor, where people view her as part of the team, not as someone who is remote and hard to understand.

Now go to your *Fix It* **Bucket List** and select the next Accountability Trait that you want to learn about.

PATH **C**
fix it in **My Organization**

ACCOUNTABILITY TRAIT 1
Obtaining the Perspectives of Others

How do you embed the practice of obtaining the perspectives of others into the very fabric of your organization so that everyone, at every level, finds it natural to "reach out to find out"? For that matter, does it even make sense to implement such an enterprise-wide initiative? According to our Workplace Accountability Study, organizations that exhibit a high-performance culture and consistently reach all Key Results also happen to score high on the Accountability Traits discussed in this book. Coincidence? Hardly. Consider these enterprise-wide suggestions.

Go Fishing

When Jack Butorac, current chairman and CEO of Marco's Pizza wished to implement aggressive growth strategies and ensure buy-in from his C-suite team down to frontline store employees, what did he do? Jack told us that he began with Accountability Trait 1, by seeking to obtain the perspectives of others. In his case, he took advantage of a fishing trip with Tom Day, group vice president of Hormel, a major player in the food space. After a day of fishing on a pristine Colorado lake, Jack asked Tom what he and his executive team should do to ensure big results. Not only did Tom point Jack to the principles you are reading about here, he taught him the value of "going fishing," or, in other words, the value of getting out of the office, out of the work environment: go to a basketball game, go bowling, or meet someone at a park or café for lunch. If you thoughtfully plan opportunities outside the office to talk to your people, you will likely get perspectives you can obtain in no other way.

Use Skip-Level Meetings

Joseph O'Callahan, manager of organizational development for Hyster-Yale Group, Inc., a designer and manufacturer of forklift trucks worldwide, employs a unique tactic for obtaining a little organizational perspective: skip-level meetings, where your boss takes a meeting with your direct reports, leaving you off the guest list. This works only for leaders who possess a great degree of humility, so people don't feel like the big boss is just trying to dig up dirt on them or handle something they are incapable of handling. Skip-level meetings help senior executives get perspective, on behalf of their directors and managers, by gathering firsthand information from the people they manage, those who typically feel less inhibited by the big boss than by their own boss. Skip-level meetings provide points of view and levels of understanding that reach from the bottom of the organization to the top, and from the top back to the bottom.

Ask Larry

Brad Pelo, cofounder and CEO of i.TV and other high-tech startups, told us about a tech-savvy program he admired and "borrowed" from Google. Apparently, Google's founders get in front of the entire company every Friday, many people joining via a videoconference, for an open, ask anything conversation with the CEO, Larry Page. The forum originates from Google's Silicon Valley office, but all forty thousand employees worldwide are invited to tune in. An online portal allows employees to type in any question they want to ask. As the questions come in, everyone votes them up or down. Larry Page just starts at the top with the most popular question of the day, and works his way down for an hour. This kind of open forum and sharing of opinions and perspectives makes employees feel relevant, which automatically promotes engagement. Pelo said that he was inspired by this "Ask Larry" idea and created his own version throughout his career where he would order pizza every Friday for employees and field any question. "A lot of great discussion ensues where everyone's point of view is heard, and they *know* it's heard."

Give Them a Heads-up

Tiffany Zakszeski, director of human resources for the endoscopy division of a prominent medical technology company, Stryker Corporation, has learned that one size does not fit all when it comes to dealing with employees. She told us that she has learned to size up people as individuals, recognizing that everyone has something they want to share, something they are burning to say, but some just don't have the courage to do it. Because Tiffany values everyone's input, she's learned the value of offering a heads-up. Tiffany will give some people a couple of days to prepare, saying that in a coming meeting, "I'll want to hear from you," or, "We'll want to know how things are progressing on the project." When someone feels fairly comfortable in their own skin, they may need only a ten-minute heads-up, or none at all, but saying, "I'm going to call on you, and I'd love your perspective in this meeting," sets the stage for soliciting a little perspective.

Look for the Quiet Ones

Chris Baldwin, president of Kohler Co.'s faucets business, openly admitted that in the past he personally struggled to overcome the temptation to make a decision and act on it without getting enough input from others when under a tight deadline. To counteract this, he's learned to listen to alternative voices, to actively solicit feedback, and to chase additional, and sometimes alternative, points of view. He consciously pays attention to the quiet ones in the room and goes after their input. "The quiet ones do the most thinking, and when teams are deep into strategizing, it's the quiet ones who can often add the most insight, but are often content to let the louder ones rattle on until asked." Make sure you hear from everyone, not because it's your job to ensure they speak up, but because it may help you do your own job better.

Go back to Page 23
PART 2

Now go to your *Fix It* Bucket List and select the next Accountability Trait that you want to learn about.

PATH **A**
fix it for **Myself**

ACCOUNTABILITY TRAIT 2
Communicating Openly and Candidly

When it comes to being open and candid, the biggest payoff will come from simply getting people comfortable with the idea of telling you what they really think. Our interviews with managers, executives, and leaders provide some practical advice about how to get that done.

Say It Like It Is

"Bad news never ages well." So says Alan Taylor, CFO of eFileCabinet and past financial leader for Helius, Adaptive Computing, Ford, and Boeing. According to Alan, something he learned long ago is that "any leader needs to be timely and straight up with employees, creating an environment where all facts are laid out." In other words, bad news gets worse if you try to hide it. Alan believes that "the sooner you come forward, the more open and candid you can be, the quicker you can then do something about it, and the less costly it will be for everyone." He instills this "say it like it is" behavior in others through experience—those who work around him know that because he consistently comes across with a "this is what's going on" approach, others learn to come to him and tell him what's happening, no matter what it is. Saying it like it is creates a two-way open and candid relationship and eliminates the stress that comes from trying to hide what's really going on. According to Alan, "Say it like it is and watch your own accountability flourish, along with those around you."

Take a Disagreement Walk

Carl Coburn, CEO for midwestern CPA firm Clark Schaefer Hackett, echoed this theme. At least once a week during lunch, Carl walks around the office, specifically seeking out those he knows have disagreed with him over the past week. He's transparent about it, asking for their input in a way that convinces them that he really wants to hear their point of view. His transparency puts people at ease, helps them feel comfortable, and lets them know that it's okay to be open and candid themselves. Everyone knows he doesn't just want people agreeing with him. Jack Butorac, CEO and chairman of Marco's Pizza, feels much the same way. "I don't want people to tell me what I want to hear, I want people to tell me what I need to know." That's worth repeating: leaders at senior levels want people to tell them what they need to know. However, opening up to "the boss" can seem risky. No one wants to tell the emperor he has no clothes! Yet in reality, the emperor really would like to know if he's wandering around catching a draft. Seek out those who may hold a differing opinion and have a one-on-one—help them have the experience that their viewpoint is respected.

Do Some Premeeting Prep

Mary Bartlett, COO for The Reserve, a professional shared workplace, told us that she likes to engage in some premeeting prep, especially if she's going to be dipping into something controversial, transformational, or anything involving significant change. Well ahead of the actual meeting, she will float a draft or an agenda to key people, letting them see what she's thinking. Even more helpful, she will often go directly to anyone she believes will offer the most resistance. She airs her concerns and allows them to candidly air theirs. Rather than dropping the bomb in a larger group session only to see the discussion go sideways, she uses the premeeting preparation to build advocacy and support. Doing so allows for a more positive, candid conversation because key players already know what's coming.

Unplug the Tech for an Hour

When Martin Lowery was senior vice president of leadership and organization development for Sony Pictures Entertainment, he shared with us that everyone needs to remember that "technology can absolutely get in the way of effective communication. We all know this can happen, it's just inconvenient to admit it." His advice now in his current role as president of OpusVertex International LLC, a provider of facilitation and leadership consulting services? "Once a week unplug the tech with your direct reports and go back to old school, in-person, face-to-face time: no computers, no smartphones, no videoconferencing, no IMing, and, most of all, no digital multitasking!" Martin adds that "it should be an hour . . . any less and you don't get beyond the superficial and into what's really going on." The amount of time is important. A full hour or more lets you drill deeper, going beyond what they're thinking and doing and into what they are truly feeling. That's when you really crack the nut and discover the benefits of being open and candid. According to Martin, getting to the feelings is critical because a person's true emotions give you the deepest insight into that person's perspective on an issue. Martin said, "Getting people to use feeling words in business is so critical, and yet it's increasingly less common due to technology." So unplug . . . to plug in to your people.

Send a Standout E-mail

To make our point perfectly clear, being open and candid isn't all about hearing the negative, it's also being open and candid about the good things people are doing. For example, Mark McNeil, president of juice bottler Lassonde Pappas and Company, told us that his former boss, Pietro Satriano, now president and CEO of US Foods, would make a point to periodically send Mark a short e-mail about some "standout" thing Mark had done that week. Not only did this make a positive deposit into the relationship-building account, it also gave Mark even more permission to be open and candid about things that weren't going so well later on. Mark said that any human being lights up when reading an e-mail from his or her boss about something they did well. It probably took Pietro all of twelve seconds to write the e-mail, but it meant so much to the recipient because the boss offered authentic praise. Mark said, "The impact of those e-mails was unbelievably powerful and I've tried to implement that in my own life and leadership." To foster open and candid communication, say something good in an e-mail!

Go back to **Page 23**
PART **2**

Now go to your *Fix It* **Bucket List** and select the next Accountability Trait that you want to learn about.

PATH **B**
fix it on **My Team**

ACCOUNTABILITY TRAIT 2
Communicating Openly and Candidly

Can a person learn to be more open and candid? Certainly anyone can. We've trained millions of people worldwide to do just that in their journey to take greater accountability for achieving results. Will developing this Accountability Trait be more natural for some team leaders and harder for others? You bet. But the good news is that the following practices provide some nuts-and-bolts techniques you can apply for helping you and your team open up in order to say what *needs* to be said so you can see what needs to been seen, an essential aspect of the See It step Above The Line.

Go Around the Horn

Casey Jones, president of tool and equipment repair company Altaquip, told us about a unique communication mechanism he uses in his meetings, where his six direct reports have been trained to take two minutes each to explain what's going on in their respective areas. The team hears quick, candid comments (there isn't time for anything else) about what's hot and what's not, with everyone taking notes. After that opening discussion, they go back "around the horn," where each team member takes one minute to comment on anything they heard from their peers that they want to explore a bit further. Now, you may be thinking that this sounds a bit too structured and limiting, but as one or two minutes don't allow much time for blathering, the structure mandates candor and demands openness. The focus on brevity grows out of Casey's twenty years in the army's Eighty-second Airborne and Reserves, where he jumped out of planes for a living. Casey told us that once you're in the air there are no do overs, so you'd better focus on what's important before you jump.

Check In by Making Sure They Have Not Checked Out

Carlyn Solomon, COO of Hill-Rom, a global medical technology company, suggested a way to short-circuit postmeeting distress disorder (PMDD), a common ailment that can plague almost any team. At the end of every meeting, Carlyn goes around the room to check in with each person in order to find out if the meeting actually caused them to check out by asking one tough question: "Was this meeting worth the time you invested in it, and if not, how can we make it better?" These questions draw lingering issues out into the open, giving everyone the benefit of the real conversations that happen for a lot of teams only in the hallways, the elevators, or the break room, where open and candid are the rule. This frankness and candor in critiquing the meeting helps people recognize that Carlyn is not intent on holding more meetings but dead serious about getting honest input. He really wants to know what his people think. Everyone knows that it's not okay to check out, because they're going to be asked to check in at the end of the meeting. Try it yourself: check in on what people think by making sure they have not checked out.

Get Real as Soon as You Can, Even in the Parking Lot

David Chapin, CEO of Forma Life Science Marketing, a promotional and marketing company targeting the life-science space, told us that he's made it a habit at the end of every prospective client sales presentation to debrief with his people as quickly as he can, quite often in the parking lot. He asks two questions: "How did that go?" and, "What could I have done better?" Though the questions might not be unique, the timing and setting are. David gets *immediate* open, often brutally honest feedback from his team. "Wait very long after meetings, and it's too easy to forget." According to David, his focus is on a real-time reaction about "what they said and how we responded. It's in that fine-grained texture of honesty and clarity of the moment where the improvements often lie." For open and candid communication, try getting it as soon as you can. Don't wait for the next meeting, or even the next day.

Start a Book Club

You may not initially appreciate how starting a book club has anything to do with being open and candid, but one director of talent and leadership development for a large energy company told us that she believes it's the relationship you have with someone that makes candor possible, so she goes out of her way to provide experiences that foster stronger bonds. For example, within their first year of participating in an after-hours book club that meets every other month, they read six books. She said that people reflect on them. They have conversations over dinner about them, sharing ideas and feelings about what they've read. The group plans to expand the club from just the senior leadership team down to directors and managers, inviting people to suggest books and lead conversations. She summarized by saying, "The book club has taken down barriers and helps everyone know that it's not all about work. It's about them as people and as leaders, and being part of all this allows them to show different vulnerabilities. I know I can challenge them a bit more because I know what their capacities are." Try changing up the routine with creative activities like a book club. They can stimulate open conversations on relevant topics that might not happen any other way.

Cater a Small Evening Dinner

Dr. Bernadette Loftus, executive medical director of Mid-Atlantic Permanente Medical Group, enjoys getting together for an informal dinner party with four or five of her senior team leaders in her office. She orders in, and after the food shows up, she and members of the medical group management team sit around the table and chat. Bernadette laughed when remembering the first few executive dinner dates. "It was very interesting. When we first started them, the new guy in the group was very nervous, in fact all of them were. They were worried that some boom was going to be lowered, so were very closed off." Valuing the importance of transparency, she actively creates opportunities like this to get her people talking. Catering a small dinner party with just a handful of executives isn't something a medical director normally does, so first-time jitters are understandable. However, Bernadette highly recommends the dinner table for getting people more comfortable because it's "something essential for dropping any barriers that might be blocking the next brilliant open and candid comment."

Go back to **Page 23**

Now go to your *Fix It* Bucket List and select the next Accountability Trait that you want to learn about.

PATH **C**
fix it in **My Organization**

ACCOUNTABILITY TRAIT 2
Communicating Openly and Candidly

If you're looking to *fix it* in your organization, then we probably don't have to tell you about the challenges of fostering open and candid communication within a corporate culture. It's one thing to make this happen on a team and quite another to proliferate openness within the entire enterprise, but it can be done. Here are some proven practices that could promote candidness within your organization's culture.

Try Weekly Breakout Calls

Bill Becker, COO of restaurateur LTP Management Group, told us that to help promote open and candid communication, he starts each Tuesday with an 8:30 A.M. call with his senior leadership team, during which they review last week's results and look ahead to the next week. At 9:30 they split up, and each C-suite leader gets on a call with a group of general managers, which involves a similar discussion, where people offer candid perspectives and feedback. At 10:30 the executive team reconvenes on a conference call to review everything the group has collected in their own calls. This communication chain, driven by smaller groups, helps people feel free to talk. According to Bill, "Over the years we've all learned to become very open and have our most effective give-and-takes when breaking into the smaller groups and calls. People are able to talk more freely in a smaller group and with a GM they know well." Candor springs from solid relationships. Weekly breakout calls can solidify good relationships and help drive openness.

Do a Brown-Bag Slide Show

Adam Porter, senior director of human resources for Edwards Lifesciences, the global leader in the science of heart valves and hemodynamic monitoring, responded to the organization's need for a more open and candid culture by initiating a once-a-month brown-bag lunch. During each session, a different member of the leadership team comes prepared to present a slide show on his or her life story. The presentation includes personal history, values, professional history, and lessons learned. Each presentation is followed by a Q&A session where everyone is expected to be open, honest, frank, and transparent. These sessions are recorded and posted to the company Web site for employees unable to attend, so that they can watch the presentation and get to know the leaders. The engagement surveys received from the employees who have attended the brown-bag lunches show that these meetings have helped promote a culture where people view the leadership as more approachable. That alone fosters openness and candor. Being vulnerable in a slide presentation allows people to feel you're approachable, particularly when breaking bread during lunch.

Establish a Leadership YOU

Mario Cajati, managing director of business development for the Central Plains District at UPS, gets his directors, sales directors, and marketing managers together once a quarter in an informal setting to focus on leadership, something they call Leadership YOU. He uses inspirational clips from thought leaders as a part of framing his people's ability to accept personal accountability for their desired results. After reading our book *The Oz Principle,* Mario decided that their Leadership YOU was the perfect venue to begin a discussion about the principles of accountability. He told us, "At first in Leadership YOU, no one wanted to speak up, but the program eventually built an environment of trust, and people learned to feel comfortable expressing themselves. Now I can't get them to shut up! It helps us share best practices and communicate far more openly than we ever have before." If you need more openness, start a discussion in your own informal university setting.

Lunch and Learn with a Wizard

Working the food theme a bit more, we'd like you to meet Jon Horn, chief human resources officer for Clark Schaefer Hackett (a large CPA advisory firm), who told us that the company holds regular Lunch and Learns from 11:30 A.M. to 1:00 P.M. People come to the preannounced L&Ls to hang out and talk accountability. The impromptu discussions are led by aptly dubbed "wizards," individuals who are trained in accountability and have a passion and understanding for the 16 Accountability Traits in this book. The wizards group consists of twelve internal facilitators taken from a cross-section of the company who have been trained by our own experts in accountability. Everyone recognizes who the twelve wizards are and knows that they attend the L&Ls to help people engage in open and candid conversations. The practice has changed the corporate culture, instilling in everyone a greater capacity for telling it like it is, while giving people thicker skins that help them *hear* it like it is. If you want all of your people to be more open and candid, try lunching with your own wizard.

Get Out of the Work Environment

Cliff Reyle, chief human resources and information officer for Youth Villages, a company committed to helping at-risk youth, told us, "As you go up the corporate ladder, there's going to be a magnetic force that pulls you away from being engaged with the people who actually do the work. C-suite and executive positions can isolate you, keep you closed off, separated from frontline employees who really know what's going on. It's a force that pulls at you, where, if not careful, you end up spending all your time with a small group of people in the corporate office." Cliff suggested we pass along his advice that by building structured ways to interact with frontline people, you can avoid the pitfalls of potential isolation, distance, and blindness. For his part, Cliff has planned retreats with employees, taken his direct reports and frontline people to training retreats, and purposely planned training events away from the corporate offices. Cliff says, "In offsite training environments, people let their guards down; they're more open and relaxed. They will talk, and tell you things they'd never tell you sitting in their cubicle."

Go back to **Page 23**

PART
2

Now go to your *Fix It* **Bucket List** and select the next Accountability Trait that you want to learn about.

(3) **PATH A**
fix it for Myself

ACCOUNTABILITY TRAIT 3
Asking For and Offering Feedback

Of all the Accountability Traits discussed in this book, this one may offer the biggest ROI (return on investment) as you strive to harness the power of personal accountability and *fix it*! And, while it may offer the biggest return, it may also feel like the riskiest Accountability Trait to implement. For most people, feedback is scary to give and even scarier to receive. But as we said in part 2 of this trait, that does not need to be the case. The more you do it, the more you want it.

Meet with People You Don't Need to Meet With

It's easy to get into ruts. Routines. Not just in your daily job, but even in terms of those you interact with, those you see, those you report to, and those who report to you. Joseph O'Callahan, manager of organizational development for Hyster-Yale Group, Inc., a designer and manufacturer of forklift trucks worldwide, has become open to getting and giving feedback from and to people he would not usually see in meetings. "When you talk to people you rarely or never see, you always learn something new." This out-of-the-box practice provides fresh new input that fills in the blanks and deepens understanding on issues he normally wouldn't see. Be careful not to solve problems and make changes without going back through your chain of command, but don't let your organization's lines of authority stop you from going after a better understanding of what's going on. Make it a standing rule to greet people outside your normal scope. When you chat with someone new, you almost always learn something new.

Just Ask for Feedback

Matt Broder, vice president of corporate communications for private brand strategy leader Daymon Worldwide, told us that he views feedback as one of the most important and vital interpersonal tools, and a major key to his business success. After such a strong endorsement, we asked him how he made feedback such an integral part of his career. He told us that all you really need to do is consciously ask for it and encourage others to do the same. Wait a minute. Time out! No gimmicks, no strategies? Just ask people for it? That's right. Matt said, "Asking for feedback is the biggest signal that you're open to it." He likes our Partners In Leadership mantra, "Accountable leaders seek feedback, and seeking feedback makes accountable leaders." Has he seen any feedback pushback in his company? Sure. "It takes time to get comfortable with it, and some people are slower at it than others, but it's just teaching people to ask, 'What feedback do you have for me?'" We couldn't have said it any better ourselves.

Use the 75/25 Rule

Ian Baines, currently CEO of the family restaurant chain Cheddar's Scratch Kitchen, told us about a notable leadership feedback practice. His secret is simple: listen 75 percent of the time; talk and explain what you're going to do with what you're hearing 25 percent of the time. He believes that if you're going to ask for feedback, then you might as well listen closely to what people have to say so that you truly understand what they think. Ian also believes that unless you get real feedback from the right people, you drastically reduce your ability to execute and actually get things done. The lesson here is to make sure you get feedback from the influencers in the organization, the go-to folks who make things happen and who mobilize the organization behind important initiatives. Ensuring that you're having an effective feedback exchange with the key people in your sphere of influence, the people who will make the biggest contributions to your success, will help secure your own success and give you the biggest return on the time you invest in it.

Engage the Nonverbal Clues

Cliff Reyle, chief human resources and information officer for Youth Villages, told us how he has committed to seeking out one person a day for a feedback exchange, a practice that better empowers him to serve the stakeholders his company helps: troubled teens. Cliff clears his calendar and goes looking for someone in the organization who he thinks needs to talk. How does he pick that person? He says that you can tell by their nonverbal signals. "I can just sense when there's someone who is working through issues, dealing with problems, either personally or business related." He pulls them aside and sincerely asks, "How can I help you?" His people know that it's not just the casual "How're you doing?" but a sincere question with the intent to learn something about them and exchange open and candid feedback. He's genuinely curious about his people, their welfare, and about what's really going on in the organization. You might try Cliff's technique: clear your calendar for a few minutes of quality feedback with someone who's sending the signal that they need to talk, and listen intently for input that might help you improve things for them both personally and professionally. You will be surprised by how effective this practice can be.

Create a Continuous Feedback Loop

Peter Hotz, industry adviser for Vynamic, a prominent health-care industry management consulting firm, adopted a practice nearly twenty years ago that still serves him well: creating a continuous feedback loop with those he works with. According to Peter, most organizations focus on feedback only once a year during employee review season. "But if you're waiting for a once-a-year review, feedback's not effective, as you tend to lose sight of it. Holding people accountable at that point is nearly impossible." To combat this, especially in today's highly dispersed, mobile, and remote workforce, Peter uses a simple one-sheet, four-bullet-point agenda that he walks through with all direct reports every month: (1) What did you get done last month? (2) What do you hope to get done next month? (3) What critical issues do we need to discuss? (4) Give me a lesson you learned this month. He uses this one-page walk-through report every month, either via e-mail or in person, as a catalyst for a crucial feedback exchange that is current and on task. The key is consistency; if it happens regularly and frequently, people get good at it.

Go back to **Page 23**

PART 2

Now go to your *Fix It* **Bucket List** and select the next Accountability Trait that you want to learn about.

PATH **B**
fix it on **My Team**

ACCOUNTABILITY TRAIT 3
Asking For and Offering Feedback

Creating a team culture where feedback is freely exchanged between team members as well as with the team leader requires a focused effort and an insistence that an exchange of feedback is not only desired but also expected. This kind of commitment and reinforcement will pave the way for making feedback "the way things are done around here."

Ask the Last Person In

Because Laura Kohler is a fourth-generation Kohler and a senior vice president of human resources at Kohler Co. (the international kitchen and bath, power, and global faucets company), she can be a bit intimidating. It just comes with the territory. After twenty-three years with Kohler Co., fourteen at the helm of human resources, she often finds that people may not have the courage required to give her the kind of feedback she wants and needs, which makes "seeing reality a challenge." What's the fix? Laura likes to quote Henry David Thoreau: "It's not what you look at that matters, it's what you see." With that firmly in mind, Laura says, "If you're a senior leader packing around inadvertent intimidation, you need to learn to ask for feedback in ways that encourage people to open up." Her favorite opportunities are talking with new people who have worked for the company between sixty and ninety days. New associates offer fresh eyes and valuable insight. She prompts feedback by asking:

- Can you tell me what you're seeing?
- What don't you understand?
- What can we do better?
- What can I do better?

Asking the last person to come into the organization for feedback is a brilliant way to extract input from those new enough to not have developed biases and blind spots, yet long enough on the job to know what's going on.

Have an Open Door

A man we'll call "Blake" was a new site vice president at a major food manufacturing facility, and he recognized that he was working in a culture where no one felt as if management wanted to hear what people really thought. He was especially concerned about solving quality issues on the manufacturing line, but he wasn't getting the open dialogue he needed from frontline workers. He wanted them to know they could come to him to share their concerns, that his door was always open. Blake decided he needed to send a strong message that he was dead serious about hearing what he needed to hear. Perhaps he would need to do something different, maybe even shocking, something to grab his people's attention and send a clear message. Blake showed up to work one morning with a drill and duct tape (not your typical messaging tools!). He then set about removing his office door from the hinges. Moments later he was duct-taping his door to the cafeteria wall, with his nameplate still on it!

The message: *Blake has an open-door policy.* Hard to miss that one. The result: feedback flourished. Dialogue that had never happened before started happening. Our advice is to find a way to let people know you are serious about an open-door policy.

Plug into the Pulse of the Organization

Don Vinci, senior vice president of human resources and chief diversity officer for electric power production company Entergy, holds regular small group and team meetings of no more than fifteen people to plug directly into important feedback. His only rule: *Those in attendance can't be his direct reports.* Taking this approach enables Don to get feedback from people many levels below him. He purposefully goes into the meeting without an agenda. Don made it clear to us that these are not meetings where people put together a laundry list of things for him to fix, but rather forums aimed at soliciting discussion, providing back-and-forth feedback, and establishing mutual understanding. We encourage this kind of joint feedback session because it greatly extends your understanding of what is going on in the organization without the overly rigid and restrictive chain of command that can get in the way of people telling you what they really think.

Make Real-Time Feedback an Important Data Point

Robert Martinez, sales manager for a California CBS/Telemundo/CW network affiliate, told us that feedback around sales targets is so key to his teams that the company generates a daily electronic report card first thing every day. "Having this kind of immediate feedback shows us the delta between where we are and where we need to be. There's no guesswork. We practice feedback on steroids around here. It comes in electronically bold and bright every day. It's hard to get better feedback than that!" The right data delivered at the right time represents a valuable source of feedback, the kind that doesn't lie! Robert said, "If people are off by themselves in any kind of job, without transparent reporting, then it's easy to get off course." The right kind of reports reveal the truth about an employee's performance and can help you calibrate what you need to do to stay on course. Robert would encourage you to not only view feedback as people sharing their points of view, which can be quite subjective, but also consider that exposure to the right data at the right time is one of the most reliable forms of feedback you can receive.

Offer a Free Lunch

Richard Pliler, former executive vice president of First Interstate Bank, served as head of all the lenders in the Pacific Northwest. With thirty-two direct reports, he made it a point to take each one to lunch once a month in order to foster the free exchange of feedback with his team. Now, you don't need a banker's mind for math to realize that there aren't enough lunch hours in a working month to accommodate thirty-two lunch meetings, so some days he ate twice. His experience, he said, taught him that "getting outside the branch created a better energy. Eating distracted from the formality of a sit-down exchange over a desk. And who doesn't like a free lunch?" While eating, Pliler would ask for feedback on what was happening in the manager's branch, and talk about the people, how everyone was getting along, and what the managers were teaching their staff. Every detail. He wanted to understand what was really going on and show that he deeply cared about who they were and what they were doing. His only goal was to make them success-ful. His key question, often asked between bites of his second salad of the day: "What can I do to help you succeed?" There's nothing like a free lunch to open up the conversation for a real exchange of feedback.

Go back to **Page 23**

PART **2**

Now go to your *Fix It* **Bucket List** and select the next Accountability Trait that you want to learn about.

(3) —————— PATH **C**

fix it in **My Organization**

ACCOUNTABILITY TRAIT 3
Asking For and Offering Feedback

A CEO client friend of ours was riding in an elevator when a front-line worker stepped in, realizing only too late who he was joining. Immediately nervous, the worker swallowed hard and asked, "Is it okay if I ride the elevator with you?" Our CEO friend was surprised, even shocked. In speaking to the employee on their ride up, he came to learn that under a prior administration, there was actually an elevator reserved for executives only. If you can't ride with them, then surely you can't speak with them. Fostering the exchange of feedback in an organization requires that you send the right signals that feedback is needed. And those signals must begin at the top.

Coach Up!

Tony Bridwell, chief people officer for Brinker International, the business behind Chili's and Maggiano's Little Italy restaurants, told us that he believes "accessible and vulnerable leaders make for more effective feedback." You can encourage this vulnerability by having someone lower in rank "coach up." At Brinker, they assign lower-level directors as coaches to the upper-level leadership team. This coaching-up practice promotes vulnerability and leadership humility, leads to candid feedback and two-way dialogue, and breaks down C-suite walls, not to mention any hint of the "executive elevator syndrome." It takes a lot of courage to do this, on the part of both the executive team and those selected as coaches, but the experience has been tremendously helpful and has led to even more timely, candid feedback exchanges that are relevant to the success of the business.

Eat and Ask

Brad Pelo, a serial CEO of high-tech start-ups like i.TV, likes to create an extremely open philosophy, represented by his current company's all-hands Friday lunch hour, where he has made it clear that people need to show up prepared to ask or say *anything*. Pelo told us, "Start-ups are always seeking funding. Rather than sit back and wonder and stew over things, I've intentionally chosen to create a culture where my employees know they can just come out and ask, 'Why didn't we take funding from so-and-so?' 'Why are we doing this stupid project for these guys?' 'I hate the decision that was made here.'" According to Pelo, "It's honest and sometimes brutal, but as long as we are an organization of integrity we can answer any question honestly and without fear of the outcome." For a little dose of high-octane perspective, add a little feedback to your salad.

Take a Weeklong Feedback Loop

Tom Simon, senior vice president of talent management at US Foods, a leading food distributor serving restaurants, health-care, and hospitality entities, told us, "In some companies you get in trouble for speaking up, but at US Foods you get in trouble for not saying what you think." US Foods promotes this mantra with something the company calls the Feedback Loop, a practice where each quarter the US Foods executive team flies around the country to the four different regions in which they do business. The executives hang around for a week, long enough to get face time with all levels of employees. It's not about popping in and out of offices or warehouses just to make an appearance. A week gives the leaders a chance to get to know people, to learn what is really happening at the ground level. It's also a time when they can share unfiltered information about the current initiatives and the company's vision with each and every layer and level of the company. Imagine what this kind of weeklong feedback opportunity, initiated from the top down, can do to close the loop on feedback from the bottom up.

Set Aside a Feedback Hour

Janee Hartcau is the first female police chief of the Minneapolis Police Department and, in fact, one of only a handful of women to serve in that role in any large American city. One program she introduced caught hold quickly. Once a month, Janee makes time for anyone to ask her any question about any topic, or make any kind of comment they want. The first hour she spends with the troops, then the second hour with the public. This establishes trust and transparency, which directly improves the quality of the feedback she wants and needs. Janee told us, "By making yourself available and letting people know they can communicate with you, it opens them up and you start to not just hear the big things, but the little things. And it's the little things that really frustrate employees." She says that it's easier to try to fix the big things, like controversial shootings, or use of force captured on video. "Oddly, it's the little things that seem to require more feedback and more focus, because they have a way of slipping through the cracks." Janee cites some good examples: "Things like the way we're handling our field training, or how officers are working with recruits for two months but not getting anywhere, even something as mundane as needing more lockers." Establishing a set time for feedback lets people know you're serious, which opens them up to getting the little things on the table.

Perform 360s from the Top Down

Gene Abernethy, chief human resources officer for consumer credit repair company Progrexion, admits to being a big fan of engagement surveys and 360s because they allow getting to the questions, answers, and actions in the safety of anonymity. Gene recalled that when working for a previous firm, after one round of 360s, he found that one of his midlevel managers with eight direct reports was making life miserable for those around him, and all eight were ready to quit. Losing all eight simultaneously would have been a disaster. In speaking with this manager, Gene was astonished that the guy was clueless. He thought people saw him as nice. Gene pressed:

Q: Do you ever just talk to your people about something other than work?

A: Never, no, there's too much to do.

Q: Do you ever ask about their weekend?

A: Well, I don't care about their weekends.

Q: Do you care about them as people?

A: I care if they do their job.

The 360s revealed some crucial input from the team, input that would ultimately help Gene encourage this leader to better understand what he needed to do in order to truly motivate and lead the team. Input discovered too late can be just as bad as no input at all. Gene added, "Then the next step is to get your culture to where people will provide all of the same information without the anonymity. Then you know you really have reciprocal trust in place."

Go back to **Page 23**

PART
2

Now go to your *Fix It* **Bucket List** and select the next Accountability Trait that you want to learn about.

PATH **A**
fix it for Myself

ACCOUNTABILITY TRAIT 4
Hearing and Saying the Hard Things to See Reality

Welcome to the last, and perhaps most intimidating, of the See It Accountability Traits. As we cited back in part 2, the See It step Above The Line is all about seeing the reality of a situation so that you make the right decisions and solve the right problems. It's difficult to take accountability for what you don't know. The more clearly you can See It, the more likely you will continue your accountability journey as you take the next steps to Own It, Solve It, and Do It. Of course, this Accountability Trait plays a strategic role in ensuring you get off on the right foot.

Ask "If You Were Me" Questions

Matt Stevens, vice president of sales and marketing for archival digital media maker M-DISC, told us there is a need for those in leadership to build the sorts of relationships that make people feel free to say what needs to be said. As he put it, hearing and saying hard things are hard only if they are tied to negative emotions. To help neutralize negative emotion, he asks "If you were me" questions. "If you were me, what deadlines would worry you?" "If you were me, why might you hesitate bringing up an issue?" "If you were me, what would you be doing differently?" "If you were me, what problems would be keeping you up at night?" Asking "If you were me's" tends to break you out of hearing the same-old, same-old input, and into hearing the harder things that people really want to say.

Give Them Some Venting Time

Another helpful practice came from Chris Baldwin, president of Kohler Co.'s faucets business, who emphasizes the value of letting people vent their emotions. Chris realizes that we're all human beings and that humans get frustrated. He recommends just letting it happen. Don't squelch it. Allowing frustration to boil to the surface can help a person say some hard, tough things they normally wouldn't say when bound up under the straitjacket of decorum, control, or intimidation. Chris suggests letting people run with their frustration for a little while, because venting feelings actually gets important issues on the table for discussion. The trick is knowing how far to let them run before turning the conversation back to constructive solutions. "If you don't allow people to be frustrated, then they feel like they aren't being heard. The genius is in finding that sweet spot, when it's time to turn it positive." It's different in every case, but allowing your people some freedom to display their frustration will certainly send the message that you care and are willing to hear whatever hard stuff you need to know in order to *fix it*.

Ask the Question You're Afraid to Ask

Denis Meade is the director of training and development for the nonprofit tissue bank AlloSource, and is also a proponent of asking questions, especially the question you are most afraid to ask. What would make you fear asking a question? Denis told us, "The scariest question is the one you don't want to hear the answer to." He suggests putting this practice to work by identifying what questions scare you the most, especially those related to (1) your team, peers, or coworkers; (2) your boss; and (3) your direct report(s). Generally the scary questions fall into the evaluation category: "How am I performing in your eyes?" "What do I need to do to improve?" "How can I do better?" However, if you're not sure about the right questions to ask, try getting some feedback from someone who knows you and your situation really well, perhaps your spouse, partner, or significant other. You might even ask the person you're meeting with, "What's the question I should ask you that you think I most don't want to ask you?" Our advice: don't be afraid of your scariest question; your boldness and courage will likely lead to very happy results.

Hang Up Technology Once a Day and Make It Personal

Joe Nilson, director of business development for Tolero Pharmaceuticals, believes that hearing and saying hard things gets easier when you shut down the technology and *make it personal*. He said that when you rely too heavily on tech for communication, you can end up with only superficial relationships. The hard things become harder to say, and hear. Tough discussions are too easily avoided. Joe said, "We've gone from the personal handshake to phones, now to e-mails and texts. Business has become less personal and therefore more cold and one-dimensional." To address this, each day he consciously replaces new school with old school. Once a day he resists the impulse to text or e-mail, and picks up the phone. Joe advises, if you'd normally make a quick call, keep your phone off and walk down the hall for a face-to-face instead. Swapping electronic for personal communication once a day will add up over time and strengthen the real relationships that make saying and hearing hard things easier.

Say, "I Don't Know"

Chuck Knutson, founder and partner at tech-based litigation consulting firm Ironwood Experts, believes that people avoid hearing and saying hard things because they don't want to be seen as inferior or incompetent. They may think that success means having all the answers instead of being able to find them. As a result, they sit confused and quiet in meetings and say nothing. Chuck told us, "We should all commit today to admit we don't know when we don't know! Speak up in your team meetings, be intellectually hungry in your one-on-ones. In reality, the realization that you don't know something should be one of the most exciting discoveries you can make." So, the confession that you don't know may be one of the most important statements that you can share. Be willing to admit you don't know something whenever the opportunity presents itself and open yourself to hard talk made easy by an expanded view of reality. Think about who you should tell right now, "I don't know." and ask, "What do you think?"

Go back to Page 23

Now go to your *Fix It* **Bucket List** and select the next Accountability Trait that you want to learn about.

PATH **B**
fix it on **My Team**

ACCOUNTABILITY TRAIT 4
Hearing and Saying the Hard Things to See Reality

Teams and team leaders who don't engage in tough talk and tough listening can suffer strategically significant consequences. Getting people to be receptive and talk to one another, saying the hard things that really need to be said, is one side of the equation for a team. The other side is getting the team to hear the hard things they need to hear. Here are a few ideas that can help your team develop their ability to say and hear the hard things.

Try Leader Assimilation

An interesting practice we learned from Adam Porter, senior director of human resources for Edwards Lifesciences, the global leader in the science of heart valves and hemodynamic monitoring, was something he described as Leader Assimilation. When a new leader joins the Edwards Lifesciences critical care business unit, the company implements a Leader Assimilation program that begins three to six months after the leader has been working in his or her new role. It takes place on one day and involves the leader's direct reports. Four questions are asked in a frank, two-way discussion that incorporates asking and saying the hard things:

- What does the team know about the leader?
- What would the team like to know about the leader?

- What concerns does the team have for the leader and the organization?
- What should the leader know about this team?

The new leader comes into the room with their direct reports and a facilitator kicks off the meeting. The leader then leaves the room while the facilitator goes over the four questions with the team. They then take a break while the facilitator goes over the same questions in a brief one-on-one with the leader. Then everybody gets back together and discusses the questions as a group. This back-and-forth on specific questions demands that "the good, the bad, and the ugly" get discussed. The hard things are both said and heard. To see things more clearly as a team, you might try a little Leader Assimilation yourself.

Set Up a Peer Team

Mike Niblock, chief of the Salem, Oregon, fire department, told us that to solicit and explore their tough issues, they have set up a Peer Team. The team consists of ten to fifteen firefighters who were voted onto it by members of the department's eleven stations. Peer Team members make a point to meet with each firefighter quarterly, just to have a cup of coffee and to offer a listening ear, providing a safe opportunity to share concerns with "one of their own." According to Mike, "There's only so much a firefighter can put in their backpack." They need someone to talk to who they can unload on, share the hard things with about how the department is being run—station life, stresses, anything that bothers them about the job. This Peer Team technique offers an avenue for saying whatever needs to be said without fear of repercussion. The peer team exists solely to ensure that the employees can get the help they need and to provide a confidential outlet. Borrow this practice from a firefighter and set up a Peer Team as a practical way to get your people saying the hard things.

Implement a Constructive Candor Ground Rule

Casey Jones, president of equipment service specialist Altaquip, believes conflict is good. They have an open and stated "Don't go along to get along" policy—no groupthink allowed. Casey believes in no boring team meetings and no glossy words, but insists instead on animated discussions where real ideas are suggested by people who are never afraid to speak their minds. He does this by leading his team meetings in the spirit of "wanting to see reality" by having people frame their comments factually. People are encouraged to take a "this is how I see it and how I got here" approach rather than the usual "I'm right and you're wrong." According to Casey, by coaching a team this way you can remove emotion and encourage candor. When you "remove emotion, people will never feel attacked, or feel like they have to attack back to defend themselves. It's *actions* and behaviors that can be inappropriate, ill advised, or less than efficient, not the *person*." Make candor a team ground rule and see how much more easily your team will engage in the tough conversations.

Take Time for "Lessons I've Learned" in One-on-Ones

Elizabeth Pimper is director of learning for Ryan, an award-winning global tax services firm. She says that she conducts biweekly one-on-ones with each member of her team as well as with colleagues who work at an equal level of management, just to make sure everyone is on the same page. Now, we realize there is nothing unique about one-on-ones, but the twist here is that Elizabeth adds some formal time for Lessons I've Learned to each session. During this part of the meeting she begins by sharing her own Lessons I've Learned since their last meeting. By going first, she sets the tone of the conversation, making the other person more comfortable, and opening them up for sharing their own lessons learned. This back-and-forth eventually brings out a candid discussion of what really matters. Minutes are kept and eventually made available to everyone on the team so that they can all learn from the past and not make the same mistakes in the future.

Deploy a Feedback Team

Because people have such a hard time saying and hearing hard things, Mark Landes, global director of information technology for the chemical and engineering company Dymax, has instituted what he calls a feedback team. "People often see problems, broken stuff, but don't *fix it* because the transition from seeing to fixing is so difficult." Mark told us that a feedback team is a group of full-time employees who have been given the extra role of surveying employees to dig up hard-to-hear feedback in a nonthreatening way. The method has proven highly effective and revealing. Quite often, people don't even know they're sharing something that would normally be viewed as hard, because it's just their friends asking for information. In this casual setting, normally tough, hard-to-hear or hard-to-say words spill out easily. The takeaways are reported back to senior management for review that helps refine their culture-building strategy. To solicit a little more free-flowing tough talk and helpful ideas, put a feedback team together and send them out to *fix it.*

Now go to your *Fix It* **Bucket List** and select the next Accountability Trait that you want to learn about.

PATH C
fix it in **My Organization**

ACCOUNTABILITY TRAIT 4
Hearing and Saying the Hard Things to See Reality

Learning to hear and say the hard things as an individual or a team isn't nearly as challenging as threading this practice through an entire organization. There may be pockets of your organization where it's working well, because of the personality and approach of a particular team leader, but hearing and saying the hard things has to become part of the culture of an organization to have any kind of lasting impact. We have found that for accountability to find real stickiness throughout a whole culture, it must start at the top. Here's what a few top leaders have suggested they do to help build a culture where everyone is capable of hearing and saying hard things so their people will consistently See It.

Tell Them You Expect Them to Be Respectfully Blunt

Mike Dufresne, regional vice president of LKQ Corporation, a national aftermarket and salvage auto parts company, reported how his company once struggled to get its spread-out workforce to adopt any kind of effective transparent communication, until it got people to be *respectfully blunt.* He said, "There's no fancy talk here now, we don't sugarcoat anything anymore, we just say, 'I want your opinion on this or that. We're having trouble here and have to know what you're thinking.'" According to Mike, people no longer tend to get defensive when hard things pop up. "We've all learned how to listen as people say things as they really are." As a consequence, their culture is far more open than it's ever been, and people are more effective at their jobs. Employees even get along better and enjoy work more because most things they once talked about in the shadows are now out in the open. Mike observed that when everyone in the company knows they are expected to be respectively blunt, even brutally honest, "it benefits us all."

Enact E-mail–Free Fridays

Sandi Guy, a partner at Carr, Riggs & Ingram, a top public accounting firm, reflected on one of her favorite practices, something she instituted back when she was executive director of human capital for BDO. At the time, her people were spread out over multiple states in multiple offices. They were suffering from a lack of effective communication. Her company relied so heavily on e-mail that people often used as many as thirty e-mail volleys to clarify something a single call could have cleared up. To create more real dialogue, the human resources team launched E-mail–Free Fridays in their department, mandating, "When you need to communicate with someone on Fridays, you must do it face-to-face if in the office, or on the phone if you're out of state. No e-mails. Period." People started walking down the hall, picking up the phone, planning quick face-to-faces. It didn't take long to show results. Once people improved with this practice, they got to know one another better, discussed issues when they came up, and resolved problems more quickly. Even the relationships between human resources and their clients improved. To promote the give-and-take sharing of hard things, try killing all Friday e-mails.

Try an Exec-Connect

David Bonnette, CEO of cloud-based software manufacturer Lanyon, created a formal company-wide communication plan that includes a weekly Exec-Connect Meeting, or Executive Connection. The meeting runs ninety minutes, only ten employees are allowed, and an employee cannot attend more than once a month. There is no agenda, and the only rule is "You can ask anything." Because employees have seen over time that their executives have been willing to hear the hard things, tough issues get shared organization-wide. People know they can readily say whatever is on their mind. And the door swings both ways. Those coming to the meeting know that they will also get to hear exactly what's on the executive's mind. A structured regularly scheduled meeting like this helps everyone understand the importance David places on a culture of the sort of tough talk that helps everyone See It.

Run a Listening Marathon

When Janee Harteau became police chief of the Minneapolis Police Department, one of the first things she did was engage in a departmentwide "listening marathon." From 6:00 A.M. to 10:00 P.M. for six days straight she set up camp in one precinct after another, making herself available to sit with people throughout the department and listen to what they had to say. She stayed there for sixteen hours a day so that she would be on hand for a sizable chunk of every shift. Before announcing her listening marathon, she half expected to be sitting there alone. But it was wall to wall. Packed with officers every day. Why? How did this practice facilitate hearing or saying hard things? It sent the message that she would be there for as long as it took to hear whatever people wanted and needed to say. When her fellow officers saw that she was serious about hearing the hard things, a lot of pent-up frustrations came boiling out. As Janee put it, it was a "nonstop revolving door, a constant barrage of tough, you should do this or that." We encourage you to try a listening marathon and send the message that you're willing to surface all the hard things you need to hear in order to *fix it*.

Introduce Straight Talk

Dave Szczupak, executive vice president of Whirlpool's global product organization, explained that his company has adopted the phrase "straight talk" to describe one aspect of its culture. Those two words have taken on such tremendous meaning and importance, with total buy-in throughout the organization, that it has become one of the company's coveted Key Results. Basically, the practice boils down to saying it like it is, whether it's hard or easy. Instead of cautiously measuring every comment, everyone within Whirlpool GPO knows they are expected to tell it how it is, regardless of level or tenure. In meetings, employees often lead with, "Let me give you some straight talk here. . . ." This signals to everyone to buckle up; they're in for a brutally honest ride. To *fix it* when it comes to hearing and saying a few hard things, engage in some straight talk. It will help you See It and focus Above The Line, especially when the truth is tough to hear.

Go back to **Page 23**

PART 2

Now go to your *Fix It* **Bucket List** and select the next Accountability Trait that you want to learn about.

ACCOUNTABILITY TRAIT 5
Being Personally Invested

As we pointed out back in part 2 of this Accountability Trait, our Workplace Accountability Study shows that 70 percent of respondents believed their success in achieving their current organizational results was "at risk" because of a lack of engagement and ownership. Wow! To help you fix any of your own ownership woes, we've gathered fifteen notable practices from some very talented people. They use these practices with great success to assist themselves, their teams, and their organizations to dive deeper into their company pool and contribute in innovative ways. High personal investment on the job is a key attribute for someone striving for accountability. It's also a key requirement for finding happiness in your work.

Make Your Investment Obvious: No Flybys

Ownership starts at the top and is contagious; that is, to catch it, everyone must be able to see it. For Dr. Bernadette Loftus, executive medical director of Mid-Atlantic Permanente Medical Group, what's worked for her is promoting the idea of being personally invested by getting close enough to the business to know what is really going on. No ivory tower for Bernadette. To her, that means being the kind of person who really knows what's going on in her world, and doing it in a way that other people know it, too. She does this by "being *up* far enough to manage, but *down* far enough to be where the work actually gets done, sleeves rolled up, to see and hear what's really going on." This inspires ownership up and down the organization. She told us, "I actually do know what we're doing, I'm not just another talking head from outer space that's doing a flyby. Really invested leaders don't just do flybys, but really know how the work gets done." The key question: "Where can I avoid the flyby and get involved in a way that others visibly see my investment?" Don't assume it's obvious; make sure it is.

Play Receptionist for a Day

Paul C. Kelly, president and CEO of Research Electro-Optics, a maker of high-precision optical components, found a way to demonstrate his investment in understanding every aspect of how his business works. He told us that REO uses a management style defined by "walking around." It's very hands-on, from the highest levels of the company. Every other Wednesday, for instance, Paul anchors the reception desk for a few hours. Yes, despite the fact that he's the president and CEO, he actually sits at the front desk, answering phone calls and greeting people. This sends everyone a clear message regarding his personal investment in understanding his company. But he also sends the message that every job is important, every job matters, and every employee needs to be invested in doing what they do as well as they can. People in his organization find this practice so powerful that it inspires everyone, down to the most entry-level employee, to get invested and know that what they do matters. Answer the phones and greet people in reception, and you just might see how it helps everyone take a giant step to Own It!

Interview Yourself Every Day

Years ago Hugh Ekberg, president of Kitchen & Bath Americas for Kohler Co., developed the practice of holding an interview with himself every day on his drive home. At the end of each workday he explicitly asks himself, "Okay, when was I Below The Line today?" Then he forces himself to answer the question as if some superior were asking it. The level of personal investment and awareness of accountability this instills is unbelievable. He knows that he's less effective, more removed, and lacking ownership when languishing Below The Line, and that by merely conducting this self-interview he catches himself early on whenever venturing down there. "When you are your most grueling taskmaster and you know that kind of interview is going to happen at the end of every day, it tends to keep you on your toes and committed to what you're doing." Help hone accountability and ownership by planning for a nightly interview with your toughest critic.

Ask, "Who Owns It?"

Johnny Priest, division president for Willbros' Utility Transmission & Distribution, told us of a time when he was promoted to his first executive position while working at Duke Power. He was conducting a town hall meeting when a friend he had started working with years before stood up in back and asked, "Can you explain how you and I came to work here at the same time, and now you're standing there as a VP and I'm still a lineman?" Johnny's answer might have offended a lesser friend when he told him: "When we first started here, you came to work for the pay, I went to work for Duke Power." His friend got it. According to Johnny, you should work as though it were your own company; don't just have an employee mentality. Mary Bartlett, COO for The Reserve, a professional shared workplace, shares this view. She got into such a habit of asking her teams "Who owns it?" that her people started referring to it as "The Mary Question." Mary told us that without someone regularly asking this question, things can quickly go adrift: "If you aren't careful and don't have an accountability culture, you can easily end up with everyone pointing at each other, particularly when things start to go wrong." We recommend you ask "Who owns it?" at every opportunity so that accountability and ownership are clear.

Make the Investment by Working Side by Side

According to Robert Martinez, sales manager for a California CBS/Telemundo/CW network affiliate, it's all about time. Time spent. Time invested. For Robert, when he sees others struggling with the ability to Own It, he's found that making the personal investment to work side by side is the fix. Going on sales calls together. Engaging in joint presentations. Robert told us that "if you have someone who's struggling or stymied in some way, and they don't know what to do and start slipping Below The Line into confusion or worse, then dig in and make an investment in helping them be successful." Think back to a time when someone invested a little time in you. Wasn't it impressive and powerful? Robert went on to say, "It's been said that even ten minutes a day spent between parent and child doing what the child wants will build enormous relationship storehouses." You can transfer the same idea to leadership and business. To infuse your downlines, uplines, or those on the sidelines with more personal investment, do a little side-by-side, peer-to-peer work.

Now go to your *Fix It* **Bucket List** and select the next Accountability Trait that you want to learn about.

PATH **B**
fix it on **My Team**

ACCOUNTABILITY TRAIT 5
Being Personally Invested

Creating ownership and investment on your team is key to making real progress. As we have said before, "Culture changes most quickly within existing teams," because the team setting is where people live and interact on a daily basis. Making sure that high personal investment is a part of the team culture is essential to building a Culture of Accountability for the entire enterprise. Try the following suggestions to move forward with the Own It step.

Make Some Investment Ground Rules

Joe Rigby, chairman, CEO, and president of Pepco Holdings, a large energy delivery company in the eastern United States, believes ownership begins with a paintbrush. Joe says that "if you allow me to help you paint part of a picture, I'm going to have a much more vested interest in loving and promoting that picture." Joe talks with his people in detail about strategy early on because he wants everyone's handprints all over the team's work. To buy in. To Own It. One way Joe accomplishes this is through some clearly stated ground rules, such as no smartphones in meetings. If someone is presenting an idea and has worked for days getting ready, they don't need someone at the table playing with their phone. You want everyone invested, not just the presenter. It's full attention. Joe has found that handing everyone a metaphoric paintbrush by making sure they are fully present in meetings contributes in big ways to being personally invested. What ground rules do you need to make?

Share Some Life Stories

Matt Stevens, vice president of sales and marketing for archival digital media maker M-DISC, told us about another practice he learned at a former job. Once a month, one member of his team was asked to participate in a "life stories" exercise. The goal was team building through human transparency, something that surprisingly promoted engagement and investment. Stevens said, "It's a natural thing, when you get to know and like the people you work with, you look forward to spending time with them, engaging in challenging goals with them." People would take thirty minutes and share a PowerPoint, pictures of kids, even "Everything I Learned in Life from My Mom." One particular standout came from a man who didn't speak about his life, but shared four stories that had made a strong impression on him. People were moved to tears. That kind of vulnerability was so rare that people came to him throughout the day to thank him for sharing. Friendships grew. Personal investment shot up. Someone even posted his presentation on YouTube for those who weren't in the meeting. If you're striving to fix some personal investment issues, try sharing a life story or two.

Ask Three Questions to Build Team Ownership

Tiffany Zakszeski, director of human resources for the endoscopy division of prominent medical technology company Stryker Corporation, loves to ask three key questions in any team touch-base or one-on-one: (1) How am I doing? (2) How are you doing? (3) How are we doing? Answering these will be harder for some people than for others, but by staying on them and insisting on an answer, ownership comes almost automatically. *How am I doing?* engages people, builds on the strengths learned back in the See It Accountability Traits, and forces people to drill down, think deeply, open up, and share. *How are you doing?* encourages people to listen and to talk. *How are we doing?* forges group ownership, a joint vision, and team and organizational unity, and makes people feel like they're playing on the same team. We invite you to fix any ownership problems on your team through a solid three-question Q&A. It's a huge ownership builder and an effective way to pool talents and thinking.

Start Your Own Ozzie Awards

Barbara Van Dine, director of talent development and learning for warehouse food and supply chain Smart & Final, told us that the sales and merchandising team created an awards show like the Emmys, something they call the Ozzies. Having derived the name from our Oz Principles, the team awards ribbons at quarterly meetings, where they recognize associates who have demonstrated extraordinary ownership for getting accountability right. The winners' names are engraved in gold on wooden plaques, which are displayed in the sales and merchandise department hallway. She believes these kinds of public recognition ceremonies plant seeds of company loyalty, commitment, ownership, and personal investment—something critical for associate buy-in. For a fun way to promote accountability, stage your own awards show and hand out an Ozzie or two.

Spend Some Time Serving Together

Matt Broder, vice president of corporate communications for retail branding and sourcing services company Daymon Worldwide, told us that they are big fans of programs that build team unity, promote engagement, and foster personal investment. One of these is team-sponsored service, a program that gives people two paid days off a year to do some community service. Various teams take advantage of these free days. For example, one team in Cincinnati has enjoyed a relationship for many years with the Ronald McDonald House. Teammates contribute time by helping families, cooking, donating items for kids, and offering financial and emotional support. This gives the team a chance to work together in a different environment, where the playing field is leveled and everyone is working shoulder to shoulder. It also helps the team feel more invested in the business as the business gets more invested in helping others. In fact, this particular team has been recognized in the local press and given awards, something that sparks the participants' loyalty to team and company. If you're looking for something to fix team investment on the job, borrow a practice from Daymon and urge your teams to perform a little service out of the office.

Go back to **Page 23**

PART 2

Now go to your *Fix It* **Bucket List** and select the next Accountability Trait that you want to learn about.

PATH **C**
fix it in **My Organization**

ACCOUNTABILITY TRAIT 5
Being Personally Invested

Developing a Culture of Accountability where people take ownership for achieving key organizational results requires a willingness
to make the link between where you are and what you have done
with where you want to be and what you are going to do to get there.
If you can't do that, then you don't Own It. In fact, you can't Own It.
Organizational cultures should inspire and encourage individuals,
teams, and other working groups to make this link a natural part of
the way they do business. Here are a few ideas, drawn from the 120
executives we interviewed, for getting this done.

Scare People Away Before You Hire Them

Hany Massarany, CEO of clinical diagnostics innovator GenMark
Diagnostics, told us that one of the keys to ensuring ownership at a
company level is to scare people away before they're even hired.
GenMark takes their culture so seriously that 90 percent of those
who don't get hired fail to land the job because they aren't initially
seen as a cultural fit. The company wants people to enter the job
with a See It, Own It, Solve It, Do It mentality. There's no room for
someone who brings a Below The Line noninvested mentality to the
job. The way they continue to ensure ownership company-wide is to
test all of this during the interview process. They pound on personal

investment immediately. According to Hany, "We try to scare people away early by emphasizing that it doesn't matter what your job description is, we have a lot to do with a 'last person out dumps the trash and turns off the lights' mentality." For a sense of ownership to spread more easily across your entire company, begin by hiring only those who show they get it—even before day one.

Create an Ownership Development Program

Suzanne Pottinger, vice president of employee experience for The Original Cakerie, a leading manufacturer of quality frozen desserts, said that one of their most effective organizational best practices to promote personal investment came about when they modified a leadership program they refer to as Crossroads (a leadership development platform broken out into six levels). The goal of the program is to deepen personal investment and capability throughout an employee's career. Employees begin moving from entry-level Crossroads 1 all the way up through executive level at Crossroads 6. The advantage of a structured program designed to develop leadership capability over years is that the structure itself fosters ownership and ongoing commitment because there's a deeply embedded long-term personal agenda. The view that "the company cares about my development and is willing to invest in me" is highly prevalent. Personal investment comes with the territory. As Suzanne explained, "During Crossroads 3, for instance, you are required to recognize those employees at levels 1 and 2, identify potential leaders in these groups, and better yourself by developing them. If you want to ascend to level 4, then you must actively aid in developing all 3s, and help them develop their 1s and 2s." It creates a web of personal investment and ownership across the entire organization. For a real answer to increasing personal investment in the organization, create an "ownership development program" that develops people over the long term.

Build a Learning Organization

Lance Boynton, COO and global director of operations for chemical engineering company Dymax Corporation, believes that continuous learning inspires higher levels of personal engagement and investment. Lance speaks highly of his firm's internal "university," which has helped Dymax to do just that. Set up for both online and in-house classes, they offer some eight hundred different courses that employees can access remotely. The classes generally run for thirteen weeks, and are taught by senior leader employee volunteers, with in-house classes occurring most often during the lunch hour. With class titles ranging from Finance to Excel to Adhesives 101, the university-type instruction has elevated and engaged employees, lighting up company loyalty. Lance insisted, "The more knowledgeable, intelligent, and familiar employees are with the latest and greatest, the better suggestions and ideas they will offer and the more committed they will be to the company." And according to Lance, it's working. "The classes help employees avoid stagnation and stay engaged. They challenge people, and when seeing their fellow employees taking classes . . . it's a positive peer pressure experience." If you're struggling with employee stagnation or can see a lack of buy-in with employee investment, stimulate ownership by starting your own "university."

Ask "Are You Doing What You Were Hired to Do?"

When Marty Smuin, CEO of Adaptive Computing, a leading high-performance cloud orchestration platform, first took over the position, he left his office, walked the halls, and started asking questions. "How's it going?" "How are you doing?" "Do you like what you do?" But the big question he has since put into regular practice: "Are you doing what you were hired to do?" Marty told us he was shocked at what he started hearing: eight out of ten people were doing things they weren't initially hired to do, something that had been directly contributing to frustration and a lack of personal investment. According to Marty, if someone was hired as a software engineer to write software and instead slipped into some sort of quality assurance role where they were now running around putting out fires, they'd more than likely come in and just wait for the clock to strike 5:00 P.M. The company had lost them. Now, in some cases the person might have liked morphing into a new role, but you must still ask the question, making sure they are doing what they thought they'd be doing in the first place.

Send Your Leaders to "the Doctor" Every Six Months

Daniel Swartz, director of human resources at Align Technology, makers of Invisalign and the iTero 3-D digital scanning system, is such an advocate of what we do to build personal investment and encourage cultural ownership that every six months they bring in two of our Partners In Leadership facilitators to spend a focused couple of days with all senior leaders. Daniel told us, "It's like sending our organization to the doctor for a twice-a-year checkup." The company investment in this kind of intimate coaching encourages personal ownership within the leaders. They see Align Technology investing in them, so it encourages substantial loyalty back. Because they are striving for double-digit growth year over year, growing internationally, and consciously striving to increase their winning culture, they can easily hit walls in confidence from the complexity of the obstacles they encounter. By bringing in those who understand how to teach accountability on a regular basis, you make ownership and personal investment believable, attainable, possible, and fun.

Go back to **Page 23**

PART 2

Now go to your *Fix It* **Bucket List** and select the next Accountability Trait that you want to learn about.

PATH **A**
fix it for **Myself**

ACCOUNTABILITY TRAIT 6
Learning from Both Successes and Failures

You probably know George Santayana's famous quote "Those who cannot remember the past are condemned to repeat it." When it comes to *fixing it*, this is exactly our goal, not only to help you avoid repeating and avoiding mistakes but also to help you discover the secrets to replicating your successes. Below are some favorite practices from our executive friends who have pulled back the curtain a bit on their own lives in order to share what they have done, and still do, to learn from a variety of life's successes and failures.

Take the Coaching

Debbie Bowles, general manager of a 600,000 square-foot Ocean Spray food-processing plant, learned early in her career not to be too direct. For instance, back when she was a senior operations manager at Gillette, a boss pulled her aside after an important meeting and said, "I want you to know that everything you said in there was correct, but I'm concerned that you may have embarrassed the person sitting at the head of the table—people never forget being embarrassed." He challenged her to meet with the senior executive, and then in the future, to get her point across while considering the feelings of others. She chose to learn from an early "failure," and today consciously practices the notion of "building the brand" of others. She does this by praising in public, criticizing in private, and focusing on trying to make others look and feel good about themselves. She said, "Brands are critical. Don't disintegrate anyone's brand. Build it up. Build them up. Have their best interest in mind." Debbie took the coaching on a failure, learned from that experience, and has now turned it into a strength.

Don't Hide It, Declare It

Ian Baines, CEO of the popular family-style restaurant chain Cheddar's Scratch Kitchen, told us that early on in his career as a chef, he took failure too personally and couldn't do anything with it, least of all learn from it. Failure back then was completely unproductive because he kept it to himself. Most important, by personally owning all failure himself, by blaming himself alone and keeping it from others, he never shared any lessons and learning. As he put it, "Failure is a good thing, it teaches. By taking it so personally, I wasn't allowing other people to fail, too." As a consequence, Ian wasn't getting the best out of everyone. They were afraid when they saw him coming because they didn't want to fail either, seeing how hard he was on himself. That kept others from taking risks. Now he recommends that when you fail you should shout it from the rooftops, "spread it around, share it as quickly and widely as possible." Sharing botched projects allows you to process the problem by creating a discussion with others that can shed light on the situation and bring new insight. When people see that happen, they know they can do it, too.

Ask About It in Interviews

"Heat hardens the steel." So said Otto Aichinger, strategic partnership manager for industry-leading, nationally recognized mortgage lenders. Like most thoughtful people, Otto has discovered in his own life that more can be learned from failure than from success, so he has made it routine to help others appreciate this by asking anyone who interviews for a job with him about their failures. "Everybody trips. Falls. Everyone fails. The trick is to learn from it. When hiring, I want to hear about their failures rather than successes to see how they've dealt with it. So I ask that they talk about them in our first interview. It's okay to say you screwed up." Otto asks whether they've ever been fired from a job, and if so, why. They talk about relationships, divorces, financial problems and how they've handled them. What they've learned. How they've grown. Otto pointed out, "I've had people tell me in job interviews that they were fired from jobs because they weren't paying attention, they showed up late, they didn't like their boss." His reaction? If you can get someone to share their failures with you early, they'll share everything later.

Learn from Others' Failures

Lance Davis, past CFO of Coventry Health Care and current CFO of Veridicus Health, an emerging online and brick-and-mortar pharmacy, told us that if you're paying attention you can learn what not to do from watching others struggle. However, Lance admitted to being conflicted about doing this. "I don't know, can you admire and loathe someone at the same time?" He told us about an unintentional mentor he admired to a point, but who was also a guy who could quickly turn you into collateral damage if you got in his way. Lance passed along the notion that it's easy, and natural, to learn from those everyone admires from the positive successes, those who lift and inspire. Just don't overlook the lessons you can gain from those who maybe aren't quite positive role models. The practice: be on the lookout for lessons you can learn by watching the missteps others make. Learning from successes and failures doesn't need to come from just your own experience. In fact, it costs a lot less in terms of pain and struggle to learn lessons from failure by diagnosing others' miscalculations.

Develop and Use a Personal Success Checklist

Dave Jennings is a performance psychology expert who understands the great benefit of learning from both success and failure, but especially success. He told us, "Taking a look at what went wrong is certainly helpful, but make sure you also identify and amplify what went right. Then duplicate it." Dave has found that there is great power in making success your teacher, so he captures that tactic by using a simple "success checklist" after every event, project, or task. For him, it works best just after a short separation from the activity, often while on a plane or in a cab. "Ask simple questions, so you get simple answers: What worked? Why did it work? How do I feel about what worked? Was it planned or luck? Is my preparation what created the win? Can I duplicate it with other clients or tasks?" Write down the answers and reflect. According to Dave, "Using a success checklist to identify why it went well will lead you to clarity and inspire higher highs and ensure you can repeat the success in the future."

Go back to **Page 23**

PART
2

Now go to your *Fix It* **Bucket List** and select the next Accountability Trait that you want to learn about.

PATH B
fix it on My Team

ACCOUNTABILITY TRAIT 6
Learning from Both Successes and Failures

Imagine belonging to a team where everyone has decided to Own It. The Three Musketeers' rallying cry "All for one and one for all!" encompasses the spirit of what makes belonging to a team fun, engaging, energizing, and empowering. Inherent in any team's culture, however, is the all-too-common tendency to blame others for perceived failure rather than owning it yourself. Basically, blame is handy because others are so close and involved. To learn effectively from success and failure at a team level, it takes real leadership and a complete lack of individual ego battles. Here are some effective practices you and your teams can implement that we know work because our contributing executives use them every day.

Try Questing

Paulette Wage, head of human resources for McDonald's Hawaii, Guam, and the outlying South Pacific islands, said she loves to use something she calls "questing," which is essentially a success and failure "scavenger hunt." When conducting a quest, Paulette gives her people index cards and sends them out to visit the competition. They go into other fast-food restaurants, place an order, and then sit and observe, taking in the successes and failures they see. They write down everything, from "What do I like about this place?" to whether they see trash on the floor or employees who are happy or grumpy. When her team gets back from their success-failure scavenger hunt, they debrief, discussing issues such as: Would you like to work there? What can we learn from their pluses and minuses? How do we apply the goods and bads from our index cards to our own operation? Seeing how others both succeed and fail can foster an invaluable learning opportunity.

Go Watch for It

Much like Paulette and her team, Jeff Schmitz, executive vice president for wireless and service provider Spirent, told us that he likes to send his product managers to customers just to observe their use of the product. This technique provides valuable insight for Spirent because it enables them to gain firsthand knowledge of the successes or failures that occur. There is nothing terribly formal about the process. It just involves sitting down and observing their customers using the company's cloud data services, IP networks, Wi-Fi, or mobile network technologies products. Jeff said that he thought he knew how their customers used their products, but after watching, he realized that he really had a lot to learn. As Jeff put it, "We've learned so much more by simply observing firsthand what works and what doesn't. It was often shocking that the customer uses the products the way they do." This practice has been so successful that Spirent is now looking to expand and formalize the process so everyone can learn from the success or failure of products in the hands of those who matter most, the customers.

Let Your People Whine

Hugh Ekberg, president of Kitchen & Bath Americas for Kohler, Co., is a strong accountability advocate and recognizes how valuable it is to learn from success and failure by letting people whine. He thinks it's healthy to allow a little frustration to creep into team meetings, and prefers it to come out in a small group setting rather than find it seeping through the halls (and culture) later. As a general rule he said, "People don't whine over wins and perceived successes, they whine over failure, setbacks, and perceived negative outcomes." For that reason, moaning in meetings can actually be healthy and solicit some robust conversation around the causes of failure—like siloed motivations or lack of communication—while promoting a freer, more transparent team culture that actually invites learning from failures. Hugh recognizes the benefits lurking in every frustrated employee and behind every exasperated comment. To enhance learning on your teams, draw a little negative out into the open, something that can invite a group to think their way out of tight spots.

Hold a Discovery Meeting

Matthew Clark, chief of police for the University of Minnesota and former assistant chief with the Minneapolis Police Department, reflected on a philosophy his department employed to deal with successes and failures—a practice where a group of accountable and experienced commanders and chiefs assembled for a "discovery" meeting. These are folks who otherwise might not come together in a team such as this. These leaders were trained in the art of nosing through failures, analyzing the causes, learning from them, and laying out a path to *fix it*. According to Chief Clark, "The meeting was a dedicated time to solve systems problems and create a common understanding." The ad hoc team would meet specifically to identify and discuss ongoing struggles or failures to discover what was not working, and then wrestle with the issues until they could turn the failures into successes. This group approach to discovery is effective because it brings the right people together out of the ordinary team structure and gives leaders an immediate first option for *fixing it,* rather than letting an issue languish or fester until it burrows itself into negative hallway conversations. Set up a time for discovery like this and give failure an immediate home so successes can grow from any failure more quickly.

Design the Team for Learning

Chuck Knutson, founder and partner of Ironwood Experts, a software technology expert witness consulting firm, believes in the philosophy of "fail fast": the idea that you should discover failures quickly enough to avoid an irreversible or costly error. What makes Chuck's advice notable and unique is how he insists on designing the team for learning by removing personal and team ego from the equation. For Chuck, it's "we," never "I." In software, you can't know what's going to work, so, as Chuck put it, "When you build any new product, there's no sure way to know if the dogs are going to eat the dog food." For that reason he says they need to criticize the tar out of things. You can't fail rapidly if you look at everything from a purely personal point of view. Failing fast involves egoless work. Egoless programming. Egoless operating. Egoless analysis. To remove ego, structure projects as a team effort. No solo acts. No product is any one person's "baby." Otherwise, people can't criticize a product without criticizing the person. To fail fast and learn quickly, remove ego and make everything a team effort.

Go back to **Page 23**

PART
2

Now go to your *Fix It* **Bucket List** and select the next Accountability Trait that you want to learn about.

PATH C
fix it in My Organization

ACCOUNTABILITY TRAIT 6
Learning from Both Successes and Failures

The challenge with learning from success or failure company-wide is that it's often like trying to turn the *Titanic* away from an oncoming iceberg. And, yes, you read that right, too often in organizations, fingers point at everything and everyone else, as if the iceberg were moving at them rather than the ship itself needing a course correction. Any organizational culture can lose the chance of learning from successes and failures due to Below The Line blame gaming, or a host of other acts of excuse making. To assist in fixing any challenges with this Accountability Trait, we invited some executives to your learning rescue.

Hold a Monday Pep Rally to Celebrate Success

Bryon Stephens, president and COO of Marco's Pizza, told us that each Monday they hold a company-wide pep rally to set the tone for the week. "These rallies have created a culture where throughout the week everyone is actually setting people up for success. The rallies are a time for recognizing people. For intentionally catching the big successful aha moments where we want everyone in the company to see that some special success has happened." To further spread the success fever, they give away financial rewards or tickets to ball games, put any accomplishments up on their employee Web site, and shout out successes in the company's e-newsletter. Bryon told us that "people like recognition and step up when knowing it's out there. So we intentionally make a big deal of the big ahas because we want everyone to see and emulate them." All the leaders in the company are actively looking for successes to share. The bigger the story, the more loudly they announce it. They want employees to "star in their own success." As a result, people who were stagnant are now leading the pep rallies. People are growing. Leaders are emerging from the practice of celebrating and learning from success.

Create Learning Groups

Brad McKain, refining general manager for a division of Marathon Petroleum, created nine cross-functional teams across his plant leadership that operate as Focused Accountability groups. Every month one of Brad's direct reports selects a learning topic for each of the groups, such as the division's Cultural Belief (a phrase we use in our training to represent a current area of improvement to emphasize on the team), "Be Heard," and encourages them to share how people and teams are succeeding in their work around that topic. Because no one reports directly to anyone in these cross-functional groups, they are more willing to voice things like, "I'm struggling with that," or, "How did that work for you?" These learning group discussions all follow the same pattern: identify a desired behavior (such as Be Heard), connect it to the results the plant is working to achieve, then tell how it was done. This kind of structured discussion, combined with focused feedback, fosters learning about any best practices or identified challenges. Brad and his division have turned these groups into a tool for improving communication, learning from both successes and areas that might need improvement, and making ongoing decisions that grow accountability across the company.

Conduct a Postmortem Meeting

Tami Polmanteer, chief human resources officer for retail branding and sourcing services company Daymon Worldwide, told us that they like to use a somewhat familiar learn-from-success-and-failure practice called the postmortem. Built into each project plan is a debriefing session focused on (1) what went well and (2) what needs to be done better. This practice of ruthlessly debriefing in order to learn from success and failure takes place in a meeting where attendees are expected to brainstorm and speak openly and candidly. The hope is that the company can learn from the past and avoid the same mistakes moving forward. Tami also explained to us that when planning subsequent projects, the project manager checks the company archives for similar, previously completed projects in order to review the previous projects' notes and learn from prior successes and failures. To improve your own company's ability to learn from either success or failure, implement your own postmortem meeting.

Ask the Customer

Gabriele Eaton, director of global talent management and organizational development for Hollister, a medical devices manufacturer, told us that employees rarely have a chance to see how their daily work succeeds or fails with the end user—the patient. Gabriele emphasized that it is easy to forget, in the routine of daily work, that the products they make help people. Because of their need to connect the lifesaving work they do with the lives they actually save, the company has adopted the practice of periodically inviting patients to speak with employees about the goods and the bads of their experiences. Patients are invited into plants and corporate meetings where company associates can learn from real people whose lives have been permanently changed by what the company does. Recently, for example, they brought in a man who had successfully received one of Hollister's artificial heart valves. The patient told them about the impact their work had on his life. The man was emotional. Grateful. This obvious success inspired everyone to do even better going forward. For some impactful hands-on learning from your own successes or failures, ask the customer.

Tell Them It's Okay to Fail

Vincent Weafer, vice president at Intel Security Group, McAfee Labs, a cyber security thought leadership company, believes that this trait and Accountability Trait 12, Taking the Necessary Risks, are closely intertwined. (In truth, all of these traits are closely intertwined, something we hope you are starting to see.) To make his point and illustrate McAfee Labs' practice, Vincent told us, "If you want to build a project that is perfect, you'll never succeed. You must allow failure, and people need to know it, so tell them." He said he often hears how people are afraid to fail, but believes that's not really the case. They just need to know that it's okay to fail, that it's all part of ultimately succeeding. Vincent encourages failure by listening to out-of-the-box ideas, approving calculated-risk projects, and letting everyone know that "You can't learn if you don't fail."

Go back to **Page 23**

PART
2

Now go to your *Fix It* **Bucket List** and select the next Accountability Trait that you want to learn about.

PATH **A**
fix it for **Myself**

ACCOUNTABILITY TRAIT 7
Ensuring My Work Is Aligned with Key Results

Everything we teach and coach about accountability is intended to point at achieving desired results. Without having a clear objective, accountability serves no real purpose, is tough to measure, hard to implement, and is difficult to sustain over time. It would be like golfing without the cup or playing football without the goalposts. Here are a few notable practices that you as an individual can use to ensure that your work, and that of those you work with, gets and remains aligned with the organization's Key Results.

Post What You're After on the Wall

Jack Butorac, chairman and CEO of Marco's Pizza, told us that he literally pins his Key Results to his office wall, where he is forced to look at them multiple times a day. Their very presence encourages Jack and others to keep all business conversations pointed at what they're all chasing. This sends a strong message about how much he personally buys in to Marco's culture and their four Key Results. Jack told us, "To reach my goals, to reach our goals, I have to demonstrate I understand them, I know them, I talk about them, and I practice them." He also immerses both new franchisees and new corporate employees in the culture before learning anything else. They are taught the Key Results and Marco's culture. Franchisees then go out into the field for six weeks of field training. After that, they come back to Toledo and revisit the Key Results and culture framework with the benefit of perspective. Jack said, "If my franchisees and employees are not practicing accountability, I failed." Pin what you're after to the walls to ensure they stick.

Be GROSS

Sandi Guy, a partner at Carr, Riggs & Ingram, a top public accounting firm, suggests you be GROSS. That's right: Get Rid Of Stupid Stuff. She believes that by committing GROSS to memory, by constantly asking, "Why am I doing this?" you might just come to recognize that you could be doing something better with your time, something that actually points more directly to what you, your team, and your organization are trying to achieve. Asking yourself, "'Why am I doing this?' is a great way to begin every day and every new task." Sandi further told us, "If I often can't find a logical reason around why I'm having to do this step or that thing, then I ask someone else to see if they know." Sandi said, "It's important to push, to peel the onion, to pull back the layers on what you're doing so you don't just keep busy, but stay effective and contributing to what your company is all about." To *fix it*, get rid of stupid stuff and spend your time only on tasks that lead to results.

Guard the First Hour of the Day

Lisa Miller, vice president of human resources for our own company, Partners In Leadership, shared a practice she learned in a previous job. According to Lisa, "The first hour of the day should be spent on more important things, never on e-mail." There must be an important call or two. A meeting. A person you can meet with face-to-face. Something you didn't get done the day before. Answering e-mails in the first hour puts you into a reactive mode, potentially making it harder for you to concentrate on what you most need to do to move things forward. Suddenly, others are controlling your destiny. Knowing that, Lisa consciously tries to start her day with activities that drive productivity in ways that align her with the company's Key Results. That calibration gets your efforts pointed in the right direction and allows you to make a difference in getting desired results. Be intentional and control your day before it controls you. Make the first hour of the day count.

Give Yourself a Renewal Day

Darryl Shiroma, assistant vice president for HawaiiUSA Federal Credit Union, believes that "in our busy, noisy, distracting world, it's easy to get pulled away from the one, three, or five main things we should be focused on." To counter this he advocates a Renewal Day, strategically planned time off when he goes away somewhere quiet. His Renewal Day begins by waking up early and driving to the other side of the island. By the time he reaches the pineapple fields of Wahiawa or the waters off North Shore, the stress is gone. All he brings is a notebook and pen. "You leave your cell phone in the car." He draws, makes lists, and engages in short reflection activities that include asking, "What have I accomplished? Am I focused on what will take me to the results I'm after? Where should I be going and how do I get there?" By the time he's headed home, he's refocused and energized. He has since espoused this practice to his employees and encourages them to do the same. He allows every employee one day a year for renewal and they get to pick the day. They don't report on where they went or what they did. Darryl believes an effective annual Renewal Day helps you focus on Key Results and makes you more efficient, both at work and in life.

Tie Key Results to the Latest Rumor

Loressa Cole, chief nursing officer for LewisGale Medical Center, likes to walk the hospital halls and chat with the nursing staff in their space. She likes to ask them: "Hey, what's the latest rumor?" By interacting with her staff on the front lines and asking a candid question like this, Loressa said, "It's amazing what you can tease from their minds, things they would never have the nerve to say in a formal meeting." Now, you may be thinking that this approach sounds more like Obtaining Perspective than Key Results . . . and you'd be correct. This is an example of how becoming proficient at one of these traits can help strengthen others. None of them is meant to live independently. In this case, after Loressa gets her nurses talking, they often start complaining and going Below The Line. At this point Loressa brings up the Key Results and how they relate to the situations the nurses are going through. This technique of sprinkling Key Results in Below The Line conversations not only keeps Loressa attuned to what's happening in the hospital but stops the Below The Line talk and refocuses everyone on their jobs, which in the case of LewisGale Medical Center literally saves lives.

Go back to **Page 23**

PART
2

Now go to your *Fix It* **Bucket List** and select the next Accountability Trait that you want to learn about.

PATH **B**

fix it on **My Team**

⬡ 7

ACCOUNTABILITY TRAIT 7
Ensuring My Work Is Aligned with Key Results

John Cuomo, general manager for aerospace distribution company KLX Aerospace Solutions, said he wants his people and company to live, breathe, and own their Key Results. For that reason he trains all his direct reports and team leaders to look regularly and literally in the mirror, in order to assess their own individual performance as it relates to leading their teams in pursuit of Key Results. We agree with John. Team leaders need to Own It and must help their teams get aligned with it. It all happens in the team setting; this is the most important place to focus. To help you enjoy a better experience with your own mirror, here are a few practices from some respected executives that may speed you along the road to results.

Get Alignment After Hours

Vincent Weafer, vice president at Intel Security Group, McAfee Labs, a cyber security thought leadership company, believes the key to getting alignment around Key Results is working with people one-on-one. Vincent told us, "Electronic communication technologies such as WebEx/Skype are okay, but if you only make yourself available at headquarters, then you aren't sending a message that 'your alignment is critically important to the team.'" Knowing that the only way to get real alignment, and then know you've got it, is by going one-on-one, he practices regular live meetings and after-hours social interaction. Here he finds people open up best, so that the real dialogue that brings true alignment occurs. In Japan, for example, he says that going out at night with the team makes a big difference. The country's culture dictates that you don't tend to say anything at work, but when you go out to dinner after hours you are suddenly free to open up about career, aspirations, bosses, or the organization as a whole. "Once you get to know people at this level, they'll come along for the Key Results ride or most anyplace else you want them to go." When it's really important to ensure that your people's work aligns with your Key Results, invest in some after-hours time.

Ask for a Team Plan

Rachael Stiles, an organizational development consultant in the energy space, shared with us one sure way to create accountability and commitment all the way through the organization. It's getting each team to own the Key Results independently. Do that and you'll achieve widespread alignment. To help with this, ask every team to formulate a plan for how they are going to help achieve the results, and then post that plan in a high-traffic area next to the team's work space. The activity creates a meaningful experience for the team members and provides concrete evidence that their leaders are sincere in changing the culture. To be effective, list the company's Key Results on the top half, with the team's explanation of how their actions and efforts will positively contribute to those Key Results on the bottom half. Rachael said, "Posters hanging outside respective team areas allow everyone from every department to know exactly what each team is doing every day to help reach the organizational results." The posters serve as a visual reminder of not only the Key Results but also each team's alignment around how to achieve them.

Help your team and organization align with the Key Results by making a plan and then putting it in a public place.

Inspect What You Expect, Often

Every other week Craig Roper, senior vice president and chief deposit officer for Bank of Utah, conducts a conference call with everyone in his direct line of report. These calls are dedicated to discussing what is and what is not working. Based on this meeting, they formulate a targeted survey that goes out to the whole company, asking, "What are you doing, or what can you do, to better accomplish the company's Key Results?" and addressing the issues raised in the initial call. This regular checkup helps his executive team focus on how each individual can be a part of the solution. Another practice Craig relies on to ensure company-wide Key Results is a monthly all-hands conference call where everyone, including the bank president, the CFO, and the deposits and lending officer, reports on what they have done in their respective teams to accomplish Key Results since the last call. The results at the bank have been amazing: record profits and record growth for the past two years. Keep the Key Results front and center by inspecting what you expect.

Begin Meetings by Focusing on Key Results

Dave Valentine, former performance and development manager for the grocery chain Kroger, told us that in the grocery industry you basically have to rebuild the business every day, due to the many perishable products they sell. As a result, Kroger employees must work fast, identifying what objectives and results are most important. Each week in team meetings they begin by reporting on commitments from the previous meeting. The remainder of their time is dedicated to answering the following questions: (1) What did you do this week to help us achieve our Key Results? (2) What were the results? (3) What are you going to do next week? Dave says they've been focusing on business agility, implementing the Key Results, and addressing these three questions for three to four years. Doing so reminds them to pay attention to the things they deem most important and not get caught up in things that don't matter. As he put it, "We don't have time." We believe everyone should have this same sense of urgency, because in reality we all deal in perishables, we all risk going stale and losing business unless we stay focused on the top priorities: our Key Results.

Invite a Trained Pro to Your Team Meetings

Denise Van Tassell, training and talent development manager at Spirent, a designer and developer of top-line network communication services, told us that one of their divisional general managers put together a team for the purposes of annual planning. It was meant to home in on Key Results. Having the wisdom to see that achieving results doesn't just happen, and knowing that Denise was a champion of accountability ever since going through our training and principles twenty years earlier, the GM made the unusual move of inviting her to attend and assist with the process. He wanted her eyes on things and her input on keeping them accountable and Above The Line. It turned out that her trained view from outside the fence provided key input and helped people see that how they think and act every day really does affect yearly Key Results. When it comes time for your annual planning and you're looking for help nailing down and executing on Key Results, consider bringing in an outside voice whose accountable input can make all the difference.

Go back to **Page 23**

Now go to your *Fix It* **Bucket List** and select the next Accountability Trait that you want to learn about.

PATH **C**
fix it in **My Organization**

ACCOUNTABILITY TRAIT 7
Ensuring My Work Is Aligned with Key Results

"The only real way to measure progress, the only real way to see if activity has any real teeth is how that activity ties to the Key Results the company is after. Activity doesn't matter, it's all about results." So says Robert Martinez, sales guru for a California CBS/Telemundo/CW network affiliate. Organizations have to be careful because even the best-intentioned individuals, teams, or even senior leaders can become mesmerized by activity, mistaking movement for effectiveness. Here are a few best practices that will help you stay focused on results, and not blinded by mere motion.

Go for Total Saturation

When we asked Suzanne Pottinger, vice president of employee experience at The Original Cakerie (a leading manufacturer of quality frozen desserts), for a favorite practice related to this trait, she laughed and said, "Just one? Everything we do is tied to our Key Results." According to Suzanne, when it comes to Key Results, they use a "total saturation" approach throughout the entire organization. They build metrics around them. Post them weekly. Display all Key Results monthly on a large graphic board. They tie yearly bonuses to them and emphasize and reemphasize them in every meeting. They convene a quarterly employee appreciation lunch where the rally cry gets even louder and more specific by offering a forum for awarding quarterly bonuses tied to Key Results, and giving everyone an all-hands opportunity to lay out where results are on track, where they aren't, and what they can do about it. A unified set of Key Results that is constantly shouted from the rooftops produces a culture where everything you do leads to desired results.

Do an On-the-Spot Quarterly

One director of talent and leadership development in the energy and gas space adopted a practice he saw his CEO perform at every quarterly meeting for team-leading managers. These meetings were designed to allow the firm's forty managers to demonstrate to the CEO just how each was executing on the company values and Key Results. He told us, "The boss would get people up right there in the meeting and put them in the front of the room. Challenge you. It made people engaged. And nervous." Though somewhat intimidating, this practice helped people realize just how important the Key Results should be for the individual, team, and company as a whole. The positive on-the-spot peer pressure filled everyone with daily accountability for results, encouraging them to reflect and to ask themselves, "Am I doing something that doesn't match with what my boss is going to ask about? If so, then I'm doing the wrong thing." It quickly became clear what the right daily activities were, and that helped everyone fix any lack of focus on results.

Make Everyone Explain How What They Do Applies

Hugh Ekberg, president of Kitchen & Bath Americas for Kohler Co., offered an interesting suggestion that may seem obvious but often gets neglected: "No one should be working on anything that isn't pointing in an obvious way to the organization's Key Results." To help make that happen, every four months Hugh sponsors an all-associates communication meeting where five hundred people show up in person, and another seventy-five hundred participate via the Web. Their Key Results are peppered everywhere on posters in the meeting room. They start the meeting by putting their strategic plan on a board, reminding everyone about the tie between the Key Results and "why we exist" and presenting a solid business case for the desired results. Following these quarterly realignment meetings, the company works hard to cascade the why-we-exist Key Results down to the individual by using them to create each person's yearly performance plan. As part of that plan, everyone at every level must be able to explain how what they do every day ties to the objectives. Hugh told us, "If they can't explain it, demonstrate it, if they're doing something and can't tie their work to the plan, then they must ask someone why they're doing it or stop."

Take It on the Road

Dr. Bernadette Loftus, executive medical director of Mid-Atlantic Permanente Medical Group, told us about a sure way to get people, organization-wide, into lockstep with their Key Results. You campaign for them. In her case, she takes their Key Results message on the road. She told us that she actually goes building by building, location by location, through all thirty-two facilities in their network, sending the message that their Key Results are mission critical. In each location Bernadette pulls out her list and campaigns for their Key Results by stressing what everyone should be doing to make them happen. She asks questions about their list of imperatives or what's happening with their strategic direction, or she asks those in the meeting to describe any emerging problems that could be hampering the progress, all placed against the backdrop of the

Key Results. For a little Key Result alignment, take *your* campaign on the road.

Drop By with a Few Coins

Mike Niblock, fire chief of the Salem, Oregon, fire department, recognized he had a Key Results problem. He also saw that his people viewed him as a threat, that whenever his frontline firefighters saw "The Chief," it meant they were in trouble. Mike decided to change all that by going out to where his people were doing their jobs; and he didn't go empty-handed. He took a bunch of custom-made, high-quality metal "challenge coins" that he gave to each of his 160 firefighters. The coins were engraved with their three Key Results. Before this his people had been viewing goals (results) as "management's deal" or as "the office staff's thing." Wanting people to connect their daily work to the results, he put a coin in every pocket to personalize them. The goal of this was to help them own it and understand that the department's Key Results were now everyone's. By dropping in at stations unannounced just to talk and hand out coins, he showed he was available and committed. To increase awareness of your Key Results and get everyone on the same page, start dropping by with a few challenge coins of your own.

Go back to **Page 23**

Now go to your *Fix It* **Bucket List** and select the next Accountability Trait that you want to learn about.

PATH **A**
fix it for **Myself**

ACCOUNTABILITY TRAIT 8
Acting on the Feedback I (We) Receive

It's one thing to get feedback, it's quite another to act on it. When it comes to feedback, the real prize is won when you use it to get better results, strengthen relationships, and achieve better outcomes all around. If you agree that feedback is the breakfast of champions, as we suggested back in part 2 of this trait, then acting on feedback provides the workout that builds the muscles. Here are a few effective executive practices for acting on the feedback you receive.

Recognize People Who Give You Feedback

Mike Dufresne, regional vice president for LKQ Corporation, a national aftermarket and salvage auto parts company, told us that just before acting on any feedback-generated idea, he first recognizes the person or persons who provided it. He said, "I find there is nothing more satisfying for people than giving them some recognition." He will also generally follow up with a gift card for a nominal amount, from twenty-five to one hundred dollars, just to let them know he's appreciated their willingness to offer input. Mike will then send a group e-mail explaining what changes they are going to make based on the feedback, why they are making them, and the champions who came up with the great idea. He's found that this helps immensely during the implementation stage. People really own it when they know feedback isn't a waste of time. Just as important, Mike always follows up with those who offered ideas that *weren't* used, speaking with them personally and explaining why it wouldn't work in that situation. Mike offered, "This keeps the feedback flow open because their next idea might be a great one!"

Act Immediately: Listen-Examine-Treat

When we asked Robert Martinez, sales manager for a California CBS/Telemundo/CW network affiliate, how he acts on feedback, he responded with one word: "Immediately." Robert said that you make feedback received your "number one priority," especially if it's what he calls "pure feedback." He defines pure feedback as "unfiltered, real, true, not dealing with innuendo or rumor." When you act quickly, you send the message to the giver that they mean something to you, and that you're taking their idea, and them, seriously. He likened it to medical terminology and protocol. "You listen, examine, and then treat. If you want healthy people and future feedback from them, then examine and treat, whatever that looks like, because you don't get too many shots to act on what you're hearing. People will shut down, then you're on your own and flying blind." The trick, of course, is that you can't take a cookie-cutter approach. You must know your people and judge how serious each one is about what they're offering, then take time to decide whether their ideas are good or not. Either way, acting immediately sends all the right messages.

Remove the Emotion by Asking a Question

Tiffany Zakszeski, director of human resources for the endoscopy division of Stryker Corporation, a prominent medical technology company, believes that the key to acting on feedback is taking the emotion out of it. "You'll rarely ever consider acting on feedback if you're all emotional about it, so remove it." Early in her career when someone was offering feedback, the situation could easily go sideways, hurting feelings and causing problems, "especially when the person offering it wasn't very good at it." According to Tiffany, "Handling constructive feedback is like navigating through the five stages of grief, because there's always something that really stings, which is what you latch on to. If you're offended, you'll never do anything with it." The key is to remove emotion, which you can do by having the discipline to remain professional and not take it personally, and by asking yourself the question that Tiffany has learned to ask from our training: "Is that the belief I want them to have of me?" If you want to act effectively on what you're about to hear, take a breath and answer that question. Doing so will remove emotion and open you to acting positively on what you've heard, promoting change, and ensuring progress.

Make It Positive in Public

Jared Bentley is senior director of global product management for the international personal care and nutritional supplement company Nu Skin. He cited being a fan of one of his boss's noted practices. Jared told us that if people can learn to give credit for good ideas and not cause embarrassment over the bad ones, they will leap far ahead in the feedback game. Recently, he offered feedback to his boss, Joe Chang. Joe thanked him and went on his way. Jared noted that when his boss believes he has heard an idea or gotten feedback that has merit, he will act on that input by bringing it up in the next appropriate meeting. He will always give the person credit when it's positive, but he also makes sure the critical feedback stays private. "Giving people credit for the good while keeping the bad hidden" is simply nice. "He doesn't call people out or put them in awkward positions. You'll never hear him say, 'Well, the other day Jared was in my office and said this and that. . . . '" Learning to act on feedback by giving credit for the positive while keeping the negative private builds relationships and encourages more feedback down the road.

Send Your Own Stuffed Giraffe

Michigan Virtual University CEO Jamey Fitzpatrick told us that whenever he observes someone "sticking their neck out through tough feedback," he sends them a stuffed giraffe. Sometime ago a young school superintendent in a rural area of Michigan wrote a provocative article that offered critical feedback to all education leaders in the state, including the urgent need for innovative changes in public education. Jamey read the article and, being an educator himself, chose to act on the superintendent's feedback by sending him a giraffe and handwritten note congratulating him for "sticking his neck out." Jamey didn't hear anything until a year later, when this man came up to him at a conference and introduced himself, saying, "That giraffe you sent me, it's sitting in the center of our conference table over your letter reminding me it's okay to speak up." Jamey's ambition to encourage people to speak up and share feedback signals to others that he wants feedback and is willing to act on it. To encourage more feedback in others, act by sending your own version of a stuffed giraffe; it just might make feedback easier for everyone in the future.

Go back to **Page 23**

PART 2

Now go to your *Fix It* **Bucket List** and select the next Accountability Trait that you want to learn about.

PATH **B**
fix it on My Team

ACCOUNTABILITY TRAIT 8
Acting on the Feedback I (We) Receive

Organizational culture is developed within the team setting. You spend a lot of time with your team. During that time, experiences are created that begin to normalize how you all work together. That's culture. It's powerful when that culture is formed around an open and free exchange of feedback that people listen to and visibly act on. In fact, we teach that accountable people actively seek feedback and that hearing and acting on feedback create even more accountable people. Getting a team to act on the feedback they receive from one another creates real traction and ensures true progress toward results. Take a look at the following practices to see what some teams have done to create that sort of environment.

Set Up an Idea Factory

Pete Hammett, managing director of human resources for Oklahoma Gas & Electric (OGE), shared with us that "the ability of our employees to process feedback that leads to action around solving problems is crucial to leading and managing a changing utility world." Knowing this, OGE created the Idea Factory to facilitate employee feedback on continuous improvement opportunities. The Idea Factory is an electronic two-way feedback portal, where employees submit continuous improvement ideas. According to Pete, "Team leaders interpret the Idea Factory experience as a 'shared accountability' that all OGE employees have for safely and reliably delivering energy to our customers." All ideas submitted to the Idea Factory are reviewed and assessed for feasibility. To ensure everyone knows that team leaders will act on feedback, team leaders meet with the submitter to get additional input. This experience sends the clear message that ideas are heard and *all ideas matter.* Pete said, "When people have the experience that feedback is heard and acted on, they build a belief that their views are valued, and feedback grows in frequency and quality." Although not all suggestions are implemented, the Idea Factory lets everyone know their feedback matters.

Start a Feedback Wall

Cinny Murray, brand president for the specialty women's fashion retailer Chico's, explained that for her, the key to acting on feedback is to be transparent and remain open about it. At Chico's, people, starting with leadership, fill out feedback and commitment cards. The cards are then posted on a "feedback wall" in a popular common area for everyone to see. The openness actually feeds action by making it part of their dialogue and promoting discussion. It's hard to not follow up on feedback and discuss how you're going to act on it when it's stapled to a wall everyone sees every day. To ensure action, employees are partnered up, with each responsible for holding the other accountable for the goals and commitments listed on the feedback cards that management has approved. What was once an uncomfortable exercise has become a valued practice. To promote acting on feedback, team up and make feedback public. The more publicized your feedback, the more people will act on it.

Create a Fun Committee

Mark Polking, director of internal audit at Transamerica, told us that, being a staunch believer in feedback, he's committed to looking for ways to prove he's really listening. That thinking led to his support of, among other things, the Fun Committee, a group specifically designed to address the feedback he was receiving about his team needing to grow closer. The Fun Committee was given their own budget, and the job to sponsor a once-a-month activity. The group had various themed lunches together, would leave the office to go bowling, catch a minor league baseball or hockey game, fill Christmas stockings during the holidays, or just stop working for an hour to engage in their own "Office Olympics." As a result of their stronger culture, internal audit has become known as a place that acts on ideas, and as a place to learn and develop, to the point that employees from other departments are often now asking to join the internal audit team. As a result of their emphasis on culture and feedback, people feel more valued because they see that they are listened to, and it makes coming to Mark on the tougher things easier.

Start Your Meal with a Color-Coded Scorecard

Stuart Fetzer, former CEO for Dura-Tuff Wear Products, a mining equipment company, told us that their feedback process was developed to help managers and employees join together to measure how well they were acting on feedback. The manager gives each employee broad categories (operations, production, customer service, etc.) and asks for feedback within the categories. Based on people's responses, the manager then inspires action around the feedback by giving employees flexibility to create their own numbers/metrics and desired results. Then each month the team manager will take the employees to a nice restaurant, where they review any action and progress. To help make it work, they use color-coded scorecards: green = achieved target, yellow = below target but within 5 percent of achievement, and red = below target but outside 5 percent. By conducting this feedback session away from the office, over a meal, and with colored grades, people see that the manager is taking the time to listen and act. To demonstrate that you're acting on feedback, try some color-coded scorecards with your lunch.

Get Hands On and Saddle Up

Richard Pliler, former executive vice president of First Interstate Bank and president of two independent regional banks, reflected on a practice he learned from his mother, Ruby, when she managed motels on the Oregon coast. She became an instant favorite with her staff because she regularly demonstrated "saddle up." For example, after getting feedback from the cleaning staff, she would make a point to jump right in and work alongside them. Being with them for a little while would help her see through their eyes and understand where they were coming from. Pliler said, "Being with them like that, hands on, helped her see what feedback was actually necessary and doable, what was actionable." Not only did this approach build relationships and encourage even more sharing, over the years it contributed to a higher business IQ, giving her an understanding of everything from plumbing and electrical to management, customer satisfaction, and all-around people skills. Pliler also adopted this "saddle up, hands on" in banking and suggests using it where possible to demonstrate the most personal form of acting on feedback.

Go back to **Page 23**

PART
2

Now go to your *Fix It* **Bucket List** and select the next Accountability Trait that you want to learn about.

PATH **C**

fix it in **My Organization**

ACCOUNTABILITY TRAIT 8
Acting on the Feedback I (We) Receive

Anyone who's played the game knows that business is a team sport. Even the brightest CEOs and C-suite teams acknowledge that they can't run everything themselves. Over and over in our combined one hundred-plus years of consulting and training experience, we have seen companies collapse under the weight of leadership isolation and blind spots, while we've seen others soar by figuring out how to think and act on feedback. The ability to encourage and then act on feedback is key to clear thinking, longevity, and success. The following practices can add a few tools to your tool belt that can help ensure that your organization gets better at acting on what you're hearing.

Encourage Your C-Suite Leaders to Invite People In

Whatever your feedback methods—scorecards, e-mail programs, suggestion boxes, or face-to-face encounters—Steve Jeffrey, vice president of corporate services for Structural Integrity Associates (a leader in the prevention of structural and mechanical failures), stresses that acting on feedback begins at the top. Because Structural Integrity is employee owned, it's probably more natural for employees there to share ideas and for management to listen, but acting on feedback still has to be learned. It still starts at the top. The CEO first embraced the concept and now regularly and randomly calls rank-and-file employees into his office to follow up on their feedback, asking straight up for their take on things. It's a big deal to be invited into your boss's office to share a little advice rather than receive a reprimand. The rest of management has followed the lead of those in the C-suite, and today they are finding that meeting in person with someone after they've made a suggestion is the best way to communicate action. Ideas are listened to. Notes are taken. Follow-up is valued. Employees can actually see the feedback process in action.

Conduct Feedback Follow-up Meetings

If you read about Accountability Trait 3 earlier in this book, Asking for and Offering Feedback, you know that Janee Harteau, police chief of the Minneapolis Police Department, is a passionate advocate of feedback. But just taking in feedback doesn't mean much unless you act on it. Chief Janee recommended, "After receiving feedback, you need to create a way to get before your people and demonstrate you heard them." In her case, she conducts follow-up meetings with officers where she lays out what she's been hearing, what isn't working, and what she plans to do. She pumps them up, thanks them for their ongoing input, then asks for their help to act on all the feedback "in order to create something they all want to be a part of." Janee further told us, "It's all about saying, 'This is where we're going. Because I heard you, we're all going to become a better version of ourselves.'" When you take the time to solicit feedback and celebrate it, and then demonstrate you're willing to act on it by conducting follow-up meetings, you tap the full power of feedback.

Focus on Feedback Fridays

Hany Massarany, CEO of clinical diagnostics innovator Gen-Mark Diagnostics, told us that all employees company-wide are encouraged to focus on feedback exchanges on Fridays. The feedback should be free flowing, unscheduled, anywhere, anytime. What does everyone do with the feedback? How do they demonstrate and encourage acting on it? In addition to every Feedback Friday, once a month the company convenes an All-Hands Friday Forum. Prior to the meeting, people submit electronic feedback cards, then they spend the first twenty minutes of the meeting getting those who submitted cards up in front of the group to share stories that specifically highlight what feedback has been received and how it was acted on, and what results have come from it. Making this an organization-wide process shows just how committed the senior leaders are to putting feedback into action. By making feedback the focus of Fridays and beyond, the company has ingrained this trait into the very fabric of the culture, something that helps *fix* accountability for the company as a whole.

Act Only on the Customer's Feedback

Darren Lee, executive vice president of Proofpoint, a mass-market software developer and marketer, told us that they prefer to process and act on product-related feedback only when it comes from customers. According to Darren, "When we have a product planning session you're not allowed to volunteer your opinion, you're only able to volunteer what you've picked up directly from a customer. You can't say, 'I want us to improve this. . . .' When people slip and couch it like that, they are invariably asked, 'Which customer told you to say that?' 'What data do you have from customers that supports that?' 'Whom did you talk to?' 'What did they say exactly?'" When it comes to product development, it's the customer's feedback that gets acted on. Why? Because when feedback comes from a customer, "It keeps the hard-charging opinions about what the product should and shouldn't do out of it." Processing and filtering customer input allows for objectivity and promises that whatever action you decide to take is more in line with market demand than with personal opinions.

Celebrate It Publicly

Brad Lee, president and CEO of Breg, Inc., a large Southern California medical device manufacturer, stressed that it's sometimes easier to get feedback than it is to act on it. In the first case, all you have to do is listen. Doing something about it can be a whole other story. "You should celebrate every great piece of actionable feedback you receive, all of it." Brad's team established a regular time each month to make those acknowledgments and to do so publicly. During their monthly all-employee meetings they recognize people and hand out gift cards to such places as Amazon, iTunes, and Starbucks. Now when people have taken a risk and offered good, usable feedback, they're rewarded for making the effort to speak up. According to Brad, "[While] employees do appreciate the gift cards, what they value even more is the peer recognition in front of the whole company." Brad has found that you always get more of what you recognize and celebrate. What better way to demonstrate that a person's feedback is being acted on than by celebrating their willingness to provide it?

Go back to **Page 23**
PART
2

Now go to your *Fix It* **Bucket List** and select the next Accountability Trait that you want to learn about.

(9) PATH **A**
fix it for **Myself**

ACCOUNTABILITY TRAIT 9
Constantly Asking "What Else Can I (We) Do?"

Asking "What else can I do?" is the very essence of taking account-ability and is the Solve It question. It's all about your ability to engage personally, and deeply, with what you can and should be doing, despite the gravitational tug from all the reasons/excuses that can drag you down Below The Line. The choice to remain Above The Line by looking at what you can control to discover solutions is key to this Accountability Trait. The following executive practices will help you get into the Solve It routine and *fix it*.

Chuck a Few Solve It Balls to Get Them Talking

You may recall the Solve It training exercise we described at the beginning of the chapter for this Accountability Trait in part 2. In the exercise, the person who gets the ball must find solutions to a problem. Mark Polking, director of tax for insurance giant Transamerica, is a big fan of this activity, so much so that he keeps a supply of red and white Solve It balls on his office desk. Mark told us, "Often when people come to me they are there to vent, finger-point, or just generally go Below The Line." Since he has never wanted to work at a place where people are afraid to talk to their boss, he goes out of his way to let people know he's always available. He also promotes a casual environment. The balls help. After hearing someone pose a problem, Mark grabs a Solve It ball with "What else can I do?" stamped on it, tosses it to the person, and has them talk through the possibilities. Having something to hold on to with the question stamped on it, something they can fiddle with and toss back and forth, promotes a casual yet productive Above The Line *fix it* conversation.

Use "The Question" to Get Along with Anyone

Most people would not readily view this Accountability Trait, or its Solve It question, as a key to interpersonal relationships. But Joseph O'Callahan, manager of organizational development for Hyster-Yale Group, Inc., a designer and manufacturer of forklift trucks worldwide, told us that for him it really does improve relationships. Asking "What else can I do?" while dealing with a tough relationship has kept him focused in the heat of the moment, provided options and clarity, and allowed him to get along with difficult people in difficult situations. According to Joseph, asking, "What else can I do?" at the first sign of trouble triggers three mental reactions: (1) it helps you consider if you are truly blameless, (2) it helps you gauge to what extent you may be contributing to the problem, and, most important, (3) it forces you to dig deep into what you can do to improve things. According to Joseph, "What else can I do?" not only supplies a vital tool for solving work-related problems, it also offers a key to solving relationship problems, at work or anywhere else.

Put in 15 Minutes More

Jamey Fitzpatrick, CEO of Michigan Virtual University, an online accredited institution, told us that early in his career, his personal version of "What else can I do?" resulted in a decision to spend fifteen more minutes working at the end of every business day. In his case, "What else . . . ?" has always meant "What more . . . ?" because, he said, "Making that kind of decision, doing something like that when young and just starting out, immediately puts you on a different path from all those who are racing for the exits at five o'clock." By always asking, "What more could I do with fifteen minutes every day at work?" as part of his daily regimen, he not only got more done, he impressed his bosses. Today Jamey tells his younger staff, "The harder you work, the luckier you get!" Asking, "What else can I do?" forces you to go the extra mile, something rare that almost always gets rewarded.

Find a Mirror and Ask "The Question"

Elaine Thibodeau, vice president of strategy and deployment for a division of Johnson & Johnson, told us that of all the Accountability Traits, this one is her favorite. Asking "What else can I do?" especially in front of a virtual mirror, forces her to go beyond her job description and deeply engage in Solving It by studying herself. A regular "What else can I do?" face-to-face checkup with a metaphorical mirror helps her. She explained, "The question, and my answers to it, limit how much I'm contributing to any negative energy. Did I do more to help this person than to bring them down?" For Elaine, "What else can I do?" helps her change her daily situation for the better. The question has even pushed her beyond the walls of her work space and into mentoring, where she gets involved in women's causes and leadership. If you want to figure out how to go above and beyond and help those around you realize their full potential, make sure you're always able to look yourself in the mirror, and while there regularly ask, "What else can I do?"

Ask the Right Question When You're Wrong

According to Chuck Knutson, founder and partner at Ironwood Experts, a consulting firm providing support for software IP litigation, "Too many people don't realize that it's okay to be wrong, that it really can be a positive, something to be embraced because it can always teach you something—if you immediately follow any setback with the right question." Asking, "What else can I do?" when you discover that you are wrong, in any situation or after suffering any personal setback, illuminates the path you need to take to get Above The Line, where you will always find the best solutions. The right questions keep you from the self-loathing that comes automatically to most people when confronted with being wrong. The right questions asked at the right time keep you from reacting negatively. For that reason, Chuck recommends making it a practice to ask the Solve It question the instant you know you've made a mistake.

Go back to **Page 23**

PART 2

Now go to your *Fix It* **Bucket List** and select the next Accountability Trait that you want to learn about.

(9) PATH **B**

fixit on My Team

ACCOUNTABILITY TRAIT 9
Constantly Asking "What Else Can I (We) Do?"

In a team setting, "What else can I do?" becomes "What else can we do?" Nothing illustrates this better than the Academy Award–winning story about the Apollo 13 crisis. It's a gripping story: astronauts stuck in space in a damaged ship with limited power; the added tribulation when the oxygen scrubbers stop working; a race against the clock to enter earth's orbit before accumulating CO_2 kills them; engineering geeks who solve problems with amazing creativity; and a breathtaking finale when everyone comes together to bring the three-man crew safely home. What we learn from this story is that good stuff happens when teams never give up, when they never stop asking, "What else can we do?"

Get Fired for a Day

Paulette Wage, head of human resources for McDonald's Hawaii, Guam, and the outlying South Pacific islands, said that in order to open her managers' eyes to new ways of thinking, she pretends to fire them for a day. After "firing" them, she sends them out looking for a "new job" with their competition. The "out of work" managers, who are in on the exercise, approach the search loaded with questions: "What else can we do that these guys may be doing?" Or the opposite: "What do they do that we do *not* want to do?" They observe these other restaurants, their cleanliness or lack thereof, how the employees behave and treat people, and the demeanor of the managers. This "fired for a day" exercise drives home the value of always asking our favorite question: "What else can we do?" It's a real eye-opener for her staff, helping them approach their own restaurant with fresh eyes and new ideas, something they take home when Paulette "rehires" them the next day.

Give Permission to Go Below The Line First

Jason Schubert, senior manager at the Kohler Learning Academy for Kohler Co.'s four business divisions (Kitchen & Bath, Kohler Power, Hospitality & Real Estate, and Interiors), told us that often the severity of a problem, or the negativity that has built up, may make it difficult for a team to ask, "What else can we do?" Such negativity can become paralyzing to people. To combat this, Jason recommends following a certain sequence, by first acknowledging the enormity of the challenge, then moving Above The Line to Solve It. Not following this simple tried-and-true sequence may slow down the problem-solving process. Jason encourages teams to maintain a structured, safe, and controlled environment to speak openly, especially during team meetings. This allows for difficult questions to be asked: "Why is this happening? It's not my fault"; "So-and-so is to blame! Who is going to fix this?" Intentionally going Below The Line first makes it acceptable to acknowledge the hard things people are dealing with, gets issues off the chest, and prepares them for the must-ask Above The Line question: "What else can we do?"

Make a Ground Rule: Ask, Don't Tell; Listen, Don't Talk

Mario Cajati, a managing director of business development for UPS, believes in this Accountability Trait so much that when he was trying to help his team bring more creativity to their problem solving, he established the motto "Ask more than tell, listen more than talk." What transforms this from a nice bumper sticker slogan into a solid practice is that solving problems for Mario and his people begins with asking, "What else can we do?" The team has learned to ask questions first, acting only after issues have been thoroughly discussed and solutions dug up and vetted. Mario believes this ground rule for his team allows them to mine the group's collective experience in order to maximize whatever solutions UPS's Central Plains District might need. The practice also stimulates "What else . . . ?" solutions by getting people to open their minds, set the expectations for how the conversation will go in the team, and ask good questions to model what he's looking for.

End Your Meetings with "What Else Can We Do?"

Debbie Bowles, general manager of a large Ocean Spray food-processing plant, uses a similar approach with her team, but with an important twist. She told us that she loves the "What else   ?" question so much that she incorporates it at the end of every meeting. By turning the question into a consistent practice years ago, her people know it's coming, so they are already prepared to drill a little deeper and think a little harder. Debbie told us that her end-of-meeting "What else can we do?" question addresses three specific areas: (1) specific issues raised in the meeting, (2) what's working and not working in the culture, and (3) any other problems the team needs to solve. Ending the meeting with the "What else . . . ?" question reminds everyone to stay engaged and is a great way to create and maintain a Culture of Accountability.

Ask "The Question" About People, Not Just Results

David Ellis, vice president of investigations for SecurityMetrics, a credit card security provider, believes that people who are happy at home will be happy and more productive at work. If someone is struggling in a marriage, then he knows they will eventually bring their troubles to the office, affecting their performance and that of the team. Dave shared a story about an employee who had gone through a divorce. After asking, "What else can I do?" Dave, knowing this was a temporary condition, eased back on his colleague's workload and encouraged the team to help the guy out. After a few weeks the coworker was happier and doing better work. "If I hadn't asked what else we could do as a group, I probably wouldn't have seen that a valuable employee was worth a little extra investment." Dave added that he doesn't consider himself a skilled manager in the professional sense, but has learned that by looking for what else he can do for others, he has been able to create a cohesive team where people feel "just short of family."

Go back to **Page 23**
PART
2

Now go to your *Fix It* **Bucket List** and select the next Accountability Trait that you want to learn about.

PATH C

fix it in My Organization

ACCOUNTABILITY TRAIT 9
Constantly Asking "What Else Can I (We) Do?"

One of our favorite authors, Victor Hugo, once said, "There is one thing stronger than all the armies in the world, and that is an idea whose time has come." For us, one of those ideas is getting everyone in your organization, all at the same time, asking the question "What else can I do to achieve the result?" When everyone gets aligned with that attitude, engaging every ounce of their intellect in problem solving, watch out, great things are going to happen. Consider the following executive practices that can help you achieve that effect in your organization's everyday culture.

Get Everyone Working on the Problem

Bill Becker, COO of restaurateur LTP Management, told us his company has achieved a lot of traction in finding solutions by making sure their employees see the company's problems. Their people attend regular meetings, break into smaller groups, and then essentially ask two questions about their list of problems: (1) Why are we experiencing these problems? (2) What else can we do to solve them? This kind of open process provides incredible amounts of buy-in, and it works because it's been seeded through the ongoing use of visuals hung backstage in all of their restaurants, including posters reminding employees of the Steps To Accountability. Bill said, "The constant visuals trigger a thinking and solution process: we use accountable language and our people are able to identify the challenge, then attack how to solve it." Everyone knows they matter and their opinions matter. That knowledge makes them eager to ask what they can do to *fix it*. Bill continued, "I don't have to come up with all the answers. There are people out there who really have come up with great ways to attack our challenges, we just have to ask the right questions and be open enough to listen."

Make It a Part of the Culture

Mike Dufresne, regional vice president for national aftermarket and salvage auto parts company LKQ Corporation, told us about the huge amount of logistics in his company. "Three hundred miles away someone might need a car part ASAP, and we used to see the part not show up on time, or show up damaged, late, or not at all because it was left on the dock. We'd hear, 'I know, but there's a snowstorm and we can't get around.' Or, 'It's not my problem, it's not my job.'" Then Mike and his managers started applying "What else can I do?" everywhere and anywhere. That kind of alignment from the management team was powerful. Before long the question sunk in and has now become a part of the organization's culture: it's just the way they do things around there. Now, according to Mike, everyone at LKQ concentrates on: "What else can we do to get our customers what they need when they need it?" Now everyone wants to be the one who comes up with the great idea: "Hey, yeah, maybe we can deliver the part by snowmobile!" By insisting everyone uses "What else can we do?" whenever they face a pesky problem, you, too, can kill excuse making and create a Solve It corporate culture.

Ground the Solve It Question in What's Most Important to You

Christina Sarabia, manager of organizational development for Exactech, a manufacturer of orthopedic implant devices, recommends that you tie the Solve It question to what's most important to your organization. Then "What else can I do?" becomes an even more powerful tool for developing your culture and promoting your brand. For Exactech it's all about being "Surgeon Focused, Patient Driven." As an example, Christina said that Exactech employees are often called upon to fill product orders for last-minute surgeries, on top of the critical shipments already scheduled for the day. Because they remain "Surgeon Focused, Patient Driven," everyone rallies around the problem and does whatever needs to be done to Solve It. That may mean delivering a needed product for a surgery the next morning by jumping in your own car, whatever the hour, and driving it to the hospital. By tying the Solve It question to what's most important to you, it sticks, takes on vital importance, and infuses more passion in the quest to find solutions.

Form a Problem-Solving Department and Change Your Culture

Karen Korytowski, general manager of Lean Operations for Smart & Final, told us that by regularly asking "What else can we do?" they looked to see what was being used elsewhere in the industry and discovered the concept of Lean Operations. "Lean" represents a group whose task it is to solicit problems, then target solutions. Having a Solve It mentality has turned them from a service group to a problem-solving group whose sole focus is continuous improvement. "What else can you do?" has helped them create an associate suggestion program, a way they can generate ideas to make things better. The group is designed to take submitted problems, then evoke solutions out of the very people who submitted them. In the beginning, a lot of associates were anonymous—they didn't want to put themselves out there. But now the associate who submitted the problem is expected to volunteer a solution, then help to implement it. Ownership is soaring. Solutions are working, already saving them hundreds of thousands of dollars a year. By asking "What else can we do?" and implementing Lean Operations, the culture is shifting from a knee-jerk focus on problems to a routine search for solutions, shedding the weight of stress and Below The Line thinking to a cut-to-the-chase mentality that gets to solutions faster.

Go Digital

In our own training and consulting company, Partners In Leadership, we have created and encouraged a Solve It way of thinking, developing our own digital tool set called PILtools, which includes a tool called The Solve It Exercise, where anyone in the company, regardless of level, can initiate an exercise and involve participants throughout the company. Anyone, anytime, can pose a question and solicit group input and contributions. Drawing on crowdsourcing technology, the solutions are then ranked by participants and commented on. The exercises have ranged from solving a problem in the shipping room to getting ideas and input on major strategic initiatives. There are a lot of digital collaboration tools out there, such as Chatter, Yammer, Slack, and Jive. Whatever your flavor, going digital allows you to involve more people at every level of the organization, through asking "What else we can do?" to Solve It! In a world where 87 percent of the millennials say that their smartphone never leaves their side, you can bet that plugging into digital connections to ask "What else can I do?" will pay big dividends.

Go back to **Page 23**

PART **2**

Now go to your *Fix It* **Bucket List** and select the next Accountability Trait that you want to learn about.

PATH **A**
fix it for **Myself**

(10)

ACCOUNTABILITY TRAIT 10
Collaborating Across Functional Boundaries

"No man is an island." "The whole is greater than the sum of its parts." "1 + 1 = 3." "It takes a village." Just what do poets, philosophers, scientists, and an African proverb all have in common? The understanding that collaboration is the key to getting it right and doing it well, whatever *it* happens to be. If you accept that business is a team sport, then you'll be interested in what some executives do to encourage collaboration across functional boundaries.

Share Stories to Bridge the Boundaries

Lois Bentler-Lampe, chief nursing officer and vice president of clinical operations with OSF Home Care Services, a division within the OSF HealthCare System, told us that with the massive changes in health care in recent years, she and her people have had to get better at seeing the bigger picture. "We now need to focus on how we are caring for people across the entire health-care continuum." Lois has found that stories are a great tool for inspiring necessary collaboration. She tells stories whenever possible to help inspire and encourage her people to want to see beyond their own tunnel vision and develop a more cooperative mind-set. "I use storytelling as a way to give people more insight into the work we all do, so I ensure buy-in to what everyone else is doing." Because stories travel, she shares success stories in one-on-ones with her direct reports, with doctors, with hospital staff, with the families of patients, and in meetings. When you regularly share stories about working together to produce the desired result (which in the case of OSF HealthCare is "Serving with the Greatest Care and Love"), you will engage and inspire collaboration across all functional boundaries.

Use Another Office

Nathan Leaman, a human resources leader for Kohler Co., a global manufacturing and service company, made it a policy years ago to rarely take meetings in his own office. It might sound a bit simplistic, but getting out of your own office actually puts you in a more collaborative frame of mind. Getting out of your own space, opening yourself up to another person's place and mind-set, forces you to collaborate across boundaries because you have physically crossed from your comfort zone into theirs. If the people you are meeting with also happen to be a bit territorial, then you might consider a third neutral location. With a change of venue, Nathan creates a different energy than the one in his office and demonstrates his willingness to engage with people where they feel most comfortable. He also says this practice gets him away from e-mail and stacks of paperwork, clearing his head. In order to collaborate across any kind of boundaries you must be willing to drop all pretense and air of authority. By doing something as simple as leaving your own office you can prepare any space for collaboration.

Spotlight Your Peers

Barbara Van Dine, director of talent development and learning for Smart & Final, a chain of warehouse food and supply stores, believes that collaboration is best served up with a dose of appreciation. For that reason Barbara loves their Spotlight program, a

Web-based initiative set up to encourage an individual to recognize anybody, anywhere, electronically. According to Barbara, "Employees use Spotlight on the computer, phone, or any mobile device. Its primary function is peer-to-peer recognition, and since day one has brought increased unity to the company." The person doing the recognizing can even recommend points with dollar values, so that the person being recognized can go to an online catalog and redeem the points for merchandise. When an individual recognizes someone, often across the divide separating functional departments, they naturally increase rapport with that person, which increases the ability to collaborate. Everyone likes an authentic compliment, and a public shout-out that reinforces working together is the preferred way to work.

Evaluate Collaboration with Minisurveys

Debbie Bowles, general manager of a 600,000-square-foot Ocean Spray food-processing plant, told us that she started focusing on improving individual and team collaboration across boundaries with minisurveys. Even before sending out her first survey it helped her personally because, as the GM, it made her think about her own answers to the survey questions. Questions like (1) How do I feel I'm doing collaborating with my peers? (2) How is my team collaborating with other teams? (3) How well do I think the company as a whole is doing when it comes to collaboration across divisions and departments? Regarding taking the survey, Debbie laughed and said, "As you would expect, as individuals we tend to rate ourselves high, the team is typically rated lower, the organization itself very low. No one ever thinks they're the problem." Debbie admits that no one likes taking surveys, but her surveys encourage discussions that lead to improvements in the way people work together to bridge functional boundaries, driving true collaboration.

Be Known as a Collaborator

Lance Davis, CFO of pharmacy benefit management company and retail pharmacy operator Veridicus Health, believes that one key to collaborating is to strive for a reputation as someone others would want to collaborate with. He told us, "You create a good example on purpose." To do that, Lance arrives at work before his subordinates and leaves after they leave, offering opportunities to chat more informally with others early and late in the day, often with people he doesn't normally work with. He also believes that his physical presence helps others see his level of commitment. "Nothing is more off-putting than those who are not working hard while you are. No one wants to collaborate with those kinds of people." We would add that letting people know you want to collaborate is the logical extension of this effort. People see what they look for—remember the last time you bought a new car and were shocked to see so many cars of that very same model on the roadways the next day? Put people on notice that you want to collaborate with them and be known as the type of person they would want to reach out to. That reputation both inside and outside your team will make all the difference.

Go back to **Page 23**

PART **2**

Now go to your *Fix It* **Bucket List** and select the next Accountability Trait that you want to learn about.

PATH **B**
fix it on **My Team**

10

ACCOUNTABILITY TRAIT 10
Collaborating Across Functional Boundaries

After Joe Rigby became president of Pepco Holdings, a large eastern United States energy concern, he found himself assisting with a management audit. The government inspector evaluating the company was extremely dismissive of the committees Joe had assembled. "Oh, you run the place by committee. So . . . nothing gets done, then?" Joe then walked the guy through how Pepco's committees assimilated and unified perspectives, how his various committees operated at high levels of internal and external cross-collaboration, and how that "committee collaboration" empowered everyone to drive results and get things done. The inspector was impressed because Joe knew how to put the right people in the same room with the same mission. You might try these executive practices to help you and your teams achieve the same result.

Encourage Collaboration by Building Social Time into Agendas

Martin Lowery, past senior vice president of leadership and organization development for Sony Pictures Entertainment and current president of OpusVertex International LLC, a provider of facilitation and leadership consulting services, is a big believer in seeding collaboration among teams through an improved social atmosphere. To do that he builds enough leeway for casual banter into every team meeting at the beginning and end of the agenda. As

Martin put it, "People aren't machines. At the basic level work among human beings is still a social exchange." Martin said that they take the first five to ten minutes just to talk casually and socially: "What are you going to do this weekend?" "How's the family?" "Do you have any plans after work on Friday?" It's a social back-and-forth. Martin believes that too many leaders feel too pressured on time, so they fill out the entire agenda with work. Spending more personal time together, especially on a cross-functional team, provides opportunities to get to know and like one another, which results in better collaboration and better results because it feels natural rather than mandated from above.

Give the "Why" and the "What"

Larry Gelwix, CEO of Columbus Travel and the most successful American high school rugby coach in history (subject of the feature film *Forever Strong*), told us, "The key to team wins is for everyone in each position to understand what the other positions are doing and why they're doing it." If teams don't collaborate effectively across functional boundaries, they lose. To create that collaboration, Gelwix makes a concerted effort to give his people the "why" and the "what." As he put it, in sports you might be teaching a player to cut right or left, but until players know *why* they are cutting right or left, they will never be exceptional. The same applies to business. Knowing the "what" becomes clearer when you understand *why* others are doing what they're doing and how all roles fit together. Gelwix said, "Sure, they may do the 'what' for you out of blind loyalty, because they are a team player, or are afraid of the boss, but their heart won't be in it until you explain the 'why.'" Armed with both "why" and "what," people will collaborate and always give you their best.

Use Culture Teams

Bryon Stephens, president and COO of Marco's Pizza, told us they have broken the company into Culture Teams. The teams consist of intentionally mixed groups, with five or six members from varying company levels on each. The teams meet for one hour every week on Wednesdays, during which time they take on activities and discussions that are meaningful to the group. A different team leader is appointed to lead the team each week and offer a report that provides a variety of viewpoints and encourages all to share in any team victories. A different team leader each week ensures that over time everyone participates and that every department and function ends up being in charge. Bryon said, "People who were shy and timid are blossoming in these more intimate team settings, and the results are wonderful." The collaboration across job and departmental boundaries thrives in Culture Teams, where ideas flourish and a greater sense of teamwork abounds.

Turn the Puzzle Upside Down

Denis Meade, director of training and development for AlloSource, a nonprofit tissue bank, likes to use a simple team exercise to develop collaboration skills and grow team creativity. He will buy a kid's puzzle, put teams into a room, and lay the puzzle pieces facedown on a table. No one can talk as team members from all departments work together to complete the puzzle while all the pieces remain upside down, showing only blank cardboard. When the teams finally get all the pieces in place, they flip the puzzle over to see that the stock picture Denis had chosen when buying it actually represents some point or principle he was hoping to get across. The metaphor is obvious: all pieces play an important role in getting the result, and you need everyone and all pieces to make a complete picture. It takes a little work and a lot of collaboration to get all the pieces to fit together, but it's worth it in the end.

Set Up a Stakeholder Team

Mary Bartlett, COO for The Reserve, a professional shared workplace, relies heavily on the concept of a Stakeholder Team, especially on large projects. She told us about one recent case where they needed some serious collaboration across departments for a major rebrand and new Web site launch. To execute the project she assembled a Stakeholder Team consisting of representatives from IT, HR, and sales, plus an executive leader. All were key players, and they needed to collaborate so the result would work for all departments. By setting up a cross-functional Stakeholder Team first thing, you encourage both early adopters and change advocates. These team members then become invested "moles" who go back to their respective departments and sell what's happening. Mary emphasized that the key to implementing an effective team is not just including senior people but bringing aboard the right people who will delve into all the dusty corners that need to be explored. Your own Stakeholder Team might just buy you a lot of collaborative insurance.

 Go back to **Page 23**

Now go to your *Fix It* **Bucket List** and select the next Accountability Trait that you want to learn about.

PATH **C**
fix it in **My Organization**

ACCOUNTABILITY TRAIT 10
Collaborating Across Functional Boundaries

Marco's Pizza CEO and chairman Jack Butorac told us that the departments of a large fast-food chain he once worked for must have spent 60 percent of their time fighting from their silos. Marketing would not follow operations on new menu items because they wanted to make operations look bad. R&D didn't want to suggest anything new for fear that operations and marketing would botch their baby. There was no company collaboration. No common Key Results. And it all seemed to start with a CEO whose door was always closed, a man who rarely collaborated with anybody. When he was finally let go, the company brought in someone who knew how to open doors. To help you *fix it* before becoming a noncollaboration casualty, try a favorite practice or two from some highly effective executives.

Get Everyone on the Bus

Vincent Weafer, vice president at Intel Security Group, McAfee Labs, a cyber security thought leadership company, reflected back on two dysfunctional departments that needed to work together. Over many months the groups had attended planning meetings, training seminars, and HR interventions, but nothing stopped the infighting, complaining, and lack of results. Then one day someone suggested they just drop everything and go bowling. (You may recall that we told this story back in part 2, but we thought it worth repeating here as a recommended practice.) Miraculously, the two groups actually made it on the bus alive, and on their way to the bowling alley they started talking. Real conversations broke out. Barriers dropped. Of the forty people on the bus, at least twenty were actually interacting, laughing, and talking shop: "Maybe we can do it this way?" "No, but what about this way?" There was so much sudden camaraderie before, during, and after bowling that on the return trip they told the driver to just "keep the bus going around in circles." They had tried to crack the code for weeks and weeks, but meetings, phone calls, e-mails, texts, and WebEx conferences didn't do it. Vincent believes that taking a bus ride regularly for some off-site social fun is one key to collaborating across any functional boundaries in your company.

Use Two Meeting Managers

Chico's is a large vertical retail women's clothing brand, where a lot of people from many different groups gather in meetings, from design to sourcing and planning, distribution, manufacturing, and beyond. For Chico's, effective collaboration across functional boundaries is more than nice to have, it's live or die. Cinny Murray, president of brand for Chico's, has tried to enhance their collaborative skills by adopting a practice where each meeting takes place with two individuals in charge, preferably from different disciplines. One employee will manage the content of the meeting, such as setting the agenda and chairing the session, while the other serves as a meeting facilitator who makes sure body language remains focused and teams stay fully aligned and on track by controlling the inevitable sidebar conversations. The meetings often involve ten to fifteen people from a variety of divisions, so opinions and interests vary. The two managers in charge aim to be efficient, to touch each issue once and then send it down the pipeline so the agenda stays moving. Two managers for every meeting just might ensure effective collaboration across whatever functional boundaries you need to bridge.

Let Goals and Money Talk

Tom Simon, senior vice president of talent management for US Foods, a large food producer-wholesaler-distributor, shared how this company practice was initiated by one of his regional vice presidents. In this RVP's case, he sponsored an e-mail contest where employees sent him stories about how they had applied the company's Cultural Beliefs in their work and personal lives. The contest created buzz and dissolved past departmental biases and boundaries, which naturally increased collaboration. Why the buzz? When the RVP received the five-hundredth e-mail, he let everyone know that he was writing a personal check in the amount of five hundred dollars to the person who sent it. Buzz! When he received the one thousandth e-mail, he again let everyone know that he was cutting a personal check, this time for one thousand dollars. More buzz! Just recently this RVP wrote a check for fifteen hundred dollars to the person who wrote the fifteen hundredth e-mail. For some inspired collaboration and unification across just about every boundary, money talks.

Incentivize Collaboration

Kim McEachron, chief people officer for Genomic Health, a highly respected global cancer diagnostics company, told us that, much like Tom Simon above, she believes collaboration comes from a consensus around common goals, which in their case means placing a major focus on Key Results to strengthen their business and thereby continue improving outcomes for cancer patients worldwide. To get that collaboration across the entire company front of mind, Genomic Health created an initiative called ACT: activate new markets, cultivate current markets, and transform our future. As part of ACT, Genomic cascaded its focus down to each business organization by requiring all groups to explain how their goals directly or indirectly contributed to ACT, thereby ensuring a collaborative effort across the company. To keep everyone's attention and focus on company collaboration, leadership tied the corporate employee bonus program to ACT. This formed a direct link between what everyone needed to deliver to be successful and the bonuses individuals and teams received. To ensure your people collaborate across any and all boundaries, recognize and communicate progress, then incentivize!

Choose One Personal Goal and Benefit Everyone

Tiffany Zakszeski, director of human resources for the endoscopy division of prominent medical technology company Stryker Corporation, told us that they hold an annual meeting designed to build unity across boundaries among company leadership. In Stryker's case, leaders from different departments come prepared to share one personal leadership expectation that they plan to strengthen in the coming year. Tiffany says that by narrowing it to just one and sharing it with a group, you can more easily demonstrate vulnerability and increase collaborative support. By narrowing it to just one, leaders leave themselves little wiggle room with respect to what they are working on, and they make it easy for joint buy-in and support across every department. An individual stating a goal publicly, where everyone across all boundaries agrees to support and encourage that effort, builds unity and contributes to the company as a whole, not just because the goal is important but also because it builds functional collaborative support.

Go back to **Page 23**

PART **2**

Now go to your *Fix It* **Bucket List** and select the next Accountability Trait that you want to learn about.

PATH **A**
fix it for **Myself**

ACCOUNTABILITY TRAIT 11
Creatively Dealing with Obstacles

The Solve It question "What else can I do?" is best served up with a strong dose of creativity. Sometimes you will find that hard to achieve. Take Charles Dickens, for example. At two P.M. each day, the famous and very creative English writer would set aside his fountain pen and go for a walk. He would walk for hours and hours, often well into the night. That downtime proved essential for Dickens's creative side. Apparently, when you stay focused for too long on a problem, you ironically can block the brain's ability to Solve It. When that happens, pulling yourself out of your daily rut can energize your thinking and get you past whatever has been keeping you from fixing it.

Get a Coach

Ian Baines, CEO of family-style restaurant chain Cheddar's Scratch Kitchen, told us that everyone should get a coach who can help them deal with obstacles. "A 'third eye' puts perspective on life's challenges." Coaches or mentors can be paid or unpaid, a friend or a hired gun. According to Ian, "The good ones teach less about structural things and more about me, and gaining a high level of self-awareness. Why I behave the way I behave." Ian says that his coaches have helped him be more successful than anything else has in his career. The right coach will help you see what is getting in the way of making progress and may help shed some light on other steps you might take to overcome obstacles. In Ian's case, he uses a life coach, someone not tied to his business efforts but who sees the way he thinks and acts more broadly. We would add that you should consider getting a different coach to play each of the collaborating team roles we described in part 2 of this Accountability Trait.

Schedule Before, During, and After Every Day

Casey Jones, president of Altaquip, a popular equipment repair company, has developed a few creative practices to help him overcome the rigors and obstacles of his role. He builds these three practices into every day: (1) Each morning after getting to his office, he engages in a little "private creative time" from 7:30 to 8:30. During this period of private reflection, he keeps his office door shut and spends the time reading, just to get his mind going. (2) Because unpredictable events can hit you throughout the day, Casey keeps himself loosely booked so he retains the flexibility to be available to react to any hurdles that might arise. For that reason he schedules himself for only half of his eight-hour day. (3) To free his mind before going home at the end of each day, he writes down the three to five things he needs to accomplish the next day and lets the rest go. Structuring your day to provide for creative thinking, like Casey does, can yield more timely inspiration.

Attack Obstacles, Don't Avoid Them

Nathan Leaman, a human resources leader for Kohler Co., a global manufacturing and service company, recalls a decision he made early in his career while working in a call center. His job in customer service was to help frustrated or even angry customers deal with a wide array of challenges related to their kitchen and bath products. His personal plan for dealing with frustrated customers was to attack the obstacles and not avoid them, plain and simple. That meant he would deliberately take the most difficult phone calls and work with the customers most of his peers avoided. Nathan told us, "Tackling any tough obstacles on purpose makes you better and comes to the attention of those over you." His advice: The more you do that, the better you will get at blasting through the obstacles that stand in your way. When most people start running from a difficult situation, try jumping into the fray instead. You will be acquiring valuable lifelong creative skills for overcoming any and all obstacles you face.

Walk the Brain

Tami Polmanteer, chief human resources officer at Daymon Worldwide, a retail branding company, suggested an effective problem-solving practice she calls Walking the Brain. People often approach problems and challenges by focusing on the "who." To deepen her ability to overcome obstacles, Tami keeps a two by two-foot chart on her office wall outlining the "what," "how," "who," and "why" of any problem she is facing. She explained that the chart allows her to Walk her Brain, guiding her thought process through "what" the issue is, "how" it happened, and "who" was involved—factors that eventually combine to lead her to a fuller understanding of the "why" behind it. Taking the time to think through these four quadrants provides some structure for looking at a problem and finding a way to *fix it*. Tami says that slowing down to analyze your obstacles will ultimately help you solve your problems quickly and more creatively. Walking the Brain gives you that edge.

Be a List Person

Elaine Thibodeau, vice president of strategy and deployment for a division of health-care giant Johnson & Johnson, admits she's a "list person," something that helps her overcome personal challenges and obstacles. Lists help you focus. They require that you think through exactly what is going on before putting pen to paper. Lists help you make sure that you decide what you're going to do about problems and where you might find solutions. To make her lists work even better for her, Elaine does not keep them to herself. She told us she uses a formalized process, especially when taking on a new role. "I review my list with my boss and key stakeholders, asking them if it makes sense, whether it aligns with our business goals, or if I'm missing anything." This list process helps Elaine know that she's consistently working on what's important to her stakeholders. She then does the same with her own direct reports. For her, lists travel back and forth, with many additional eyes bringing fresh perspectives that spark creativity. If you start to feel a bit overwhelmed by obstacles or tough issues, try using a list to put a fence around a problem and bring multiple people on to help you *fix it*.

Go back to **Page 23**

PART 2

Now go to your *Fix It* **Bucket List** and select the next Accountability Trait that you want to learn about.

PATH B
fix it on My Team

ACCOUNTABILITY TRAIT 11
Creatively Dealing with Obstacles

The very best teams all have one thing in common—their members share a common purpose and feel accountable for a common outcome. Of our study respondents, 50 percent stated that the single most descriptive reason for why they found it difficult to hold others accountable was that they were not sure *how* to do it in a way that yielded good results. Not knowing how trumps a lot of other reasons, such as avoiding confrontation, not wanting to lose rapport, or even believing that no one else in the organization is doing it, which could make you look like a bad guy. Creating accountability on the team requires knowing how to unlock people's creative juices to solve pesky problems. Try these barrier-busting ideas with your team.

Do a Quick Brainstorm

Krista Stafford, vice president of human resources for KLX Aerospace Solutions, a leading full-service provider to the aerospace industry, says that one of her favorite team mechanisms for dealing with setbacks or roadblocks is something they call the "quick brainstorm." This creative approach to problem solving can happen anytime, anywhere, with anyone. She and her people will corner others in the hall, office, lunchroom, or parking lot and use the "energy of spontaneity" to brainstorm about a specific looming project or issue that's causing struggles. The brief meeting involves a minimum number of people in a casual situation—just a quick back-and-forth of shared ideas. Krista likes to write everything down as fast as she can with no attempt to reach final decisions. It's all about collecting a whole bunch of ideas from others into one big list. As she told us, "The topics can be anything from more serious issues related to integrating new policies to this year's Halloween costumes." If an obstacle has got you stuck and you need some fresh ideas, try a little quick brainstorming in unusual places with some unexpected people.

Sponsor a Regular Friday Potluck

Otto Aichinger, strategic partnership manager for industry-leading mortgage lenders, told us, "If you want your teams to bring more creativity to your desk, first have them bring some food to the table." Otto has found that people contributing their food to a potluck gets them in the mood for contributing "food for thought" to a problem. They need to put themselves out there for both. The food they bring, and the ensuing banter about how they cooked it or how good it tastes, breaks the ice for any business discussion that really needs to happen. The consistency of the potluck schedule is what brings the magic. Over time, people become better acquainted with the program and one another and are more willing to open up with what they really think. Individuals also discover personal and often surprising insights into one another, little facts about their lives that might draw two people together for ideas that they never would have discovered otherwise. Schedule a periodic potluck with the people you want to see contributing to solutions, and get ready to feast on the ideas they can generate.

Enjoy Instant Recess and a Little Walk and Talk

According to Sheree Chiang, senior vice president of human resources for the American Heart Association, her people promote good heart health and trigger more creativity by unleashing a little fun and physical activity on their problems. Her practice of Instant Recess can involve something as simple as someone due for a scheduled break jumping up from their desk and yelling, "Okay, we're going to do instant jumping jacks now!" On other breaks someone will click on a YouTube exercise video for a minute or two. A creative fitness break like Instant Recess gets people moving and thinking differently, bringing a more energetic vibe to problem solving and the daily routine. Sheree also loves to take her team deliberations on the road, going outside for a Walk and Talk, a practice that also infuses a physical component, something that helps mentally, emotionally, and physically. Sheree encourages team leaders to factor in good health and some physical movement to help stimulate the greater creativity needed to break through any barrier.

Form a Business Book Team Study Group

Terri Longbella, senior director of worldwide human resources for Quantum Corporation, an expert in scale-out storage and data protection, said that her HR team "seems to always work hard developing everyone else, but we rarely spend time broadening our own ability to overcome the obstacles we face." To attack the problem, Terri said they started a business book study club where once a quarter a different HR team member picks a book to pitch, suggesting how it might provide new insights, ideas, and best practices that could help them better serve their clients, not to mention overcome obstacles they face every day. Every month they get together on the phone or in person and talk through the previously assigned pages from the selected book. They highlight the aha moments, those passages that conjure up creative solutions. For Solve It solutions from the outside that can help fix your inside problems, make *Fix It* your first choice and start your own study group.

Meet in the Hallway

Debbie Bowles, general manager of a large Ocean Spray food-processing plant, believes in the creative problem-solving power inherent in spontaneity, informality, and tight hallways. Every day at 9:00 A.M., Debbie will hold a stand-up meeting with her team of twelve to fifteen people in the hallway outside the cafeteria in front of a six-by-nine-foot whiteboard. The group includes her safety manager, human resources manager, operations manager, quality manager, supply chain manager, engineering manager, and others who want to be involved or just happen to walk by. Debbie told us, "The daily 9:00 A.M. meeting is intentionally held standing in a busy hall so people are encouraged to walk through, stop, make comments, or just be a fly on the wall and listen." She believes this casual meeting leads directly to creative solutions. By the time the meeting ends, they will have used a red marker to scribble down the right side of the board their obstacles, current or ongoing problems, and issues requiring immediate action and follow-up. They also write down possible solutions. At times, an offhand suggestion by one interested participant offers a key to the right solution to a problem.

Go back to **Page 23**

PART 2

Now go to your *Fix It* **Bucket List** and select the next Accountability Trait that you want to learn about.

PATH **C**
fix it in **My Organization**

ACCOUNTABILITY TRAIT 11
Creatively Dealing with Obstacles

You always want to be creating a Culture of Accountability where people at every level of the organization, especially the front line, take accountability to unleash their creativity against all obstacles and problems. Creating this Solve It mind-set requires an overt, intentional, and formal invitation for everyone to jump in with their ideas and suggestions. It can't be just *okay* to make suggestions; it must be standard operating procedure. Here are a few executive *fix its* that can help create that kind of culture.

Listen, Observe, and Ask Questions

Mark McNeil, president of international juice bottler Lassonde Pappas and Company, loves to visit his facilities, observing, asking questions, and listening—three simple steps too often overlooked when it comes to solving problems. For example, soon after taking over as CEO he knew the organization needed to resolve issues like low morale and brand loyalty among some employees. He had been keeping an eye out for a creative solution to the problem. Then, one day at a lunch town hall at one of their plants, he happened to notice that many of their people were drinking a competitor's sodas and drinks. This prompted him to ask the obvious: "Do we not have our own cold single-serve juice available to employees?" The company was a juice bottler, after all. The answer: "No, we've never done that."

Mark, recognizing an opportunity to boost morale in a creative way, immediately asked for cold-juice vending machines to be installed in all their plants, so that employees could be drinking their own product and not some competitor's. And what was the result of that simple and creative step? It pumped up his people and increased loyalty to their own brand, providing a boost to morale. Mark believes that you can find the creative genius needed to deal with obstacles right in front of you. Just get out there and observe, ask questions, and listen to those who already know how to *fix it*.

Question the Norm

Richard Pliler, former executive vice president of First Interstate Bank and president of two regional banks, told us that back in the 1960s, the bank operated like the military, with everyone focused on titles, position, and rank. That created a real obstacle to unity, with employees more focused on their own careers than on customer needs. To address the problem, Richard began doing what he described as "questioning the norm." You see a problem, you question the same old way you've always dealt with it. He would start with the obvious by asking, "Does it have to be done that way?" or, "Why do we do it this way?" This often caused people to redefine the problem and the way they went about solving it. For example, one day during a meeting in a manager's office, Richard found himself staring at his coworker's desk nameplate, title and all. That glance convinced him that the focus on titles was sending the wrong message. Soon after he told his people to remove their existing nameplates with their various "Senior" this and "Manager" that, and replace them simply with "Salesperson." Deemphasizing titles and reemphasizing the customer was a creative move that drove a major mental shift. The all-about-me career culture became less about self and more about customers. To overcome old and new obstacles, question the norm and redefine the problem.

Don't End the Meeting Until Everyone Speaks

David Chapin, CEO of Forma Life Science Marketing, a promotional company in the life-science space, said he strongly believes that someone, somewhere in his organization, can offer the solution to their problems and obstacles. This belief has promoted a company culture where decisions are often delayed until all pertinent people have chimed in. Even if they need a quick decision, David will wait until the last minute to decide, "because I believe there's something each person can add." He has seen that his people are capable of solving almost every problem. Expecting participation and engagement from everyone in the meeting creates even more accountability, as people anticipate that it is safe to speak their minds. If you believe problems get solved from a wide range of input, then try tapping those sources before the meeting ends.

Launch a Pilot

Matt Stevens, vice president of sales and marketing for M-DISC, an archival digital storage maker, cites an organizational practice used while he was director of sales for FamilyLink, a family-oriented Facebook app. He told us that a wonderfully effective and creative way to deal with obstacles is the often-used practice of conducting pilot programs. Running a pilot allows you to experiment with an idea within a small sampling of the organization. According to Stevens, "Internal pilots provide creative input and show you how to make improvements, conquer obstacles, and learn important lessons for ensuring effective implementation, before the idea goes organization-wide." These test-drives can reveal a lot about potential solutions. Often pilots also provide proof of concept, but Matt thinks they do even more: "Use a pilot to test for solutions to tough obstacles." There's nothing like a real-life simulation to get a creative bead on what it's going to take to make something really work.

Plant Early Seeds for Increased Creativity

Sandi Guy, a partner at public accounting firm Carr, Riggs & Ingram, suggested that in a problem-solving meeting you delay offering your own opinion on a possible solution. "If I lead out early in a meeting with my ideas, employees tend to seize up." When employees seize up, they stop thinking and stop problem solving. So now, before any important meeting, she will often confer with key players and discuss the idea with them first, planting some subtle seeds. Then, during the meeting, these same people will often contribute additional ideas and creative solutions, independent of her opinions, because they've enjoyed some time to think about it themselves. Because the idea isn't coming from Sandi or another leader, people start talking with more freedom. Sandi says that this technique creates a fascinating dynamic as peers freely float solutions to obstacles versus blindly accepting what the boss says. Planting early seeds is a creative and healthy way to let an idea live or die on its own merits, free of leadership bias.

Go back to **Page 23**
PART 2

Now go to your *Fix It* **Bucket List** and select the next Accountability Trait that you want to learn about.

(12) — 🧍 PATH **A**
fixit for Myself

ACCOUNTABILITY TRAIT 12
Taking the Necessary Risks

Solving It almost always requires a certain amount of risk taking. You will always be required to place your bets on new strategies, tactics, and solutions that will be key to "winning the day." Committing yourself to a steady course is essential to success, even when you can't predict with certainty what the outcome of those efforts will be. If you are afraid to take risks and continue to push yourself forward, then there will be some obstacles you will never overcome. Operating Above The Line eventually requires some amount of disruption, stepping out and putting it on the line. Consider these executive practices as you contemplate taking the necessary risks needed for success.

Intentionally Step Out of Your Comfort Zone

Hugh Ekberg, president of Kitchen & Bath Americas for Kohler Co., is adamant about getting and staying outside his comfort zone, and he advocates that others do the same. Hugh told us, "There is no 'easy button' when it comes to beating the competition. Success is simply about working hard and delivering results and staying uncomfortable." So take risks. Push boundaries. While most hunker down in the security of their comfort zones, Hugh insists on stepping out of his. "Intentionally look for opportunities and make choices that will take you outside your comfort zone. And do this every day." For example, he strongly believes that people should never consciously act in ways simply designed to preserve their job. Fear keeps people from the risk associated with doing their best. Hugh told us that one day he reached a turning point where he decided that he would never again allow fear of losing a job to drive his decision making. "I have to be honest and true to myself and risk doing what's right." He recommends three things: work hard, don't allow job preservation to drive behavior, and stay uncomfortable.

Take a Risk and Promote Someone

Nathan Leaman, a human resources leader for global manufacturing and service company Kohler Co., uses nearly the same philosophy as Hugh Ekberg. This is significant because it demonstrates how these Accountability Traits can become broadly cultural within companies. Even though the two men work in different divisions and don't interact directly with each other, they practice similar philosophies, which includes the way they think about promoting people. Nathan told us that from his perspective, "There are too many in leadership today who are not willing to promote midlevel executives due to the risk that those they promote could eventually rise up and take their job." This perceived risk, grounded in fear and a lack of confidence, keeps other people suppressed. Lack of risk on the part of leaders drives potentially rising stars into the arms of other companies, taking with them their passion, skills, talents, and potential to help get results. Nathan advocates forgetting your own self-protection, taking a risk, identifying talent, and promoting those worthy of it, so that their talents benefit all.

Display Curiosity Early

Denis Meade, director of training and development for nonprofit tissue bank AlloSource, suggests that those seeking leadership roles should learn to take a little personal risk by displaying more curiosity, especially about information that runs the risk of getting personal. Denis told us, "A lot of managers don't like to ask employees, 'How can I be a better manager?' Most managers don't want to hear it. They're afraid of opening that door." Denis said that most people find it awkward at first and need practice, but it's healthy to put ego aside and allow for a little personal imperfection. The problem with not learning to show a healthy curiosity about how you can improve early in a career is that the further up the ladder you go, the more you shut down and don't think you need it. The same holds true for a new role or job. The earlier you show curiosity about how people think you're doing, the better. He suggested, "It's really an accomplished leader who can embrace risk and ask, 'What's my role as a leader? How can I do better?'" It doesn't need to be any more complicated than that.

Break the Routine by Seeking New Roles

Lois Bentler-Lampe, chief nursing officer and vice president of clinical operations with OSF Home Care Services, a division within the OSF HealthCare System, told us that she's a risk advocate. That attitude manifests itself in her passion for disrupting her own routine and seeking new roles and new opportunities. She reaps real rewards from taking such risks. According to Lois, "Whenever you work yourself into a new position, you are forced to put yourself out there and ask questions. Because you're new, it's easier for people to be bolder and give you advice, even if there's some big title in front of your name." Such risk not only gains rewards, it fuels personal growth. Now, a new job may not often present itself, but if you're working for any business, you can find ways to break with routine and take on new duties and new assignments. Lois encourages you to chase these opportunities in order "to stay unstable and insecure and purposely move around." As you do, taking a risk will come more easily, and so will the rewards.

Disrupt Schedules and Show Up in Unexpected Places

Loressa Cole, chief nursing officer for LewisGale Medical Center, told us she periodically makes time in the middle of the night to visit nurses. The risk is whether her sacrifice for extra night duty will result in a tangible payoff (a risk/reward analysis we all must take when we invest our time doing something new). In Loressa's case, it's a very big deal to work through the night, but worth it. Showing up unexpectedly is constructively disruptive, because night shift nurses don't expect to interact with top leadership at that hour. By appearing in the middle of the night, Loressa stumbles on information that a CNO would never know otherwise: how one nurse put in extra hours to become certified, how another attained an additional degree, that someone else recently got married. Her night shift duty attracts attention, builds morale, provides insight, and helps her build a Culture of Accountability in the department across all shifts. By providing Solve It coaching moments with her staff, Loressa has found opportunities to disrupt schedules and show up in unexpected places.

Go back to **Page 23**

PART
2

Now go to your *Fix It* **Bucket List** and select the next Accountability Trait that you want to learn about.

ACCOUNTABILITY TRAIT 12
Taking the Necessary Risks

Risk taking at the team level always requires clear accountability. It's all too easy to hide behind the team or someone else, and that can lead to irresponsible risks or no risks at all. The CEO of a major Fortune 100 company we worked with often taught the following: you don't hold teams accountable, you hold team *leaders* accountable because someone must step up and take ownership for the ultimate decision that leads to solutions. While we agree with this notion of accountability, creating a culture of team accountability is essential to involving the entire team in taking the necessary risks. Here's what some executives do to foster risk taking in their teams to Solve It.

Say "Yes, We Can"

David Ellis, vice president of investigations for credit card security provider SecurityMetrics, told us that when the company first started, it was like any start-up, small, hungry, and bold on the outside, but a bit insecure on the inside. He remembers people asking questions such as "What am I missing?" "Do we have the tools?" "How are we going to pull this off?" According to Dave, ultimately his team "made the decision to choose risk and chase any job that presented itself, especially those ahead of our experience curve." Dave said that when they started getting calls from larger companies, asking if they could supply and service the needed computer forensics, or document evidence, or teach people how to testify, "We made it a practice as a team to just say, 'Yes, we do,' 'Yes, we can.' Then we'd hang up the phone and scramble to figure it out." That kind of necessary risk taking was essential for success and growth, and it eventually brought his team bigger jobs. Using "Yes, we can" will stretch you beyond smaller opportunities and on to greater potential.

Tell the Stories

Sheree Chiang, American Heart Association senior vice president of human resources, told us her firm celebrates risk taking. In meetings, employees are encouraged and given time to share stories that involve risk taking, even if the venture didn't work out. According to Sheree, "It's all about the transformational growth for people." When we pressed her for an example of a story, she told us about Sean Maloney, former Intel executive and now a member of their board. Sean suffered a devastating stroke in 2010 and lost his mobility on the right side. Out of sheer will, he made enough of a recovery that he committed to a coast-to-coast bike ride and raised a million dollars for the Heart Association—a journey that might seem too risky even for the healthiest and strongest riders. Risk-oriented stories, especially from one of their own, serve to inspire. Sheree believes that sharing stories that model necessary risk taking, especially those about people inside the company, motivates and unifies the team.

Do Something Different

Otto Aichinger, strategic partnership manager for industry-leading mortgage lenders, thinks it's important for leaders to take a little personal operating risk for the greater good. To disrupt how his people think about a leader's role in engaging with the team, Otto intentionally risked some lofty leadership perks, and perhaps some rapport with peers who might be expected to follow his lead, by choosing one of the smallest cubicles in his team's work area. He took this risk because he knew it would send the message that their leader wanted to engage with the team to solve problems and get results. Disrupting expectation and accepted norms provides an experience that gets attention and shapes beliefs. Otto does admit that this kind of disruption to accepted practices is risky because management must maintain a level of respect, and that other leaders may not want to copy his approach. But he counters that building a rapport with his team allows them to engage and solve problems together much better, greatly benefiting the customer. To disrupt how your team collaborates, try abandoning your fancy office, sending a clear message that you're playing on the team to win it.

Let Them Solve It on Their Own

Jared Bentley serves as senior director of global product management for Nu Skin, an international developer of personal care and nutritional supplement products. Jared told us that they try to demonstrate necessary risk taking in their teams by consciously "letting people solve their own problems." Management helps people conquer this final Accountability Trait in the Solve It step by empowering them to pitch team solutions to problems they encounter. Jared said, "To the extent possible, I try to get teams to solve their own problems and be rewarded for their own solutions." The risk for him? If they fail to find a solution, he will be accountable for any lack of progress. However, as people jump in and engage, the payoff can be dramatic. He observes that too often supervisors are too quick with a solution, often because they want to remove the risk in a team environment. However, he believes that those closest to the problem will come up with the best solutions, and that relying on the team is a necessary risk accountable leaders must take.

Make It Part of Your Leadership Brand

Krista Stafford, vice president of human resources for full-service aerospace industry provider KLX Aerospace Solutions, believes that the power of disruption inherent in risk is vital, but before you can implement any risk strategy, you must clarify your leadership brand. That brand must reflect an action-oriented style that errs on the side of getting results. She's worked for companies where there has been no clear leadership brand, as well as no vision, few values, and a dearth of common causes. Without a strong leadership brand that signals the organization's style favors necessary risk taking, people will not feel comfortable taking any kind of risk at all. For example, at a previous employer, a simple logo change helped to clarify the brand. When her people saw the compelling new logo they knew what it meant. It captured her description of the more aggressive leadership brand she was working to create. It created alignment and purpose. To quote Krista, "When your leadership brand is clear to people, they become inspired and empowered to do what is needed to get the result."

Go back to **Page 23**
PART **2**

Now go to your *Fix It* **Bucket List** and select the next Accountability Trait that you want to learn about.

PATH C
fix it in My Organization

ACCOUNTABILITY TRAIT 12
Taking the Necessary Risks

Organizations spend a lot of time managing risk, often striving to minimize or entirely eliminate it from the business. Legal eagles spend countless hours fleshing out all the contingencies for any given situation, then they develop policies that mitigate even the most remote negative possibility from occurring. Given that tendency, it may seem counterintuitive to talk about how to get people within the organization to be disruptive and take more risk, but that is exactly what is required to fully engage people Above The Line. Here's how some execs work to get that done.

Sponsor a Risk Night

Jamey Fitzpatrick, CEO of an online virtual learning institution, Michigan Virtual University, let us know that as a company they sponsor an annual employee appreciation party. The most popular of these was Vegas Night. For the event they hired a professional gaming company, gave everyone five hundred dollars in fake money, and cut them loose. Not only was the activity different and exciting and gave employees and their spouses an opportunity to build friendships, it actually allowed everyone a look at their own risk-taking capacity. After the evening, everyone got together, debriefed, received prizes, and, most important, discussed what they had learned about themselves, both individually and collectively as a company. It identified the risk takers, the gamblers, the unadventurous, the ultraconservative, and the too freewheeling. If a gambling theme doesn't appeal to you, the same goal can be accomplished with other competitive games or athletic events. Whatever you choose, implementing a "risk night" not only builds camaraderie, it can also reveal a lot about your people's risk-taking aptitude.

Always Ask "Why It Can't . . . ?"

Darren Lee, executive vice president of Proofpoint, a mass-market software developer and marketer, told us that software development is a risk-oriented business where the company must constantly strive to develop the next "new thing." To succeed, they must create a propensity toward the sort of disruptive thinking that helps generate a constant flow of new and different ideas, ideas that might at first seem too risky to bring forward for fear of failing and being blamed for it. Early on, Darren implemented a software "scrum" designed to expose a bright idea and then let the engineering team gang up on it—to vet the risk associated with the innovation. To help with this, they engage in a Why It Can't exercise, taking time to find every reason why it *can't* work. The Why It Can't game encourages the generation of even more innovative ideas that might not otherwise be brought forward for fear of the risk associated with them. At Proofpoint, everyone knows that the very best naysayers will thoroughly test every idea before it travels any further up the development pipeline.

Try Going First

Darryl Shiroma, assistant vice president for HawaiiUSA Federal Credit Union, recalled a practice from a previous employer, one of Hawaii's largest and most prominent local banks. According to

Darryl, following a difficult period, a new CEO was brought in to turn things around. The CEO did that by demonstrating a few disruptive tactics, both organizationally and personally, that taught Darryl some vital lessons about company loyalty. The new CEO did not implement any across-the-board pay cuts, something many people were expecting. That was disruption number one. Disruption number two came when he promised to take no personal salary for three years. This leader then propped up the bank by investing millions of his own dollars into buying the bank's stock (disruption number three). And disruption number four: the new CEO asked his executive team to take a 20 percent pay cut. Essentially, the CEO and his leadership team led by example. Darryl understood through their actions that Solving It *always requires risk,* sometimes very personal risk, and that an organization's leaders need to demonstrate the value of disruption by going first.

Reward Risk

Erin Trenbeath-Murray, CEO for Salt Lake's Community Action Program and Head Start Program, believes that because CAP and Head Start are federally and state funded, it's easy for a sense of paranoia to arise when any minute they could lose their funding if they step out of bounds. This created a highly risk-averse culture, as everyone felt cornered by self-imposed restrictions on their creativity. Erin, knowing it needed to stop, threw a disruptive monkey wrench into their machinery, involving both an indirect and a direct approach to rewarding those who did some risk taking. Erin directly and publicly encouraged more risky decisions by bringing up examples of necessary risk taking in meetings and public forums, praising those responsible. Indirectly, she rewarded risk by consciously doing everything she could to implement her people's good ideas. This conscious decision to disrupt the existing culture and reward risk encouraged more risk taking and fostered a culture of creative thinking that over time has reduced any worry of Big Brother snatching away their livelihood.

Start with a Minimum Feature Set

Matt Stevens, vice president of sales and marketing for archival digital media maker M-DISC, mentioned to us that the companies who succeed most in his business are at first "just willing to get subpar product out there, then let the market guide them until they hit." The key is to get comfortable with this kind of risk by offering up what the industry calls a minimum feature set. With MFS, it's ready-fire-aim, it's jump into the market with *good enough,* be disruptive, take a risk, get input, then adapt and improve as quickly as possible while on the move. Speed to market provides a tactical advantage in getting early clients' input as well as creating a strategic advantage by staking out a space ahead of competitors. Many risks could probably be framed in much the same way. Start asking, "What does the MFS look like for us here?" Establishing the practice of looking for the MFS just might trigger even more creative thinking that will drive the Solve It mentality, as people think more incrementally about the problem and the risk associated with Solving It.

Go back to **Page 23**

PART
2

Now go to your *Fix It* **Bucket List** and select the next Accountability Trait that you want to learn about.

PATH A
fix it for Myself

ACCOUNTABILITY TRAIT 13
Doing the Things I (We) Say I (We) Will Do

Doing what you say you will do sounds like a no-brainer. So why haven't we made it the first Accountability Trait in the Do It step? Because it's *not* easy to do, yet it's absolutely essential to creating a Culture of Accountability. While anyone might fall short due to someone else's malicious intent, conscious neglect, or willful dishonesty, that rarely happens. It's generally more about juggling multiple priorities and over-the-top overcommitment. To help firm up your Do It muscles, consider adopting the practices of these "can do" executives.

Find Your Balance

Matt Broder, vice president of corporate communications for retail branding company Daymon Worldwide, believes that to be effective at doing what you say you're going to do, you need to develop the kind of staying power that allows for consistent performance over time. For him, that comes with maintaining balance in his life. Matt cites three anchors that help him keep balanced: (1) family, (2) work, and (3) an outside passion. His passion is competitive rowing, something he walked away from thirty years ago but came back to recently because he found he needed that third anchor. He now works out almost every day, and on the days he rows he's on the water at 5:30 A.M. To further feed his balance, he has become a fan of flextime, saying, "Sometimes you have to be in the office in a suit, other times working from home in blue jeans." It's the balance that allows him to maintain a consistent performance and not flame out after cyclical spurts of high energy. To empower yourself with the stamina needed to consistently do what you say, find your balance.

Hold the Own It Conversation

Dr. Bernadette Loftus, executive medical director of Mid-Atlantic Permanente Medical Group, told us that her number one standout mentor was her father. "He taught me the importance of commitment, of doing what you say you're going to do. It really isn't complicated. If you say you're going to do something, you do it. If you don't plan on doing it, then don't overcommit." Dr. Loftus reminded us of the simple idea that resides in every accountable person: *Mean what you say, do what you promise.* If it looks like your plate is getting too full, hold Above The Line discussions that will help you realign your schedule. As we mentioned back in part 2 of Trait 7, at Partners In Leadership we call this the Own It Conversation, a dialogue you should personally conduct with the right people when you may not be able to deliver on what you've promised, or on what you may be asked to promise in the future. Holding that conversation early, clearly, and continuously helps you gain a reputation as a "doing the things I say I will do" person.

Make Your Word Your Bond

Nathan Leaman, a human resources leader for Kohler Co., a global manufacturing and service company, believes that much of the conviction and follow-through needed to do what you say you're going to do consistently is "born out of a deep commitment to the value of personal integrity, the quality of being honest and true to what you believe." To us, it includes keeping your word. There was a time when folks did business on a handshake and your word was your bond. Marcus Lemonis, CEO of Camping World and star of the reality TV show *The Profit,* says that's how he built his $3 billion business, by rolling over one hundred smaller businesses into his brand on just handshake deals. He said, "I'm a big believer that a person's word and handshake are the best signature you can have." Nathan agrees, believing that when you realize your reputation for integrity is on the line with every commitment to do something, then operating with a "my word is my bond" approach will establish a Do It reputation that will serve you well throughout your career.

Build Your Personal "Do It" Brand

Given that there are bumps in every road, Hany Massarany, CEO of clinical diagnostics innovator GenMark Diagnostics, told us that he's taught himself never to let hurdles stop him. Hany remains confident and committed to what he says he will do, by (1) choosing to see beyond the bumps and hurdles to the goal and (2) remembering why it's important. His personal brand is one everyone should build. Being known as a go-to person who delivers on what you say you will do is valuable currency in today's competitive marketplace. According to Hany, "There are always challenges that make things go sideways. It's not whether hurdles happen, it's about your response. You need to see beyond all that, to see beyond hurdles to the real goal, despite the hills and mountains and pain along the way." Developing a personal brand that represents solid follow-through will differentiate you from the crowd. A favorite saying that keeps Hany on course: "If it can be done, then we'll do it. If it can't be done by us, then no one can do it."

Self-Assess to Make Better Commitments

Elaine Thibodeau, vice president of strategy and deployment for a division of Johnson & Johnson, told us that she holds a personal debriefing session after any significant experience, a self-examination intended to identify her own natural strengths and weaknesses displayed during that experience. Knowing yourself can create a type of "can do" and "don't do" commitment system, a yes-no filter. Such a filter guides your initial commitments, "energizing you around the skills you have that are ready to bring to the table." When you reflect on past struggles, Elaine suggested you might say, "I failed because I really don't like doing X. I don't naturally have the skills for X." This doesn't mean you avoid a challenge; it does mean that knowledge of your own strengths and weaknesses helps you prequalify those activities and projects to which you should readily commit versus those you ought to reconsider before jumping in. Keen insight into your limitations helps you filter what you say you're going to do, a practice that will tip the scales of success more strongly in your favor in the future.

Go back to **Page 23**

PART 2

Now go to your *Fix It* **Bucket List** and select the next Accountability Trait that you want to learn about.

PATH **B**

fix it on **My Team**

ACCOUNTABILITY TRAIT 13
Doing the Things I (We) Say I (We) Will Do

In a perfect world, teams should be the ideal incubator for account-ability and ensuring a "doing what you say you will do" culture. Culture develops within the team, among the people who work to-gether on a regular basis. And, unlike organizations, smaller units like teams do not allow Below The Line hiding places to exist for very long. This "not too big, not too small" dynamic of a team pro-vides a perfect setting for this Accountability Trait . . . if you can get everyone on the same page and going in the same direction.

Keep an Open Chair

The management team headed by Denis Meade, director of training and development at AlloSource, a nonprofit tissue bank, believes that their organization's mission is the greatest driver behind help-ing people do what they say they'll do. For Denis and the manage-ment team, their source of motivation springs from the people they serve, which explains why their team culture includes keeping an open chair in their management meetings. The open chair offers an ever-present reminder of the donor, donor's family, customers, and recipients. It's easy to get caught up in the day-to-day turmoil at work and forget those people you're really serving. Remembering this has helped make AlloSource a front-runner in its industry. As the organization helps to heal severe burn victims, providing bone grafts and even tendon grafts to hundreds of thousands of patients every year, its leaders keep the patient front of mind, an act that seeds them with a sincere motivation to keep doing what they say they will do. After all, their work really is a matter of life and death. To experience a little increased commitment, try dedicating an open chair in your team meetings to those who mean the most to you.

Reinforce with Accountability Language

David Chapin, CEO of Forma Life Science Marketing, a promotional and marketing company targeting the life-science space, told us that getting people to do what they say they're going to do requires deliberate team training. They have successfully encouraged people to follow through by adopting "accountability language" learned in *The Oz Principle* Accountability Training. Otherwise, people naturally fall Below The Line. David and his teams make this happen with four defined steps: First, modeling. It starts at the top with the team leader. Second, bringing Do It language into public view by agreeing to catch any Below The Line talk. Third, praising people whenever they use accountability language. And fourth, putting up accountability charts and sayings everywhere as constant reminders. According to David, "Everybody wants to be accountable, they see it as a desirable trait, but don't know how to get there." Training helps ingrain a language of accountability into the group culture, something that extinguishes excuses for not doing what you say you will do while igniting an all-out effort to get it done.

Commit the Team to Be All In

Sandi Guy, partner at Carr, Riggs & Ingram, a top public accounting firm, told us that because she's such a raving college football fan, she likes a sports analogy: "We're a team. Some are a coach, some a kicker, a quarterback, a lineman. We're all important, and we all just need to get in and do whatever our position calls for." For this team approach to win consistently, everyone's got to be all in, fully committed to do what they say they will do. Sandi shows that she's all in by making it easy for colleagues to get hold of her anytime, anywhere. She observes no set hours. Everybody knows her cell phone number. That doesn't mean she works 24/7; it just means she's "available and comfortable doing administrative stuff from [her] couch at home." Ensuring that your team commits itself to thinking and acting all in will create the right foundation for people to do what they say they will do.

Put People in Charge

When we asked Robert Martinez, sales manager for a California CBS/Telemundo/CW network affiliate, about any team practices he uses to help his people do what they say they'll do, he mused about the growing performance gap he sees in today's workforce. Over his twenty-five years on the sales side of broadcast media, Robert has discovered that to close the gap, leverage employee engagement, and get people to make good on promises, you should "put them in charge of something. Get them up front. Out front. Make them team leaders. Force them into accountability with visible and regular responsibility." Robert has found that when people rise up and get behind doing what needs to be done, it's much harder for them to slide down and hide and not produce the results they need. Leadership increases accountability because it's visible. Leadership forces people to lead, to do what they say they'll do. Otherwise teams fail, and eventually the whole house of cards can come tumbling down. To fix any lack of doing, put your people in charge.

Make Mistakes More Acceptable

Dr. Sandra Massey, chancellor at Arkansas State University–Newport, explained to us that when she stepped into her position, she inherited a culture lacking a sense of empowerment. People were hesitant to take initiative. She took the time to sit with each member of her team and explain how she understands that everyone makes mistakes. She made a point to talk about all their new initiatives, and how it is inevitable that the team will drop the ball from time to time. Of course, she was talking about what we refer to as a type 1 mistake: a mistake from which you can recover. On the other hand, you should avoid type 2s at all costs, because you can't recover sufficiently from those. Dr. Massey explained that when you talk about how you expect type 1 mistakes, you open people up to do more with their day, to increase commitments. Growing at ease with type 1 mistakes empowers people to do what they say they're going to do because the fear of failure does not freeze movement, it actually increases what people say they'll do in the first place.

Go back to **Page 23**

PART
2

Now go to your *Fix It* **Bucket List** and select the next Accountability Trait that you want to learn about.

PATH C
fix it in My Organization

ACCOUNTABILITY TRAIT 13
Doing the Things I (We) Say I (We) Will Do

In part 2 of this trait, we highlighted how personal integrity includes doing what you say you will do. Here we want to introduce an idea that we presented in our book *How Did That Happen? Holding People Accountable the Positive, Principled Way:* the notion of "organizational integrity." It's the idea that a group of people shares the value of being *true to their word* with one another. This means that the entire group makes it their rule to do what they say they will do. When that happens, you can reduce the time and energy spent following up and inspecting your team's work, investing instead in innovation and ensuring that the work is aligned with the mission of the organization. These executive practices can help you do just that.

Put It on the Wall

Stuart Fetzer reflected on a practice he used as CEO of Valdez Machining. In order to encourage and motivate people to make good on doing what they said they would do regarding their development, they created an organizational chart on a five-by-five-foot board, which they hung on a common wall. The board listed all the major categories of job roles and responsibilities. Within each category appeared levels of achievement from a career path perspective. The board also included nameplates of Valdez employees. When people accomplished what they had committed to do, their names moved up the chart. As an example, for "Machinist," all employees could see who was moving from beginner to journeyman to master. To further help with people development, company managers took responsibility for providing training. The visible tracking board served as an effective way to prioritize work commitments and Do It, encouraging people to do what they had committed to doing.

Discover the DNA of Success in Their Motivation Jeans

Mark McNeil, president of the international juice bottler Lassonde Pappas and Company, told us that "every culture is different and you have to dig until you find what motivates your particular people into really 'doing what they say they're going to do.'" Mark eventually got the input he needed to create an incentive that rewarded people who hit their numbers with the right to wear jeans for a month. He said that this simple gesture offers an important leadership lesson: you need to understand what motivates employees to *want* to do what they say they'll do. When he shared his jeans practice at a large food conference, other industry leaders couldn't believe that something so simple really worked. He promised them it did. Everyone in his company anticipates the first PowerPoint slide that pops onto the screen at each end-of-period meeting. When a green check mark appears next to the picture of a pair of jeans, the room erupts in applause. Zero investment. Unbelievably high return in terms of getting people on the Do It bandwagon!

Show a Token of Your Appreciation

Johnny Priest, division president at Willbros Utility Transmission & Distribution, an energy infrastructure contractor, told us they use a token to motivate their people to make good on what they say they will do. When field supervisors see an individual performing well, they can reward them with a two- to five-dollar poker chip. These chips add up, and once people earn at least twenty dollars' worth, they can either trade them for time off or cash them in at the end of the year. Tokens of appreciation work great as an accountability tool, not just because they tangibly recognize people for their efforts but because they help keep the idea of fulfilling commitments front of mind for both leaders and employees. It puts something in their hands for their Do It actions, currency that shows how well you do what you say you will do. Of course, tokens can take the form of vouchers, gift cards, or cash. Whatever the reward, a little reinforcement goes a long way in creating a culture that follows through.

Remove Warts with a Culture Committee

Jamey Fitzpatrick, CEO of the respected online accredited institution Michigan Virtual University, told us that his organization has established a Culture Committee, aimed at building teamwork and identifying the "warts" in their company, those dangerous habits and ways of thinking that will only get worse if not diagnosed and removed. The committee involves a one- to two-year appointment, an amount of time that allows for training members to spot what they're looking for. This committee approach to rooting out a company's unwanted behaviors and practices not only puts more eyeballs on the problems but also increases the resources for fixing them. As more and more people serve on the CC, they all gain a greater appreciation for the need to help everyone do what they say they are going to do, collectively building a Do It culture from the inside out.

Spotlight "Do It"

John Cuomo, general manager for aerospace distribution company KLX Aerospace Solutions, has assigned separate months to See It, Own It, Solve It, and Do It. An executive leader sponsors each of the categories of accountability each month. When it's Do It month, for instance, the company dedicates the Culture section of its newsletter to stories about individuals who are exemplifying Do It. This heavy emphasis on accountability at the company level sends the message down the line to teams and individuals that everyone doing what they commit to doing is important, and that their leaders won't quit talking about it. When people don't feel alone in their practice of accountability, they will more eagerly engage with it. Casting this kind of wide cultural Do It net encourages everyone to do what they say they're going to do. Find ways to broadcast the word to your masses and watch the empowerment of Do It spread throughout your entire culture.

Go back to **Page 23**

PART **2**

Now go to your *Fix It* **Bucket List** and select the next Accountability Trait that you want to learn about.

PATH **A**
fix it for **Myself**

ACCOUNTABILITY TRAIT 14
Staying "Above The Line" by Not Blaming Others

After making all of the effort in your journey Above The Line to acknowledge reality and See It, discover your involvement and Own It, identify creative solutions and Solve It, you are now ready to execute flawlessly and Do It. Beware of one big danger, however: the gravitational force Below The Line is so strong, it constantly works to drag you down, tempting you to stay stuck. After all, it appears the "safe place" to be. Avoiding this trap and staying Above The Line will make all the difference at this final stage. Consider some executive safety tips for keeping Above The Line and staying on the road to real results.

Use a By-When to Stay Above The Line

Denis Meade, director of training and development for nonprofit tissue bank AlloSource, told us about a mentor who taught him the value of always using a By When to keep him Above The Line and away from finger-pointing. When Denis worked as a paramedic and started an emergency medical service (EMS) program for a local hospital, he reported to a VP whose mantra was "Always say what you're going to do and the time you'll be doing it. You hold yourself accountable, or I will." Denis said, "It's as simple as saying, 'I need X by Y,' or, 'I will have it to you by this date and time,' a By When." He's followed that advice ever since. "There's something about

By Whens. Using them makes it easy for me to avoid blame and stay on task and Above The Line." Commit to this simple idea (one we use in our Accountability Sequence training) and make it a regular practice throughout your own day. You'll get the job done with fewer excuses and better results.

Get an Accountability Coach

Rachel, David, and Laura Kohler (of the Kitchen & Bath, Power, and golf Kohlers) stay Above The Line by working together as a team and serving as one another's coaches to help maintain accountability. Laura told us, "We commit to keeping each other accountable and Above The Line." She believes that people should adopt a code of conduct and get an accountability coach, someone close to you—coworkers, family, or other mentors—who can help to hold you accountable. She cites her family's Sibling Code of Conduct: "We commit to always keep each other Above The Line by intentionally investing the time and behaving conscientiously. We will first seek to understand one another. We challenge our own assumptions about each other's intent in a timely manner." To stay Above The Line, consider developing a code of conduct and enlisting an accountability coach to help you keep it.

Wait-Wait-Wait, Listen-Listen-Listen

Daniel Swartz, director of human resources at Align Technology, makers of Invisalign and the iTero 3-D digital scanning system, told us that one practice he's found very effective when helping colleagues stay Above The Line is to think to himself: *Wait-wait-wait, listen-listen-listen.* As director of human resources, he regularly deals with sensitive issues. When people come to him with a problem, he's learned to bite his tongue while they venture down Below

The Line and complain and vent until they literally exhaust themselves. He just lets them go without getting sucked into the issue himself, until they finally say something like, "I've been talking this whole time, don't you have anything to say?" This is the moment he's been waiting for, the point in the discussion where he might say, "I'm hearing all these different reasons why you can't do something, but what do you think you should do?" It's amazing how this approach yanks people right back Above The Line. To stay Above The Line, use a little "wait-wait-wait, listen-listen-listen."

Adopt an Above The Line Attitude

Johnny Priest, division president of Willbros' Utility Transmission & Distribution, an energy producer-distributor, is matter-of-fact about a practice he uses to reinforce this Accountability Trait. He simply *chooses* to show enthusiasm. "You can't get down. You must work hard on how to manage emotion yourself." He acknowledges that the going will get tough from time to time, and often it will take awhile to work through issues. For Johnny, it's mental. "It always reverts back to attitude." He tells people that he hasn't had a bad day in his life since walking out of the jungles of Vietnam. "If nothing is trying to eat me, then I'm in pretty good shape. Everything is manageable." Johnny suggests you mentally repeat something like this: "I'm going to work at a place I love, in an industry I love being involved in because of the challenge and excitement. Live it, breathe it, understand it, research it, study it. Learn every day." It might sound a bit simplistic, but it works.

Embrace a "Bloom Where You Are Planted" Philosophy

Janee Harteau, police chief of the Minneapolis Police Department, sees people drop down Below The Line when they are passed over for a promotion or assignment. It's easy for them to get discouraged, sulk, and even stop trying to contribute. For those who do access enough accountability to say, "I want to achieve this," or, "I want this job title," Chief Janee advises that they stop focusing on the next step in their career or they won't do great work in their present role. "It's good to have goals, but don't wait to be the chief to act like a chief." For Janee, leadership doesn't mean rank or title, it's the way you live your life. It's what you're doing *now*. She thinks of it as a "bloom where you are planted" philosophy, an attitude that can do a lot to keep you Above The Line. To get ahead, focus on what you are doing now and do it so well that no one can ignore your success. This down-to-earth practice has served her well. She became the first female chief of the Minneapolis Police Department, and only one of a handful of women to serve in that role in any large American city.

Go back to **Page 23**

PART
2

Now go to your *Fix It* **Bucket List** and select the next Accountability Trait that you want to learn about.

(14) — PATH **B**

fix it on **My Team**

ACCOUNTABILITY TRAIT 14
Staying "Above The Line" by Not Blaming Others

How does a team stay Above The Line? Short answer: the rising tide of positive peer pressure can lift all boats. The trick is to make sure the team has agreed to operate Above The Line. To do that, everyone needs to understand the Steps To Accountability and receive training in the concepts and tools. When that happens, the team can make a conscious effort to be vigilant in not blaming others when things go wrong, but rather focus on what else they can do. Agreeing to behave according to our accountability model makes it easier to coach one another, exchange feedback, and conduct the conversations that are needed to work through difficult challenges and ensure progress. Here are a few executive practices that can help you do that.

Adopt a No Plops Rule

Joe Rigby, chairman, CEO, and president of Pepco Holdings, a large energy delivery company in the eastern United States, adheres to a No Plops rule. That means no one can just come into a room and plop their problems down on a desk or conference table, saying, in effect, "Look at that problem!" Joe told us, "If you allow that in team settings, it becomes contagious." No Plops means that anyone wishing to present a problem or complaint must come prepared with at least one solution. "No one is allowed to hijack meetings without putting something in the accountability kitty." By ingraining this practice into your culture and tying solutions to every problem, you can reduce the amount of problems you hear about in the first place, because half the time your people will Solve It on their own before a problem ever gets to you. Try a little No Plops rule yourself, and watch the team get back Above The Line without you having to say much at all.

Post It Everywhere

Barbara Van Dine, director of talent development and learning for the warehouse food and supply chain Smart & Final, told us that they have set up a number of small programs to help bring living Above The Line to the top of everyone's mind. According to Barbara, "For me and my team, since we are responsible for training throughout the company, it's not just how can we pick up a tidbit to get someone through this problem or that, but how can we develop a common language that is accountable." To help with that, they used the Partners In Leadership training, which allowed them to prominently display our accountability posters in their break rooms as a reminder to live Above The Line. They also printed stickers listing their Key Results, which every employee stuck to the back of their name tag, to serve as another constant reminder. For Barbara, it's not any one thing that makes a difference for her team; it's a lot of little reminders coming together to shape an entire Above The Line culture.

Take 5

Lance Boynton, COO and global director of operations for chemical engineering company Dymax Corporation, says that he understands the need for people to vent, to express frustration, and to get things off their chest when dealing with challenging obstacles. With that in mind, they coined Take 5, which allows five minutes at the beginning of every meeting to moan and whine and go Below The Line. While this may sound like an added burden to the agenda, it actually limits the time that can get absorbed focusing on circumstances seemingly beyond their control. And because they are consciously establishing a Culture of Accountability at Dymax, they can trust the process and know Take 5 won't hijack their entire meeting or their current thinking. They acknowledge that going Below The Line is perfectly normal, and that allocating a short time where it's a planned part of the meeting is actually healthy. Lance did point out, however, that a few rules apply: you can't go to any subsequent meeting and gripe about the same issue. The key to success with Take 5 is that the Below The Line venting must involve accountable language, language that leads to Above The Line problem solving, empowering everyone to go out and *fix it*.

Let the Newest Employees Vent First

In a slight twist on Dymax's Take 5 practice, Elizabeth Pimper, director of learning for Ryan, an award-winning global tax services firm, schedules regular team project meetings with a five-minute block of time allowed for going Below The Line. Because some projects come with a lot of frustration, and pretending that it doesn't exist only increases time spent Below The Line, it pays to get it out in the open quickly. What gives this practice its twist is that they give newer employees the first crack at venting. This ensures that everyone feels free to give honest comments, without the intentional or unintentional influence of senior leaders. Elizabeth believes this approach allows for fresh perspectives from young talent, while saving the experienced viewpoints of senior employees for the end. For some effective Below The Line to Above The Line meetings, try letting your newer people go first.

Stick to the Plan

Why do teams go Below The Line and become less productive? Dr. Bernadette Loftus, executive medical director of Mid-Atlantic Permanente Medical Group, has learned from experience that it's because they don't stick to the plan. All too often, Bernadette sees everybody come to a team meeting, develop a great group-oriented Above The Line plan, cheer, fist-bump, backslap, and shout, "Yeah, we're going to do this!" Then they leave with the assumption that everyone *else* will stay positive and follow through. When the needle doesn't move, the whole group drops Below The Line and starts firing off the excuses. To fix that, Bernadette recommends a "continual reminder mind-set," which involves regular and frequent check-ins from the top down: an e-mail, text, phone call, Post-it, or carrier pigeon that comes from the boss. Creating concrete milestones and a plan for checking in and checking up allows even a half-decent team with a half-decent plan to stay Above The Line and succeed.

Go back to **Page 23**

PART 2

Now go to your *Fix It* **Bucket List** and select the next Accountability Trait that you want to learn about.

PATH C
fix it in My Organization

ACCOUNTABILITY TRAIT 14
Staying "Above The Line" by Not Blaming Others

Companies are notorious for becoming siloed, with too little communication between functions or departments. It's not anyone's fault, it's just the way it goes, especially in larger and more complex organizations. Of course, silos create a virtual breeding ground for blame. Division of labor tends to bring with it a division of responsibility that can distance everyone from the one factor they all share: results. Confusing activity for results can cause people to feel successful when they get *their* job done, even if that does not add to the achievement of the ultimate organizational result. This does not happen when an organization creates a Culture of Accountability. The trick to righting any sinking ship stuck in Below The Line blaming is maintaining Above The Line accountability. By putting concrete practices into your daily culture, you reduce the silo effect and increase accountability. These tips can help you do that.

Master Line-of-Sight Accountability

Paul C. Kelly, president and CEO of Research Electro-Optics, a maker of high-precision optical components, told us that they keep people Above The Line through developing and supporting a strategic plan aimed at the achievement of the Key Results, a company plan that maintains line-of-sight accountability, clearly connecting individual objectives from the bottom to the top of the organization. He holds twenty meetings per year with key contributors, from the bottom of the organization up to the executive team, where each key contributor describes what they need to do over the next few years to help accomplish the company's strategic plan. They augment this with monthly town hall meetings. In each meeting, Paul highlights different areas of the overall plan, discussing what is working and what's not. He also regularly takes the plan out to customers and asks them for their input in defining what key strategies and actions should take place. The plan is posted in people's cubicles, on office walls, everywhere. No one can escape it. This all adds up to total immersion in what they want to achieve as a company. Total line-of-sight accountability keeps them Above The Line, while such constant clarity removes most reasons for blaming others.

Hand Out "I Work Above The Line" T-Shirts

Mike Dufresne, regional vice president for national aftermarket and salvage auto parts company LKQ Corporation, suggested that "'I Work Above The Line' shirts are cheap and effective." Although this practice is simple and to the point, Mike didn't want that to detract from how effective it has been for them. He told us that they've seen great results in Above The Line awareness and overall accountability talk, just due to the message on printed T-shirts. Every GM has a stack of them. If one of their employees gets "caught" being accountable, they call him in and give him a couple of shirts. "It's reward and reinforcement. You can see people wearing them on any given day." Managers make sure they hand them out only when warranted so they really mean something. The shirts are badges of honor. Because of that, people wear them proudly, as everyone knows they were earned for adding to their accountable culture. Walking around wearing "I Work Above The Line" can't help but contribute to the individual, team, and organizational goal of maintaining Above The Line attitudes and actions.

Use a Trigger Word

Mark Neave, owner at NSM Construction, a California construction company, told us that Partners In Leadership was instrumental in helping him and his people transition to an accountable mindset, and for inspiring them to discover a fun and effective tool for keeping them Above The Line. He believes that you must recognize when you're Below The Line before you can get above it. To do that, they have adopted the trigger word "Omaha!" They borrowed the term from NFL quarterback Peyton Manning, who, when calling audible signals at the line of scrimmage, frequently uses "Omaha" to warn fellow players that he's changing the play. At NSM, people shout out "Omaha!" when they want to call someone out who just went Below The Line. According to Mark, "This is done by simply saying, 'Omaha!' or, 'That was an Omaha comment.'" Using a trigger word has helped everyone in the company become more aware of Below The Line antics and take steps to get back Above The Line.

Let People Know Their Work Matters

Pete Hammett, managing director of human resources for Oklahoma Gas & Energy, shared with us that "achieving results isn't simply a by-product of the actions employees take, it's about the culture embedded within the organization." Pete said one of the ways they create the culture they need is by letting employees know they are valued as individuals and that their work matters. Hammett said, "OGE is like most companies: we become so involved in achieving results we sometimes forget to pause and recognize those who made the results possible." To promote emphasis on the individual, the company has published a newsletter designed to highlight the uniqueness of people in the organization. Video clips are often shown to recognize member accomplishments, share successes, and promote OGE's inclusive culture. Additionally, they promote Above The Line thinking and recognize accountable actions through storytelling, occurring informally in regular team meetings, and formally in corporate communications. "Stories inspire and engage, prompting people to reflect on how they can personally take accountability for the role they play in creating our desired culture." To encourage Above The Line thinking and acting, get the word out that your people matter.

Use an Accountability Mirror

John Cuomo, general manager for aerospace distribution company KLX Aerospace Solutions, told us that for a long time their organization had neglected to emphasize developing their senior-level managers. Recently, however, John said they started a new executive-level initiative called Look in the Mirror. He asked his direct reports to join him in regularly taking a look in the mirror and assessing their own individual performance, along with that of all the other senior-level managers. This senior-level introspection deepens when they share their observations in their meetings and describe how they hold one another accountable for staying Above The Line for what they see in the mirror. This candid back-and-forth is repeated at the highest levels of upper management. John has asked executives to keep Key Results and company goals front and center in their minds when looking in the mirror, asking, "Do I live it, breathe it, and own it?" Developing senior leaders in this way may be one of the most important practices you can use to create a Culture of Accountability and accelerate your journey through the Do It step.

Now go to your *Fix It* **Bucket List** and select the next Accountability Trait that you want to learn about.

PATH **A**
fix it for **Myself**

ACCOUNTABILITY TRAIT 15
Tracking Progress with Proactive and Transparent Reporting

Going public can make all the difference between keeping a commitment and failing to follow through. That kind of transparency announces to the world that you are committed and willing to close the back door on backsliding. It's important to be transparent, not only about your level of commitment but also about the progress you are making toward achieving it. Doing that proactively is what this Accountability Trait in the Do It step is all about. To better operate Above The Line, consider these practices from the executives we interviewed.

Track Progress at Home and at Work

Tom Cromwell, group president-power for Kohler Co.'s worldwide power business, told us that he is personally quite meticulous in tracking progress, both at home and at work. He breaks business life and personal life apart, looking at them individually, saying, "Okay, what was it over the last year I've done well? What am I missing? What do I need to change in my roles in work and family?" Then sometime over the winter holidays, he and his wife conduct a personal evaluation around what they hope to accomplish in the coming year, and they then establish a budget. Once the budget has been agreed to, the whole family tracks expenses by turning in receipts. Those receipts are entered into a family budget-tracking spreadsheet monthly. Tom stated that "this tracking is about being thoughtful and accountable to how money is spent," and that his wife is better at it than he is. This kind of detail and transparency in reporting in his family life is mirrored at work, allowing him not only to track progress but to remain highly accountable. If you want to Do It, then you need to track it. Remember, if you can't measure it, you can't move it.

Manage How You React to Bad News

Terri Longbella, senior director of worldwide human resources for storage and data protection company Quantum Corporation, told us that one way she has chosen to promote proactive transparency is to manage how she reacts to bad news. It's been said by her co-workers that no matter how much stress she's under, "Terri rarely, if ever, allows it to be heard in her voice. There's no crisis too big. She's really great at instilling confidence that everything is going to be okay." Why does this matter? When those around her know she won't explode, they feel free to open up and report what's really going on. Terri takes this practice to the next level by asking, "What's on your plate today?" She's made it a pattern not to add one more thing to another's plate before asking that question. If people are overloaded, Terri suggests choosing someone else, or waiting a day or two. Until a confidence bridge is built between you and others, most will never be totally open, transparent, or report what's really going on, all necessary traits for effectively tracking progress.

Take It to Your One-on-One

Krista Stafford, vice president of human resources for full-service aerospace industry provider KLX Aerospace Solutions, made it clear to us that she has a standout favorite meeting: the one-on-one with her boss. This gives her a chance to go to them and proactively report. A chance to "make clear what I am accountable to do and By When. To be open and visible. To track myself on a regular basis around how I'm doing." Krista thrives on the one-on-ones where she's able to report what's needed, obtain clarity, and ensure alignment. She happens to work for a boss who allows her to keep things informal, so there's no set agenda. They typically meet out of the office and over lunch. "It's a time to share, to make sure we both get out what we need." She reaffirmed, "It's just nice when you can walk out with a level of alignment, to know you're going in the right direction." Proactive reporting doesn't hamper her independence, it actually empowers her so she can Do It even better.

Try "Last Three, Next Three"

David Bonnette, CEO of Lanyon, a leader in global meetings, events, and hospitality technology, told us that he believes in making reporting easy by keeping the process simple. When you want meetings to be transparent and reporting progress to reflect what people are actually doing, long meetings only dilute what you're talking about. By keeping the meeting simple, you make it easy to report. You also increase the likelihood of accuracy with fewer items to report. David feels that reporting shouldn't feel like some big test every time people touch base. One way he accomplishes this is to use a format where he covers just the top three things his people did in the past week, and the top three they are going to do in the upcoming week. Last Three, Next Three. For him, this type of focused meeting works best because it more easily aligns everyone's actual work efforts. Human nature being what it is, the temptation is to start reporting on everything. Our observation is that organizations tend to report on too much, making it difficult to keep everything actionable. By keeping agendas simple and prioritizing the most important, you will encourage real reporting that reflects what people are actually doing and what they are planning on doing.

Get People to Report Fast and Often

Tim Robinson is a serial entrepreneur, past chief marketing officer, and current managing director of TMR Media Services, a social media and marketing services company. With experience in marketing and knowledge of the software space, he has personally developed a *"fix it* fast" philosophy. According to Tim, "In software, you don't want to release a huge chunk of code only to find out something's wrong with it. You release small bite-sized chunks so you can pick up problems quickly." His idea is to do the same with reporting. The best way to track progress is with frequent check-ins where people report often on progress since the last review. It's a practice that can be ported into almost any functional discipline, not just software engineering. In his world, this practice allows team members to rewrite a line of code here or there, fixing problems as they go. Tim's view of frequent reporting: "If you can learn about mistakes fast, then fixing it is generally fast, and not as costly in time, money, and resources."

Go back to **Page 23**

PART 2

Now go to your *Fix It* **Bucket List** and select the next Accountability Trait that you want to learn about.

(15) PATH **B**
fix it on **My Team**

ACCOUNTABILITY TRAIT 15
Tracking Progress with Proactive and Transparent Reporting

It's easy for a team to get stuck in a form of groupthink where they start managing to opinions instead of managing to the facts. Tracking progress with proactive and transparent reporting for a team must be fact based and data driven. Only then can you truly create real accountability, because you will be dealing with real numbers, real facts, and real results. Your best insurance policy against coming under the spell of a Phantom Reality is to get the facts and study the data. To help you do this, consider these practices from a few accountable executives.

Focus on Leading Indicators

Denis Meade, director of training and development for AlloSource, a leading nonprofit tissue bank, told us, "What gets measured gets attention. So to have your teams and company do better, find the right metrics and start measuring and reporting." Basic to that is how "most organizations pay the majority of attention to lagging indicators, when it's more effective to focus on leading indicators." By way of example, according to Denis, "If you want to lose weight, what do you end up doing every day? You jump on a scale and say, 'Well, great, I've lost ten pounds.' This is a lagging indicator. You're looking at a lost pound here or there. It's better to train your teams to pay attention to the leading indicators, pay attention to the calories, the amount of exercise you get every day." Lagging is after the fact. Leading is before. Lagging manages the result. Leading makes it happen. To make consistent progress that is more easily tracked, focus on leading indicators and respond proactively to any early warning signals you may see.

Hold a Daily Stand-up Meeting

Executive vice president Darren Lee, of software developer and marketer Proofpoint, told us that one of their most effective team practices for tracking progress is the ten-minute daily stand-up meeting. Keeping it to ten minutes eliminates the casual "How was your weekend?" They stand before a whiteboard and get right to it, discussing posted To Do cards. If a task is accomplished, the person responsible moves the card along. If not, he or she can't move the card but is expected to straight-up explain, "No, I didn't finish it. I'll fix it by tomorrow." The team then helps by identifying the blockers, whatever might be standing in the way. Everyone agrees to these blockers, and to when and how they will move the blockers out of the way. That's it; they don't get into the politics or make it personal. By holding this short, fast stand-up meeting, everyone on the team can tell whether progress is being made.

Give Reported Numbers Context

Brad Pelo, a serial CEO of high-tech start-ups like i.TV and Folio, has found that in order to track progress more effectively, you should provide context as to why the numbers you are tracking are important. Brad said, "I used to just ask my teams to get me this report or populate some spreadsheet, but came to learn that if they don't know what the numbers are for or how those numbers inform decisions, they can deliver on it, but will likely be very passive and the reporting incomplete." Instead, Pelo recommends giving the numbers context, something like, "We are trying to decide which region to move into next as we grow our sales force and need these numbers to help determine that." Context gives the numbers sizzle. Instead of some bland report, people now understand how their numbers make a difference and are tied to their goals, what they're trying to accomplish, and how reporting those numbers affects them and their own job and even their compensation. Help everyone understand how reported numbers hit close to home and you'll get better numbers and more engaged reporting.

Implement a Monthly Check-in

Janee Harteau, Minneapolis Police Department's first female chief, told us she has developed a reporting routine for her supervisors where they do a monthly check-in to regularly track and manage progress. After she meets with her team leaders, the check-in practice trickles down, where her supervisors then meet with their people. Making this reporting system routine loosens people up over time, reduces blind spots, and establishes a structure for reporting. She shared that their framework is built around three talking points: (1) expectations, (2) performance, and (3) feedback. The specific dialogue is left to the supervisors, but by establishing a framework for the discussion, Janee has seen proactive reporting increase. In fact, she conducted an employee survey after initiating these routine check-ins and there was a dramatic improvement in proactive reporting among all teams, with more honest reporting due to closer and more comfortable relationships. With this type of structure and routine, supervisors are also forced to actually be supervisors, making everyone more accountable.

Find Your Weekly Cadence

Alan Taylor, CFO of eFileCabinet and a serial financial leader in companies like Boeing, Ford, and Novell, reflected on a time in his career when exceptional proactive reporting and tracking progress were critical to his success. As a young director of finance in the aerospace industry, with a team of nineteen plant controllers reporting to him, his job was to make sure they were on track, on budget, and hitting targets. To make that happen, he discovered that routine was a must, specifically "establishing a weekly cadence for meetings." Same day. Same time. Same duration. In Alan's experience, "Human beings are built to desire and respond to daily and weekly cadences; something in our nature resonates to daily and weekly routine. For a team, monthly is too far apart to be effective." Alan concluded, "When you know you'll be facing yet another agenda with your name next to an action item, that kind of pressure will drive some very healthy accountable behavior."

Go back to Page 23

PART 2

Now go to your *Fix It* **Bucket List** and select the next Accountability Trait that you want to learn about.

PATH **C**
fix it in My Organization

ACCOUNTABILITY TRAIT 15
Tracking Progress with Proactive and Transparent Reporting

For any organizational practice to work its way deep into the culture of your organization, it needs to start at the top. If tracking progress with proactive and transparent reporting around the most important objectives is happening at the top, odds are it's happening at the bottom as well. This creates line-of-sight accountability throughout the organization: clear accountability from the bottom to the top on well-defined results the organization needs to achieve. To check that, try sampling a few people at different levels of the organization. See if they are tracking and reporting what management is most concerned about. If they are not, you don't have line-of-sight accountability. Here are some ideas to jump-start your efforts on this Accountability Trait.

Open Your Books

Steve Jeffrey, vice president of corporate services for Structural Integrity Associates (a leader in the prevention of structural and mechanical failures), told us their CEO has an open-book style when it comes to tracking progress and reporting results. This practice makes their budgets, financials, and other important information available to employees. The company spends a lot of time tracking and reporting, which they do consistently and deliberately for everyone's benefit. To facilitate real engagement and true ownership, they make sure everyone knows what's going on. This data transparency increases buy-in and promotes transparent reporting all the way down to entry-level employees. In an effort to openly report to the entire company, they do several things, including the following:

- Sending out a CEO report each month, offering regular, candid updates on everything the company is doing.
- Producing quarterly all-employee telecasts to further loop everyone in.
- Making sure each of the business units sends out a quarterly newsletter company-wide, so everyone knows what every other unit is doing.

Using this kind of public reporting breaks the silo curse and serves to engage everyone by distilling important performance metrics that otherwise might be held confidential.

Conduct a Yearly Audit with an Outside Coach

Bill Becker, COO of restaurant operator LTP Management, shared that at least once a year they will have one of our PIL field practitioners come into their organization to meet with their owners, executive team, managers, and senior staff. In a series of meetings, they will go through an accountability "audit," where they develop and refine Key Results, track and measure progress, and hone their ability to report each week. Bringing in someone from the outside applies a healthy pressure to prepare while putting fresh eyes and a fresh perspective on how well they are creating line-of-sight accountability with their Key Results. It's this face-to-face with an outside expert that pushes capability in this area to the next level.

As a result of this accountability audit, they will print and post the takeaways (along with regular sales and profit reports) backstage of their restaurants in conspicuous areas where employees can't miss them. This yearly audit holds company leaders to a high standard of transparency and reporting, something that trickles down, making everyone more accountable and more productive.

Make It Visible with a Quarterly Town Hall

Lance Davis, CFO of Veridicus Health, a pharmacy benefit management company and retail pharmacy operator, told us that town halls certainly aren't unique to them, but he didn't want them overlooked as a tool for promoting transparency. Once a quarter, Veridicus will bring in something to eat and conduct a company-wide lunchtime forum for asking questions. The Q&A is a visible and regular effort to provide transparent reporting on the important strategic initiatives they are tracking. Their philosophy: "Everyone in the organization should know how we are doing as a company." Lance pointed out that a fringe benefit from these meetings is that it tends to shine a light on those employees who aren't engaged with where the company is heading. According to Lance, "There will always be those who don't engage with corporate openness, don't ask questions, don't want all the details, they just want their check, and many companies just put up with them as long as they're doing their job." The reality, however, for Veridicus, and any Above The Line organization: anyone not engaged and not on the accountability train really isn't doing their job.

Measure and Track Everything Important to You

Kim McEachron, chief people officer for global cancer diagnostics company Genomic Health, told us there is real company-wide alignment around how they implement, measure, and then track progress relative to evolving their culture to support growth plans over the next three to five years. Some might think this is too subjective to really measure, but not Genomic Health. They use a system of short assessments called the Pulse Check. This program is built on a set of regular surveys for employees, where they can report on their perception of progress relative to the culture change. The Pulse Check provides a simple tool that encourages reporting. Loaded with all the information from the survey, management then puts together trackable action plans to promote the change effort further. To date, the system has been a huge success, with 90 percent of employees offering actionable input. By providing this kind of reporting structure for something many would consider subjective and hard to measure, everyone feels greater accountability to ensure progress and success.

Use a Stoplight and Make It Obvious

Karen Korytowski, general manager of Lean Operations for Smart & Final, told us that they are big believers in proactive and transparent reporting. That's why they do it every day at the beginning of every shift. Company associates working on the floor present the "numbers for the day," how many cases per hour they've been pulling and shipping, shortages, damages, and injury metrics—progress made relative to their daily-weekly-monthly goals. These reports are consolidated and given a grade, and are reported by a large stoplight showing red, yellow, or green. A yellow or red motivates them to up their game and get back to green. Barbara Van Dine, director of talent development and learning and someone who works with Karen, told us that because everyone, from senior management down to entry-level associates, has been trained in the Oz Principle

Accountability Training, they understand the importance of reporting and measuring progress and know exactly how the stoplight impacts the company's Key Results. Hanging a stoplight from your ceiling might not be subtle, but it's a good example of a way to track your progress publicly, so everyone knows where you stand.

Go back to **Page 23**

PART
2

Now go to your *Fix It* **Bucket List** and select the next Accountability Trait that you want to learn about.

PATH **A**
fix it for **Myself**

(16)

ACCOUNTABILITY TRAIT 16
Building an Environment of Trust

As we discussed in part 2, one of the important outcomes of getting accountability right is that it produces an environment of trust. Accountable people can be counted on to do what they say, to not blame others, and to listen carefully to their colleagues, all essential ingredients to building trust. Often, when people set out to Do It, they quickly realize that they can't do it alone and that they need the help of others to get it done. Making things happen through others is an important Above The Line skill. Check out these ideas from our executives on how to do that in a way that builds trust.

Allow a Flesh Wound or Two

Hany Massarany, CEO of GenMark Diagnostics, a clinical diagnostics innovator, admitted to us that early on in his career he struggled with extending trust to people, for fear of their making mistakes, something he now knows robs a person of learning and growth. As Hany put it, "It's too easy for those in leadership to see just how to do it and micromanage everything and everyone in order to avoid flat tires and pitfalls. It takes a lot of patience and understanding and maturity to allow people to mess up, and then learn from it." When younger, Hany didn't want to sit back and watch his people make mistakes. By intervening, though, you don't let the individual, team, or even organization develop as it could, and should. The best attitude: "If it's not fatal, if it's just a flesh wound, then sometimes you have to let the wound happen." Hany recommends just biting your tongue and being patient. Allowing people the ability to make flesh-wound errors does more to establish trust than empowering them to make only safe choices that don't allow for the risk of mistakes.

Share a Personal Story

Ian Baines, CEO of family restaurant chain Cheddar's Scratch Kitchen, told us that he's made a career out of being a turnaround artist and fixing organizations. His first *fix it* tool in the trust tool chest? *Share your stories.* "How do I get a manager I'm eating with in their restaurant to open up? I share my own history, the good and the bad. Sharing personal stories promotes vulnerability." Ian will often go back and walk people through his rise from an entry-level caterer to where he is today. He'll be open about his scars, his war wounds. "Sharing stories breaks down leadership intimidation and builds trust. I don't see myself as intimidating, but my role is intimidating." When it comes to opening up, people are always concerned about whether they can share candidly and maintain job security. "Trust opens people up to give you the truth, rather than just telling you what you want to hear." If you're struggling with trust and need to *fix it,* try sharing a vulnerable personal story or two.

Focus on Being with Those You're With

Sherry Moore, human resources director for Ocean Optics, a leader in modular spectroscopy technology and manufacturing, described how a candidate had recently gone into a hiring manager's office for a potential job interview, and while there, one employee after another kept interrupting. What was scheduled to be a ten-minute interview turned into a forty-five-minute convoluted waste of time. Sherry's point: "The best way to build trust . . . when you are with someone, is to really be with them." She reflected on when she worked with a controller in accounting whose computer was against the back wall of his office. If someone was sitting in front of his desk, they would often be talking to the back of his head because he was always turning around to check his computer. Nothing breaks trust faster than feeling devalued, underappreciated, or ignored. It's really about putting aside your work stuff and giving someone your undivided attention. Close your laptop and look at the person. Put your cell phone in a drawer and listen. Mutual trust will develop when you focus on being with those you're with.

Bait and Switch with Full-Size Candy Bars

David Ellis, vice president of investigations for SecurityMetrics, a credit card security provider, reflected on a time when he was a commander with the Oakland Police Department. According to Dave, "Cops at a certain level are noncomplex creatures. It sounds silly, but to build relationships of trust I would keep a bowl of candy on my desk, with the door open. Officers would walk past and be lured in. Invariably I'd hear, 'Chief, can I have . . . ?'" Before they could snag a candy bar and run, Dave had them going in conversation. Because it wasn't an official sit-down where they were afraid he might come down on them for something, it made talking easier. The candy made him more aware of the day-to-day line-level issues. How they were really doing. Things that were really on their minds and important to them. Relationships expanded. Trust grew. But the key, according to Dave: "It has to be full-size candy bars. M&M's

won't do it." He continued the same practice in the private sector at SecurityMetrics. Still full-size candy in his office. Still trusted relationships built at the cost of a few calories.

Coach Others to Eliminate Your Own Job

Hugh Ekberg, president of Kitchen & Bath Americas at Kohler Co., believes one sure way to foster greater trust in people is to help them see that you as a leader are doing everything possible to make them better, build them up, and promote them. Hugh practices a "Forget self and become a coach" personal mantra, something instilled in him by an early mentor whom he saw consciously turn his attention from his own career and actively start coaching subordinates, grooming them for advancement. This selfless style of leadership and investment in others can't help but infuse huge amounts of trust into a relationship. Hugh told us, "To elevate others, you want to try to constantly eliminate your own job by teaching it to subordinates, so you don't have to do today what you did yesterday." This takes a high degree of self-confidence and mutual trust, along with an understanding that it's all about the business and not about any one person. To increase trust and achieve a great deal of job satisfaction, start replacing yourself by coaching others on how to do it.

Go back to **Page 23**

PART
2

Now go to your *Fix It* **Bucket List** and select the next Accountability Trait that you want to learn about.

PATH **B**
fix it on **My Team**

ACCOUNTABILITY TRAIT 16
Building an Environment of Trust

People will work hard for people they trust. Teams will work harder as a unit when they feel mutual trust and mutual respect. We've all been part of teams where trust is absent, dysfunction reigns, and gossip and infighting rule the day. But team leaders can make a difference. Mark McNeil, president of juice bottler Lassonde Pappas and Company, told us, "If someone asks who I've worked for I always give them people's names. I've worked for five great people in my career and could tell inspiring stories about each." We are all in the driver's seat to leave that kind of legacy in our teams and organizations. It starts with trust.

Ask "Do You Want to Be Part of a High-Performing Team?"

According to Mary Bartlett, COO for The Reserve, a professional shared workplace, trust happens by talking about it and promoting it. She insists on high-performing teams and told us that you get there only through trust, so trust is a drum she's always beating. Whenever she is asked to lead a new team, she'll go through a basic exercise that begins by simply asking, "Does everyone in the room want to be part of a high-performing team?" Seems pretty rudimentary, but she said, "Most assembled teams don't ever think to ask the question, let alone intentionally decide what they want to be. People are usually just thrown into a room and start working." Getting everyone to set their expectations on how they will work together and consciously think about what it will take to create a high-performing team will yield huge dividends. To build team trust, make sure you talk about it.

Personally Recognize Everyone

Mark Polking, director of tax for Transamerica insurance, said that a few years ago he and his team endured a nightmare yearlong project. Despite the tough situation, the team pulled together, working through many overtime hours and untold stress. It was an entire team effort, and by the end Mark knew his people needed his gratitude. So he pulled them into an auditorium and said, "When I call out specific items, stand up." One by one, Mark cited a specific contribution that each individual had made to the team win. By the end of the meeting, all sixty-five members of his team were standing—he had gone through all sixty-five! Tears peppered the team's eyes and Mark himself was breaking down. Team trust was forever ingrained due to his leadership. He really did know and care about every member of the group. Mark said, "I want people I work with to remember me as a leader, as a mentor, and as a friend. Remembering this truly shapes how I think and act." When people believe you care, trust is automatic.

Assign Partners

Christina Sarabia, manager of organizational development for Exactech, manufacturers of orthopedic implant devices, told us that they've adopted the practice of assigning a partner to every person who attends their leadership team meetings. These ongoing partnerships between team members eventually produce a strong bond and trust among team members that was never there before. The trust built within these partnerships encourages and promotes an open exchange of ideas that has led to new action items that directly seed accountability. As trust grows in the partnerships, the back-and-forth expands. The practice became so successful at Exactech that they extended team meetings by thirty minutes in order to give the partners more back-and-forth time. In subsequent meetings, the assigned partners then share whatever action plans came from their previous meetings, as well as any successes. If you want a better exchange of ideas and a more vibrant team culture, try partnering people. The eventual freedom will open minds and mouths and improve your culture and results.

Practice Active Listening

Denis Meade, director of training and development for tissue bank AlloSource, told us that a key best practice for him in building team trust is "active listening." This means making a conscious decision to show people you're listening with intent to act and aren't just waiting to shut them down with your own opinions and ideas. He believes much of team dysfunction and lack of trust rests in the simple inability to get people's personal agendas out of the way, in trade for a little real listening. Denis recommends simple mirroring and paraphrasing skills like, "Do I have this correct?" or "Is this what you mean?" explaining back to the person with as many of their own words as possible, so they can then come back to you immediately if you're missing it. When people feel listened to, they feel trusted and keep talking, dropping their guard and letting others in. That's when you really gain team momentum, because there are fewer secrets. To build team trust and eliminate dysfunction, try a bit more active listening with your people.

Participate in Leading Training

Cliff Reyle, chief human resources and information officer for Youth Villages, a company devoted to helping at-risk youth, shared a story about a time he attended a leadership summit where former GE chairman Jack Welch spoke. Jack was running one of the most complex organizations in the world at the time, but would still go to "GE University" every four to six weeks to train and lead a session personally. Cliff was able to ask Jack, "Did you ever have a board member question why you'd spend your time in that way?" Jack immediately responded, "Of course not, what more important thing could I be doing than investing in our future leadership?" The respect, admiration, and trust that develops for a leader who engages like that is hard to measure. Today, Cliff makes a point of personally leading their once-a-month six-hour team training sessions. He loves it, "because in a normal office setting people are more on guard when the chief whatever walks in." Allocate time to participate in training others on a regular basis. You are not only making an investment in developing talent, you are also building trust with more familiarity and discussion.

Go back to **Page 23**

PART 2

Now go to your *Fix It* **Bucket List** and select the next Accountability Trait that you want to learn about.

PATH **C**
fixit in My Organization

ACCOUNTABILITY TRAIT 16
Building an Environment of Trust

The primary purpose of Creating a Culture of Accountability is to establish a working environment that motivates people at every level to take accountability to overcome problems, find solutions, and get results. Doing so will help you to discover every possible option, tap every available resource, and look for every conceivable way to make results happen. Act like this and you will plug into every person who can help you produce the desired result. Connecting with people and energizing their efforts toward the desired goal can be done only when accountability is clearly defined. Then, and only then, can you engender the necessary trust to align and mobilize an entire organization to do whatever it takes to Do It and get results. For some final *fix it* tips on how to make this trait work for you and your people, try a few of these executive practices.

Ask Guiding Questions

When Jim Arnold was senior vice president of Nexen Oil Sands, he explained that in the past he and their senior-level managers were holding on too tight, making too many "contributions," and spoon-feeding solutions to stifled employees, all in an effort to guarantee success. It wasn't working. Then Jim and the management team changed their approach to asking Guiding Questions rather than impatiently dishing out their own solutions and ideas. Jim explained that it was initially difficult for senior-level employees to trust, pull back, and ask questions such as "What do you think we should do?" "Would path A or path B be better?" "Have you thought of a solution?" With the new approach, trust grew and newfound freedom from Guiding Questions began paying big dividends. The once-silent lower-level employees started opening up, discovering breakthroughs and creative solutions, all of which began to make a real difference. Jim advised, "When you guide and don't tell, people may fail a bit more, but they will also grow more, learn more, have more ownership, and bring more results to the company table."

Give Them More Rope

Joe Nilson, director of business development for Tolero Pharmaceuticals, told us that early in his career he remembers working for a place that had little room for trust. Leadership micromanaged most everything. Before making decisions, you had to ask for permission. According to Joe, "We were handheld. You couldn't think for yourself, you couldn't move without permission. As soon as you were thinking for yourself, you were stepping out of bounds." The result was stagnant company growth, vegetating employees, and flatlined innovation. The polar opposite is true at Tolero, where, according to Joe, they trust their people and practice "giving people as much rope as they need." If there's a problem or challenge that needs to be solved, the attitude from leadership is, "Great, we trust you. Go do it and report back. Just do it." When you're in a risk-averse environment, like Joe's earlier employer, when someone is watching everything you do, Joe said, "you lose all confidence in yourself. But when someone says, 'Just go do it, we trust you, so trust yourself,' that's empowering and produces real results."

Move Your Desk and Listen

Kevin Thissen serves as design engineer manager for Chart Industries, a cryogenics manufacturer and natural gas processor-distributor. According to Kevin, they experienced the traditional "cross-functional dysfunction" between engineering and manufacturing. The engineers would stay in their office and shuttle drawings down to manufacturing, expecting the work to be completed exactly as drawn. Manufacturing would then pull their hair out, knowing changes were necessary based on customer need. Engineering and manufacturing weren't talking. Silos were alive and well. Mutual trust? Impossible. Then one day Kevin moved his desk from his office two hundred yards to the shop floor. For an entire week he spent his days chatting with the frontline manufacturing workers (the welders and supervisors) about how the engineering team could better support them. Talk about a trust play! A practice with enormous benefits! The manufacturing employees were blown away that Kevin was willing to go to such lengths to understand their frustrations. Communication improved. Silos crumbled. Trust grew. Kevin would tell anybody to "move your desk and listen." Doing so will build trust and make everyone Do It better.

Leapfrog to Coach Instead of Manage

Mike Gummeson, president and CEO of National Diversified Sales (NDS), a leader in water management solutions, told us they are consciously striving to open up relationships and get team trust and team communication flowing better. They've had great success by shifting leaders' views of themselves from "managers" to "coaches." There's something about coaching versus managing that builds relationships and promotes trust, especially when your coaching philosophy is driven by helping to make employees successful, rather than just telling them what to do. One example of how they promote trust is Leapfrog Coaching Calls. This practice involves "leapfrogging" direct reports and interacting with employees a few levels down. Mike said Leapfrog Calls help him "focus on being a resource to the person I am coaching, since I'm not talking about their results (which is what they discuss with their boss), but rather about opportunities or challenges they're facing. I'm also able to provide additional insight about company direction and initiatives." This builds relationships that don't normally exist and encourages trust, from lower-level employees to company leaders. To increase organizational trust, coach instead of manage.

Start a Leadership Outreach

A director of talent and leadership development for a large energy and gas supplier shared a terrific trust-builder practice used by a past CEO. It involved an ongoing leadership outreach program consisting of ten junior leaders from the company who were recruited directly by the CEO—those he was impressed with and wanted to know better. The group would meet every week for six weeks for breakfast or lunch to talk about leadership principles. As part of the outreach, each person was assigned a principle to research in order to lead a discussion about it. The trust and respect for this CEO grew exponentially. And the company as a whole greatly benefited, as the initiative became a real motivator for those not chosen to work harder in order to be considered next time. The director told us, "We had to perform and he was able to challenge us and build relationships without our direct-report leaders in the room. Trust from and for him jumped tenfold." Try a regular outreach for some solid trust building.

Now go to your *Fix It* **Bucket List** and select the next Accountability Trait that you want to learn about.

Remember to check out **www.fixit book.com** where you can add your own favorite accountability practices to the growing database of solutions posted by *Fix It* readers.

About the Authors

Roger Connors and Tom Smith are cofounders of Partners In Leadership, Inc., a leadership training and management consulting company recognized as the premier provider of Accountability Training and Culture Change services around the world. They have coauthored the groundbreaking series of bestselling books on workplace accountability, including the *New York Times* bestsellers *The Oz Principle: Getting Results Through Individual and Organizational Accountability; How Did That Happen? Holding People Accountable for Results the Positive, Principled Way;* and *Change the Culture, Change the Game: The Breakthrough Strategy for Energizing Your Organization and Creating Accountability for Results.* Their most recent *New York Times* bestseller is *The Wisdom of Oz: Using Personal Accountability to Succeed in Everything You Do.*

Their books have been translated into several languages and have appeared as the top leadership books in their category on numerous bestseller lists, including those compiled by the *Wall Street Journal, USA Today,* The Associated Press, *Publishers Weekly,* and Amazon.com, among others.

These popular books provide the basis for the Three Tracks To Creating Greater Accountability, the comprehensive and coordinated management consulting and training service offered by Partners In Leadership. The Three Tracks methodology helps organizations create a Culture of Accountability for individual, team, and organizational results. Many of their clients rank among the most admired companies in the world, and they include almost half of the Dow Jones Industrial Average companies, all of the top twelve pharmaceutical companies in the world, and nearly half of the Fortune 50 largest companies in the United States.

Tom and Roger have appeared on numerous radio and television broadcasts, authored articles in major business publications, and delivered keynote speeches at major corporate conferences. They have also led consulting engagements and major organizational interventions throughout Europe, Japan, North America, South America, Southeast Asia, and the Middle East. Respected as trusted advisers to senior executives and recognized as the worldwide experts on the topic of workplace accountability, they and their team of executive consultants and facilitators bring extensive expertise to help management teams facilitate large-scale cultural transition through their Three-Track Accountability Training. Both authors hold MBA degrees from Brigham Young University's Marriott School of Management.

Joining the writing team on *Fix It: Getting Accountability Right* is thirty-year veteran writer and practitioner Craig Hickman, a coauthor of *The Oz Principle* and a partner with Partners In Leadership. Craig is the author of more than a dozen books on management and leadership, and his consulting and training experience includes American Express, PepsiCo, IBM, Procter & Gamble, Frito-Lay, Nokia, Ernst & Young, Unilever Bestfoods, Halliburton, Hormel Foods, and many more. Craig is a keynote speaker for the American Society for Training and Development, the International Society for Strategic Management and Planning, the Society for Human Resource Management, the National Association of Manufacturers, and numerous other industry and professional associations. Craig received his MBA with honors from the Harvard Business School and a BA in economics from Brigham

Young University. He lived in Brazil for five years and is fluent in Portuguese.

Tracy is a senior partner and president of Partners In Leadership's International Division. He has more than twenty years of experience in the leadership development and consulting industry, facilitating executive and management teams with such notable organizations as Precor, GMAC, BP, Clorox, Brinker International, Ventana, American Airlines, Internal Revenue Service, United-Health Group, McDonald's, and Petronas. He is known as a vital partner in helping clients achieve unprecedented performance and has assisted organizations throughout the world to achieve Key Results. He has been featured at CIO conferences and as a member of numerous panels as an industry expert. Tracy received his bachelor of science from Brigham Young University in international relations. He has lived abroad and is fluent in the Spanish language.

Marcus Nicolls is also a senior partner for Partners In Leadership. Marcus works extensively with executive leaders, principally in Fortune 500 companies, providing coaching to the CEO and entire C-suite with such organizations as AT&T, Alaska Airlines, Cigna, Hilton, Kroger, Louis Vuitton, Nestlé, Northwestern Mutual, Oakley, Sony, Starbucks, US Foods, and Walgreens. He has been a keynote speaker for many organizations, including Sony, Nestlé, and the International Association of Amusement Parks and Attractions, and has the distinction of providing a keynote address at the MGM Grand in Las Vegas to an audience of twenty thousand people. Marcus received a bachelor of arts in international relations from Brigham Young University and an MBA, with Pacific Rim focus, from the UC San Diego School of Global Policy and Strategy (GPS). He is conversant in Chinese.

Considered worldwide experts on the subjects of accountability and change, Roger, Tom, Craig, Tracy, and Marcus, along with Partners In Leadership, have provided Accountability Training and conducted organizational transformations in thousands of organizations reaching millions of people. Their work has created billions of dollars of shareholder wealth and hundreds of thousands of jobs and has resulted in some of the best workplaces in the world.

You can learn more about their books, workshops, and training by visiting www.fixit-book.com.

Acknowledgments

Fix It: Getting Accountability Right has been twenty-five years in the making. Built on the foundation of our multiyear Workplace Accountability Study, we must offer sincere a thanks to our more than forty thousand respondents who took the time to not only participate in the study, but were willing to be open, candid, transparent, and quite real with their answers.

Additionally, as you have or will soon discover during your reading of *Fix It*, there are 240 highly practical and proven Executive Practices that were gleaned from 120 personal interviews with successful executives. Each of these skilled, talented, and time-tested leaders took the time to speak with us one on one as a give-back, offering you the reader practical insights into how they actually make accountability work for them personally, their teams, and their organizations. You have here at your fingertips amazing secrets, what proven professionals in accountability do every day to See It, Own It, Solve It, and Do It! The value of these noted practices from top-level executives can't be overstated and will be a resource you can turn to again and again. To all of these wonderful clients and friends, we offer a profound "Thank you!" If you happen to know any of these superb leaders, give them a shout-out and thank them for taking the time to pass along what works.

To our friends at Portfolio Penguin Random House, Adrian Zackheim, Will Weisser, Jesse Maeshiro and Leah Trouwborst and the entire team, we are thrilled to have your continued support and passion for our work on accountability over the years. Your belief in how we teach these principles has made the worldwide distribution and success of our books, workshops, and coaching possible.

Special thanks go to David Pliler who offered tireless and ongoing support to help move a project of this magnitude forward. His creative talents and contributions played a major role in bringing our vision for this book to fruition, including his numerous interviews of the executives who contributed to this book.

We also offer a hearty and respectful nod to our longtime agent and collaborator, Michael Snell, a great friend and true professional. He continues to assist us in our ongoing work of spreading the message of greater accountability to the world.

Even with five authors, a work of this scale takes a vibrant and engaged behind-the-scenes team. We would like to give a shout-out to some of our own: To Pete Theodore and his team, we give a collective high-five for their thoughtful creative and design work. To Michael Christensen for his executive interviews. To Brett Walker and his marketing staff for their assistance with helping get this book into your hands. We also thank Mark Grosser and team for their early support in gathering research, and Spencer Taylor for his critical and ongoing support in helping make sense of the statistics within the Workplace Accountability Study. And to all of our colleagues, coaches, consultants, and support personnel here at Partners In Leadership who rallied to help us help you *fix it* . . . thank you.

Finally, we offer unending gratitude to our wives: Gwen, Becky, Laura, Diane, Joy, along with our children and grandchildren, their tireless encouragement over countless miles and across every continent makes the joy in our work possible.

The Authors:

Roger, Tom, Craig, Tracy, Marcus

About the Workplace Accountability Study

The Partners In Leadership Workplace Accountability Study is the most comprehensive study on workplace accountability ever conducted. The purpose of the study was to understand the impact of attitudes and actions associated with workplace accountability on the ability of individuals, teams, and organizations to fulfill their purpose, achieve their mission, and deliver on expected results. The study looks at both accountable and nonaccountable actions and attitudes and how they impact the performance of the organization.

The study itself was a three-year study conducted from 2012 to 2015 and involved more than forty thousand respondents. Respondents were sampled from a wide variety of industries and job titles, from front line to C-suite personnel. The data was collected via live online surveys and during live webinars hosted by Partners In Leadership. In almost every case, the webinars were conducted by author Roger Connors. Each survey was introduced by the webinar presenter and questions were asked in the context of the topic then being discussed. The content of the webinar surveys primarily focused on personal and organizational accountability and the impact of these principles on the workplace.

The data from the study has been independently reviewed and certified by Dr. Chris Barker, who reviewed the quality of the data and determined that, using a 95 percent confidence interval, the margin of error rate (MOE), ranging from 0.24 to 4.22 with an average of 2.45, was acceptably low, fully supporting the quality of the data. For specific MOE information on any one or more questions, please contact Partners In Leadership.

Mr. Barker endorsed the study as "an exemplary and trustworthy asset of Partners In Leadership." He has a PhD and twenty years of experience in statistics in several industries, including the pharmaceutical industry; he is also an adjunct associate professor of biostatistics—University of Illinois at Chicago School of Public Health.

Index to Executive Practices

In addition to the 240 practices below, we encourage you to check out www.fixit-book.com, where you can contribute your own favorite accountability practices to our growing database of solutions constantly added by your fellow readers.

TRAIT 1: Obtaining the Perspectives of Others

TRAIT 2: Communicating Openly and Candidly

TRAIT 3: Asking for and Offering Feedback

TRAIT 4: Hearing and Saying the Hard Things to See Reality

TRAIT 5: Being Personally Invested

TRAIT 6: Learning from Both Successes and Failures

TRAIT 7: Ensuring My Work Is Aligned with Key Results

TRAIT 8: Acting on the Feedback I (We) Receive

TRAIT 9: Constantly Asking "What Else Can I (We) Do?"

TRAIT 10: Collaborating Across Functional Boundaries

TRAIT 11: Creatively Dealing with Obstacles

TRAIT 12: Taking the Necessary Risks

TRAIT 15: Tracking Progress with Proactive and Transparent Reporting

TRAIT 16: Building an Environment of Trust

INDEX TO EXECUTIVE PRACTICES

Additional Copies of
the *Fix It* Assessment

We have included two additional assessments for you to use to follow the other two paths in your exploration of the Accountability Traits that you have not yet taken.

As you did on your first journey through the book, use the assessments by doing the following:

- First, determine the path you will take: "for myself," "for my team," or "for my organization." Your chosen path will determine your focus when taking the assessment. Select the box at the top of the assessment corresponding to your path to help remind you of which path you've chosen.
- Second, take the assessment by sorting the Accountability Trait number into one of the three buckets on the page opposite the assessment that best fits the description. This will produce your *new Fix It* Bucket List.

After completing the assessment, go to Part 2 of the book and begin reading about the Accountability Traits in your *Fix It* Bucket List. Just remember to come back here to reference your current Bucket List, instead of page 23 as you did in your previous read.

Your efforts here will lead to lasting and significant results for you personally, your team, and your entire organization!

The fix it Assessment

My path: ☐ 🧍 Self   ☐ 👥 Team   ☐ 🏢 Organization

SEE IT	Obtaining the Perspectives of Others	①
	Communicating Openly and Candidly	②
	Asking for and Offering Feedback	③
	Hearing and Saying the Hard Things to See Reality	④
OWN IT	Being Personally Invested	⑤
	Learning from Both Successes and Failures	⑥
	Ensuring Our Work Is Aligned with Key Results	⑦
	Acting on the Feedback We Receive	⑧
SOLVE IT	Constantly Asking "What Else Can We Do?"	⑨
	Collaborating Across Functional Boundaries	⑩
	Creatively Dealing with Obstacles	⑪
	Taking the Necessary Risks	⑫
DO IT	Doing the Things We Say We Will Do	⑬
	Staying "Above The Line" by Not Blaming Others	⑭
	Tracking Progress with Proactive and Transparent Reporting	⑮
	Building an Environment of Trust	⑯

Put the trait number in the spaces provided for each bucket.

Must fix it

Needs work

Do pretty well

Do pretty well

These are the traits that you do pretty well. They could deserve some tuning up but are not the most important to focus on now.

Needs work

Working on these traits will prove useful, but we're going to encourage you to focus on the must fix its.

Must fix it

These are the traits that you most need to improve to get the results you are looking to achieve. This is your *Fix It* **Bucket List**, items to fix now before it's too late! Refer to these numbers as you continue reading.

GO TO PAGE →23

The fix it Assessment

My path: ☐ 🧍 Self   ☐ 👥 Team   ☐ 🏢 Organization

SEE IT	Obtaining the Perspectives of Others	①
	Communicating Openly and Candidly	②
	Asking for and Offering Feedback	③
	Hearing and Saying the Hard Things to See Reality	④
OWN IT	Being Personally Invested	⑤
	Learning from Both Successes and Failures	⑥
	Ensuring Our Work Is Aligned with Key Results	⑦
	Acting on the Feedback We Receive	⑧
SOLVE IT	Constantly Asking "What Else Can We Do?"	⑨
	Collaborating Across Functional Boundaries	⑩
	Creatively Dealing with Obstacles	⑪
	Taking the Necessary Risks	⑫
DO IT	Doing the Things We Say We Will Do	⑬
	Staying "Above The Line" by Not Blaming Others	⑭
	Tracking Progress with Proactive and Transparent Reporting	⑮
	Building an Environment of Trust	⑯

Put the trait number in the spaces provided for each bucket.

Must fix it

Needs work

Do pretty well

Do pretty well

Needs work

Must fix it

These are the traits that you do pretty well. They could deserve some tuning up but are not the most important to focus on now.

Working on these traits will prove useful, but we're going to encourage you to focus on the must fix its.

These are the traits that you most need to improve to get the results you are looking to achieve. This is your *Fix It Bucket List*, items to fix now before it's too late! Refer to these numbers as you continue reading.

GO TO PAGE →23

About Partners In Leadership

For nearly three decades, Partners In Leadership (PIL) has delivered proven, sustainable approaches to achieving results by creating greater personal accountability and transforming organizational culture. Recognized worldwide as the experts on workplace accountability, PIL training and consulting services have enabled thousands of companies and millions of people to achieve dramatic results, reporting billions of dollars in improved shareholder wealth, saving hundreds of thousands of jobs, and helping to create some of the best places to work in the world.

New York Times Bestselling Books

Discover deep insights into the power of personal accountability and culture change—available from booksellers everywhere.

The Oz Principle: *Getting Results Through Individual and Organizational Accountability*

Change the Culture, Change the Game: *The Breakthrough Strategy for Energizing Your Organization and Creating Accountability for Results*

How Did That Happen? *Holding People Accountable for Results the Positive, Principled Way*

The Wisdom of Oz *Using Personal Accountability to Succeed in Everything You Do*